CHARLES M. JOHNSTON, MD

NECESSARY WISDOM

Meeting

the Challenge of a

New Cultural Maturity

ICD PRESS
SEATTLE, WASHINGTON
in association with
CELESTIAL ARTS
BERKELEY, CALIFORNIA

Cover design by author with Thomas Schworer and Dianna Slack

FIRST PRINTING, 1991

Library of Congress Cataloging-in-Publication Data

Johnston, Charles M., 1948-
  Necessary wisdom: meeting the challenge of a new cultural maturity.
  / Charles M. Johnston.
        p.   cm.
  Includes bibliographical references and index.
  ISBN 0-89087-650-9
  1. Conduct of life. 2. Philosophy. 3. Polarity. 4. Civilization,
  Modern—20th century—Psychological aspects. 5. Psychology and
  philosophy. I. Title.
  BJ1581.2.J64   1991
  303.49—dc20   91-6749
                                                                      CIP

1   2   3   4   5   6   7   8   9   0   /   95   94   93   92   91

In memory of my sister, Jody.

WORDS OF THANKS

Much of this book was born from long lunches and late night discussions with friends and colleagues. In particular I am indebted to members of the core group at the Institute for Creative Development—Pam Schick, Sandy Wood, Larry Hobbs, Ron Hobbs, Peggy Hackney, Jeff Bickford, Marsha Leslie, David Moore, John Palka, Tom Schworer, Tom Engle, and Michele Naylor—along with Dean Elias, Leo Johnston, Peter and Trudy Johnson-Lenz, Dianna Slack, Colleen Campbell, Susan Taylor, Susan Willson and Dee Davidson.

Special thanks as well go to my patient and committed editors Carol Orlak and Peggy McCauley, to Dianna Slack for coordinating book design and production, to Stephen Herold for design and publishing consultation, and to Tom Schworer for creative collaboration in the design of the cover.

CONTENTS

CHAPTER ONE

HOLY WAR IN THE POLITICAL AVIARY...
AND OTHER TALES

*"If I am right, the whole of our thinking about who we
are and what other people are has got to be restruc-
tured.... The most important task of today is to learn to
think in a new way."*
—Gregory Bateson

*"An American Renaissance is taking place in all the
disciplines, breaking the boundaries between them,
transforming them at their farthest reaches, where they
all converge."*
—Max Lerner

*"Do I contradict myself?
Very well then, I contradict myself.
I am large. I contain multitudes."*
—Walt Whitman

The most exciting—and unsettling—periods in culture are those
uniquely creative times when humanity's fundamental story becomes inadequate to its critical questions. By all evidence, ours is
such a time.

Through the course of this century, the story that gave rise to
the wonders of the industrial age has come under increasing scrutiny. Today, the need for a more complete story presents itself not
just as a question for philosophical debate, but as a cultural imperative.

From every direction, we find ourselves confronted with potentially overwhelming challenges. We have an environmental crisis, a drug crisis, an educational crisis. There is a crisis of confidence
in government. Our medical care system is in crisis. The family is
in crisis.

The sheer number of these crises would in itself be enough to overwhelm. But the numbers remain secondary to something more basic: The new challenges, wherever we find them—from love to politics, education to economics—seem universally unresponsive to familiar kinds of solutions. Just trying harder at what we already know, however good our intentions, fails to get us where we need to go.

The concerns that define our time require much more than just better policy. They require whole new ways of understanding and whole new ways of being. They require that we re-ask the most elemental questions about who we are and how our world works, that we step forward into a new chapter in the human experience.

My interest here is to bring the challenges that define this new chapter into focus and to explore with the reader the new maturity they ask of us. Our task will be not just to understand, but to create together the "new story" on which our future depends.

Bridging Polarities

"Life is a constant oscillation between the sharp horns of a dilemma."
                                                    —H. L. Mencken

As a futurist, I am constantly on the lookout for guide posts—images, ideas, metaphors—that can help us make sense of the territory ahead. This book centers around one such guide post, a simple yet immensely powerful observation. If we look at ideas big enough for the emergent questions, we find a fascinating common characteristic. Universally, new ideas take things that before seemed separate, even opposite, and invite us to think in terms of some larger, more dynamic whole.

Throughout this century, such "bridgings" of once established distinctions have more and more confronted and reordered our understanding. Matter meeting energy in physics ushered in the nuclear age. The bridging of traditional definitions of maleness and femaleness has transformed every aspect of our lives, from the bedroom to the boardroom. The growing interpenetration of mind

Ideas adequate to today's critical questions "bridge" traditional assumptions. ("Footbridge in Central Park," photo by Thomas Schworer.)

and body in medical thinking increasingly redefines our most basic concepts of health and disease. And a new, emergent "remembering" of the inextricable relationship of humankind and nature offers growing promise that we may stop short of irreversibly destroying our planetary home.

The recognition that new ideas and sensibilities inherently bridge traditional assumptions presents a powerful tool for making our way in the territory ahead. Bridging polarities is a simple notion, conceptually a "single brushstroke." Yet, it has the capacity to lead us in a quite complete and elegant way toward the larger understandings being demanded of us. This book is structured like a fugue, taking this deceptively simple theme and weaving it through the various realms of human passion and endeavor.

A few brief stories set the stage:

Not long ago, I was invited by a friend, a political science professor, to sit in on one of his classes. The topic for the afternoon's discussion was written in bold letters on the front blackboard—"Peace: Is it possible? How do we achieve it?"

It was a spirited group of students, full of fire. The discussion began richly. A woman in her forties commented that, as she saw things, war on any major scale had ceased being an option. Changes in the technology of warfare had made it simply no longer consistent with anyone's survival. A young man, leaning forward, shared his fears that world peace might be just a utopian dream, that the making of war might be just part of who we are.

As the discussion progressed, my friend said, "Okay, we seem to agree that peace has become an imperative. If that is so, how do we go about achieving it?"

As the students struggled with the question, the mood in the room began to change. Voices became more strident. Stances hardened. Soon our "peacemakers" were engaged in their own kind of holy war, those who leaned toward more dovish solutions set against those with sentiments of a more hawkish sort.

At first a certain excitement fueled the intensity of the conflict. But soon it was clear that something had been lost. For all the sparks, the fire of inquiry had largely disappeared. For all the pushing and shoving, little headway was being made.

At this point, my friend turned to me and said, "Charley, roll up your sleeves and dive in here. This is your kind of stuff. Play creative consultant for us. Get us past this logjam."

I appreciated my friend's timing. The moment was ripe with possibilities, though I wasn't sure quite what to do. I got up from my chair and walked slowly toward the front of the room, hoping that by the time I got there an idea would arrive as well.

As I got close, I turned and invited the students to get up and come forward with me. I shared that while I often enjoyed a good fight, I had to agree with them that somehow we had lost track of what was important. I asked the students to try something with me. It wasn't going to be easy to get unstuck, but by using our imaginations, we just might be able to do it.

"I'd like you to pretend," I said, "that we have been invited to go together to a planet in another galaxy. A battle is going on there between two groups of beings who see their worlds very differently and often end up in conflict. Actually you've already begun to make their acquaintance. One group calls themselves the hawks. They live over there on the right side of the room. Over there on the left side live the other group, the doves. We've been invited here as intergalactic anthropologists and ombudsmen. Our task is to find out as much about these beings as we can and help them work toward peace."

I suggested the students begin by going over to the right side of the room, the domain of the hawks, and finding out everything they could about these people's world: to move as hawks, to breathe as hawks, to sense what they felt there, to notice what they valued, to see how they experienced both themselves and others. After four or five minutes, I suggested that they might try speaking from that place of "hawkness" and notice what words seemed to want to express themselves. Soon the room was filled with strongly upright postures and resolute voices.

I then asked people to return to the front of the room, and to share what seemed most interesting, what had most surprised them. One of the original doves commented that she had always assumed hawks really wanted war. What most surprised her from this place was that, while she had very different ideas about how to achieve peace, she felt like she wanted peace as fully as before. A man who had originally expressed strong hawkish sentiments commented that in the past he'd associated his stance with simple courage and strength. He shared with us how he had felt this strength, but also a lot of fear, even paranoia, and how there was more to understand than he had assumed.

I suggested then that we move to the other side of the room and explore being doves. Again our task was to notice all we could—feelings, body posture, values, how we experienced the other people in the room—and finally to speak. The postures were softer here and the voices quieter.

Again we returned to the front of the room. Once more there was a tempering of previous differences. Reflecting, one of the original hawks shared his feeling that having experienced "doveness" from the inside, he now had more respect for it. He had felt caring there and had seen that it wasn't just weakness, that it took guts to speak from that place. One of the original doves explained that while he still identified with being a dove, his experience certainly made him step back and reflect. He had to admit that some of his proposals seemed naive when he listened closely to them.

Turning to the class I commented, "Well, the fire is back, isn't it? Things feel alive again." After a pause, I said, "Okay. Now here is the important question, the question that all this has been about. If the hawks are over there, and the doves there, who are we here? What is this place, this place from which you can appreciate the postures of both the hawks and the doves, from which you can see the larger picture? Take some time to explore who you are here. What now are the feelings, values, body qualities?"

After some time, people again shared their observations. "What most strikes me about this place," said one student, "is how tricky it is to stay in it. I get it for a moment, then I lose it completely. The only way to hold it is to make a lot of room in my body. It sure is easy to get scared and go someplace else."

"To be here, I have to be willing to let go of easy answers," said another. "It demands a lot of subtle weighing, and often between contradictory things, between apples and bananas."

Another commented, "What I'm most aware of is feeling that this place is asking in some fundamental way that I grow up, take a larger kind of responsibility, accept a bigger kind of reality than I've really understood before."

There was a pause, and then one student expressed what many were feeling: "I think it is possible to have peace only if we can think and act from this more complete and mature place."

Listening, I responded that I agreed, and that as I saw it the significance of this place was even greater. "It is not just that it is key to realizing peace," I said, "it is key to any practical understanding of the concept of peace. Only from this larger kind of perspective is it possible to discern realistic, workable images for what we are striving to achieve."

Effective political decision-making in the future will demand a new cultural maturity. This involves a growing capacity to step beyond a multitude of common polarities. As demonstrated here, one such polarity is the political left and right. We will need as well to bridge ally and enemy, and even, as we shall see, war and peace as we conventionally conceive them.

Let's turn now from this traditionally very "outer" world of the political to the more "inner" world of the psychological.

Tom was forty-six when he entered therapy. In his words, said half jokingly, half seriously, he had come to work on his "midlife crisis." Tom was a respected university administrator. He was married with four nearly grown children. He had been successful at most of what he had set out to do in his life. But for the last couple of years, something had not been right. The old drive and enthusiasm were gone. "You know," he said, "most days, if you pressed me to tell you why I'm doing what I'm doing, I couldn't answer."

One session, about a month into the work, Tom came in looking particularly frustrated and out of sorts. "I feel like I'm fighting with myself," he said. "I have no idea over what. My gut feels like someone is using it for a punching bag."

"Stay with the image," I suggested. "Who is that someone?"

After a moment he chuckled. "Just a kid," he said. "Looks kind of like Huck Finn—a real rascal, but kind of lovable too. Every now and then he just hauls off and hits me, then runs and hides."

"What does he want?" I said.

"I don't know."

"Why don't you ask him?"

At that point I got up and brought a chair into the room for the boy. I suggested Tom take a moment to sense what he most wanted to ask the boy, ask it, then go over to the boy's chair and let the boy respond.

Tom asked the boy what was bothering him.

"You're becoming an old stuffed shirt," he said. "We don't have any fun anymore. All work and no play. You think what you do is *sooo* important."

Returning to his chair, Tom turned to me. "He's really pissed," he said, sounding defensive and a bit irritated. "He doesn't see what I've done for him."

"Tell him," I suggested.

Tom again turned to the boy's chair. "What I'm doing is important," he said. "And I'm only doing it for you. If I wasn't working, you wouldn't have anything."

At this point I turned to Tom and said, "Listening to you, I feel that the you that is speaking isn't the whole you, but another character. Try something with me. Here is another chair. Come sit here, then look back and see if you can make out who it is that has been speaking."

Another pause…and another chuckle. "He's a king, seated on a throne. He's a good king. He's done a lot for his people, but he looks awfully tired. He's lost touch with his subjects and feels unappreciated by them. The way he's used to ruling just isn't working anymore."

I asked Tom if the king knew the little boy. Once they had been quite close, he said, but it had been a long time since they'd really even talked. There was estrangement, antagonism.

That first conversation was a good beginning, and thoughts about the boy and the king played in Tom's mind throughout the week.

Arriving for the next session, Tom expressed a desire to have the king and the little boy actually interact. We set up the chairs so that could happen, with Tom in his third chair serving as facilitator for the exchange and with me as consultant when needed.

As the conversation unfolded, changes began to happen in each of the characters. The king recognized that while he had been a good leader, there were new things that were important to him now. He realized he was tired of always having to be the responsible one, always on top of things. And he realized he really did want to get to know the kid again. He proposed that maybe they could go fishing together.

The kid saw that while he had never acknowledged it, there were times when he had been grateful for how hard the king worked and how he took charge. If he had always had his way, many things that were now important to him would not have been accomplished. He told the king that he'd be willing to take over now and then if the king needed a break. And yes, going fishing might be nice.

It was a moving dialogue, one that eventually extended into several months of work.

Following these initial exchanges, Tom's attention gradually shifted from the chairs of the two characters to a fascination with who he was in his own chair. He still talked with the kid and king, but now it was more just to check in. He'd bring questions that he was exploring—about something that was going on in his marriage, a decision at work—and he'd consult with them to see how it looked from each of their sides, but it was clear that the important action was now with the third chair.

In one session he shared some of what he was discovering there. "I feel different from this third place," he said. "In one sense it's just me, but it's me in a larger sense than I've known before. It is not always easy to be here. Life is bigger from this place, much more demanding and in ways that are often very hard to put my finger on.

"In one way it's more ordinary. At least it's less charged with questions of self-importance. But also it's more profound. I'm ultimately more powerful from here. More and more it's okay for me to be just myself, to ask what's important to me in the largest sense. I don't think I really understood what maturity was about before.

"A lot of very interesting things are changing in my life, many of them quite unexpected. I'm feeling purpose and direction again. That's what I'd wanted. I think it disappeared because it was time for me to live from this larger place. I wasn't quite ready.

"I've been spending more time with my kids (...laughs). We even went fishing. I've been with them in a different way. When I'm with them now my inner kid is there too. Sometimes I let them be the adults. My relationships with them had become strained. This is what was missing."

Tom smiled and relaxed in his chair.

"So lots of changes, all connected in some curious way. I'm becoming a better administrator and teacher, more willing to be just who I am. And believe it or not, I'm taking some classes myself. Never would have risked being one-down like that before."

In one session, reflecting on the multiple levels of change that were taking place in his life, Tom said, "You know, Charley, a lot of this is just my journey, my growing up. But a lot feels like more, like it's part of something larger than just me. Like how I'm being as an administrator, more open, more simply a person. It seems very connected with what people are writing about the need for new thinking about management. And with my kids. It's less that I was screwed up before and now I'm doing it right, than that I'm helping scout out new territory. I think the whole culture is looking for more mature ways to be."

Like the students in the political science class, Tom had begun to glimpse a future that was asking new kinds of questions. In the personal, as in the political, our times challenge us to bridge, to realize a new maturity and wholeness.

The focus of a third story is interpersonal, exploring the question of love and what it now seems to be asking of us.

I was walking on the beach in front of my home when I saw two people waving to me in the distance. Getting closer I saw Ben and Michelle. Old friends, they had moved to the East coast four years ago and we had lost touch.

We greeted warmly—smiles, hugs—and sat down together on a nearby log. Several rich hours of catching up followed.

At one point I asked about their marriage. Before they left they had been doing a lot of questioning about how they wanted to be together. Traditional marriage roles, being each other's "better half," had stopped working for them. They were looking for ways to be more fully "whole people" together. I'd had a lot of respect for the way Ben and Michelle had been exploring these issues together. I was curious about where their relationship had gone.

"It's been four good years, Charley." Michelle looked out over the water. "We've come a long way. I got out of the house and started my career rolling again. I speak up, feel more assertive in our marriage. And I've made friends that are not Ben's and let it be okay for Ben to have friends that are not mine."

Ben leaned forward, scooping up a handful of sand and letting it fall. He spoke. "Remember that I said I'd take a more active role in parenting. It's really part of my life now. I also took a hard look at the 'fast track' mindset I'd had in my work. It never really was me. Other things are just too important—time with Michelle and the kids, time by myself, time to read, find out about things. Remember how I always wanted to paint? I've started doing it."

"We've had some surprises too," Michelle said. "Last year wasn't easy; we learned a lot. You might enjoy hearing about that."

Ben leaned back, chuckling. "We thought we really had it worked out. We made the changes we'd talked about. Everything should have been perfect.

"Then one day we looked at each other and knew there was a serious problem. For all those good intentions, that hard work, somehow the old spark was 'puffft!'—gone. We didn't know what the matter was.

"We tried talking it through...talked and talked...but got nowhere," Ben said. "For quite a while we feared that the direction we'd taken had been a bad mistake. Then one afternoon some big new pieces fell into place. Each was a surprise."

"The first new piece had to do with that 'spark,'" Michelle reflected. "We saw that we simply needed to accept some of the loss of intensity we were feeling. Before, we had been like two poles of a magnet. I realized that while I still loved Ben, I no longer saw him as the handsome prince who would bring me eternal happiness. And I was no longer just his fair maiden. Some of that old reflex magnetism was quite rightly not going to be there anymore.

"It's funny," Michelle went on, "as soon as we acknowledged this, much of the passion returned. We began to recognize the deeper, more mature love that was growing between us. We saw that it could offer a new kind of passion—subtler—but one that in time would mean a whole lot more."

"The second new piece equally surprised us when we first recognized it," Ben went on. "There had been a critical flaw in how we'd been looking at being whole. We had confused equality with being the same."

"It's pretty embarrassing to admit," Michelle put in, "but sometimes I found myself longing for the old Ben. I had wanted him to be softer, and now that he was, often he wasn't very attractive to me. I cringed thinking it, but sometimes I just wanted him to be 'more of a man' again. And I wasn't fully happy with myself either. I was trying so hard to be Supermom—full-time career woman, mother, and lover all rolled into one—that I lost touch with myself and what I really needed."

"It's terribly tricky stuff," said Ben. "I'm sure what is right for other people must be quite different. But we had to accept that if we really wanted to be whole, that meant letting go of new 'liberated' roles as much as traditional ones. It was scary, like leaving behind the last safety net. We saw that it was quite possible that being this fully whole could lead us in opposite directions. But we had no choice, not really. Not to do it would diminish who we were. And ultimately our love."

"So, one more formula down the drain," laughed Michelle, "and a whole new world of possibilities."

Ben and Michelle had bridged to a new completeness in themselves and, with this, in their love. As for Tom's psychological insights and the students' more political ones, these bridgings had to do not just with new personal possibilities, but new possibilities critical to all of us.

CHAPTER TWO

WHEN ONE PLUS ONE EQUALS MORE THAN TWO

*"We shall require a substantively new manner of thinking
if mankind is to survive."*
—Albert Einstein

*"For to say that opposites are polar is to say much more
than that they are far apart: It is to say that they are
related and joined—that they are the terms, ends, or
extremities of a single whole. Polar opposites are
therefore inseparable, like the poles of the earth or of a
magnet, or the ends of a stick or the faces of a coin."*
—Alan Watts

*"Out beyond ideas of wrongdoing and rightdoing there is
a field. I'll meet you there."*
—Rumi

Robert Frost once wrote, "It almost scares a man the way things come in pairs." It seems in our nature to view reality as composed of polar parts. We divide our world into sacred and secular, true and false, friend and enemy. We see some things as objective—real and concrete—and others, such as feelings and imaginings, as subjective. Some people are men and do men's things, others are women and do women's things. There are virtuous acts and there are sinful acts.

Or perhaps, more accurately, it has *been* our nature. Today's critical questions demand a "softening" of old hard and fast distinctions. Setting "us" against "them," in our increasingly global world, becomes less and less a reliable formula for glory. Scientists and spiritual thinkers find themselves sneaking glimpses over the once impenetrable wall separating their realms. And role-defined hierarchies of all sorts—teacher and student, doctor and patient, manager and worker—are giving way to a rich array of more dynamically creative relationships.

Softening, which suggests mushy compromise, is actually not the best word. Enlivening comes a bit closer. Bridging doesn't neutralize polarities; rather, it animates them, fires living sparks across their points of difference. We see a growing capacity, and I would suggest an imperative, to grasp life in terms of the larger living processes that circumscribe the either/or's of our customary assumptions.

We find an intuiting of the dynamic of bridging in the increasingly popular notion of "wholeness." We hear of the importance of being "whole" in relationships, the need for "whole person" health care, and the imperative of thinking in "whole system" terms about the planet and our place on it.

At a first level, wholeness is a fairly obvious concept—to be whole is, well, to be whole. But if we explore more deeply, we find that wholeness confronts our assumptions at every level. Grasped with any completeness, it propels us into a qualitatively larger reality than that to which we are accustomed.

We get a glimpse of this larger complexity if we take a moment to ask just what it means to be a whole person. Does it mean being complete in oneself? In one sense it does. But at the same time, nothing is more obvious from a whole-person experience of the world than one's fundamental relatedness—to others, in culture, and within life's entirety. Biologist Lewis Thomas offers the other side of the paradox of individual wholeness with these pointed words: "There is no such creature as a single individual; he has no more life of his own than a cast-off cell marooned from the surface of your skin."

Emergent reality presents a reality of interplaying whole systems. The questions of how such a reality works are today's critical teachers. In them lie the sensibilities and understandings we will need to survive and thrive in times ahead.

Joining the Two Hands of Truth

"There is a green field between the scholar and the poet;
should the scholar cross it he becomes a wise man;
should the poet cross it he becomes a prophet."
—Kahlil Gibran

In Seattle I direct a think tank, the Institute for Creative Development, that brings people together to address critical cultural questions. We work with the concept of bridging in a variety of ways. Some of the work is more inwardly focused, more psychological, and some more outwardly focused, more socio-cultural. One of our time's pivotal bridgings links inner and outer experience; they can no longer be kept fully separate.

Tom's dialogue with the king and the little boy nicely illustrates both "inner work" with polarities and this work's common "outer" implications. Before doing this work, Tom often talked about new concepts in management, but such ideas were really just words to him. When he stepped into his role as administrator, he became the king. Only after he found a new, more whole relationship with the parts in himself did ideas of whole-person leadership begin to have real meaning.

Recently, I had a friend guide me through a similar dialogue with the artist and scientist parts of myself. Both parts are strong, but they have not always understood each other. The conversation became powerful. The scientist saw that the kind of science that was becoming important to him—science that was sensitive to ethics, science that embraced the mystery in life as much as the objectively provable—required the artist as an integral presence. The artist saw that if his art was to be much more than just decoration, if it was to have the kind of potency and relevance he was just discovering to be possible, he would need the scientist's clarity and perspective. Like Tom, as I worked I realized this dialogue concerned not just questions of personal possibility, but questions of possibility in the whole of culture.

Much of the effectiveness of the Institute as a think tank comes from the fact that its members have all done a lot of work with the polar parts in themselves. They can quickly spot when their personal psychology has them side with one hand of truth against the other—"us" against "them," masculine against feminine, the artist against the scientist—and lose sight of the larger body of experience that joins truth's two hands.[1]

As often, work with polarities focuses specifically on questions of our evolving "cultural psyche." I work frequently with groups from different domains—educators, religious leaders, scientists, artists—helping them envision their professions in ways more in keeping with a vital future. Often, I begin by having people list the polarities that in the past have most defined understanding in their field. Here are a few examples of such lists:

Education
teacher/student
right answer/wrong answer
intellect/feelings
school/not school
young/old
   etc.

Medicine
physician/patient
health/disease
mind/body
personal/environmental health
haves/have not's
   etc.

Business
management/labor
business ethic/human ethic
work/play
logic/intuition
business/community
   etc.

Religion
God/humankind
sacred/secular
virtue/sin
body/spirit
us/them
   etc.

Once we've made our lists, we take time looking at each polarity, trying to understand the larger process at work. We often take several hours—sharing feelings and telling stories of moments that seemed to bridge. Simple formulas never capture it. But given time, important common themes and sensibilities begin to emerge.

---

[1] Appendix I includes instructions for people interested in exploring psychological work with polarities more personally.

A brief glimpse into such a dialogue—here among a group of educators—gives a feel for what takes place:

> "I think future education needs to emphasize not just learning, but thinking—and thinking innovatively and personally," offered one teacher. "We've got to bridge our old cut-and-dried distinctions between 'facts' and things like feelings and imagination."
>
> "If we want that to happen," added a second teacher, "we'll have to bridge between the old roles of teacher and student as well. A one-way, 'pitcher and cup' model of education works fine for facts and skills. But thinking and questioning require an environment in which teachers are willing to question and explore along with the students—and where students feel empowered."
>
> "I'm struck by another polarity that has to be bridged here," offered a third, "that between school and the larger world. It only makes sense to talk about empowerment when there is some way for that power to manifest. The walls of schools need to be much more permeable: students doing projects in the community, people from the community coming in to share what they are doing."
>
> "We are talking about students as if that means just kids," added a fourth teacher. "I think we need to bridge as well between young and old. In the future we will all have to be active learners throughout our lives."

As the discussion develops, we draw together the different bridgings with which we have been working. We explore the larger, more dynamic patterns that, taken as a whole, these bridgings seem to create. We look at the reorderings of understanding they suggest. And we look at what they seem to be saying about needed changes both in what we do and the kinds of structures and institutions in which we do them. The experience is always rich and provocative.[2]

---

[2] Appendix II presents a more extensive list of domain-specific polarities.

A Play of Polarities

"The whole crux of life...is that it constantly requires the living reconciliation of opposites which in strict logic are irreconcilable."
—E. F. Schumacher

I find a simple image useful for grasping how identifying and working with polarities can help us move toward the kind of understanding the future demands. The image depicts a doorway offering entry into the new and necessary understanding. Polarities are like pillars on either side of the threshold of that doorway.

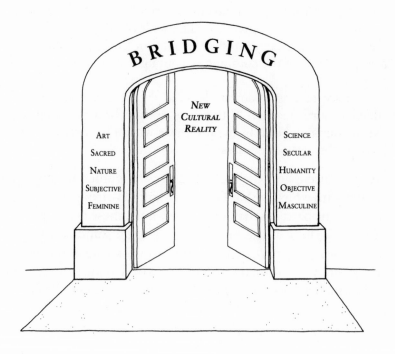

Fig. 2-1: The Conceptual Doorway

Just recognizing polarities doesn't in and of itself take us over the doorway's threshold: More than seeing that matter and energy are related was needed for Einstein to arrive at $E=mC^2$. But it's a start. It gets us moving in the right direction.

If we can do more than this, if we can actually bridge in our thinking, our ideas begin to take on the needed new magnitude and character. Whenever our understandings and actions in some way describe or embody the larger relationship of past polar assumptions, those double doors open further to give us new access to the territory ahead.

This recognition of the power that lies in understanding and bridging polarities will serve as our place of departure for the explorations in these pages. With each chapter, we will focus on a particular sphere of experience—relationships, politics, philosophy, morality, health, leadership, the environment, the sacred—using the polarities that before have defined it as entryways into the new terrain. We will look at perspectives that take their inspiration from beyond that conceptual threshold. And we will examine what these more integral notions seem to say about how we must learn to think and act if our future is to be a healthy one.

It is important to emphasize as we step forth that this book is about directions, not final answers. As Poet Wallace Stevens said, "It is necessary in any originality to have the courage to be an amateur." In the task of engaging the new, larger reality ahead, we are all amateurs—toddlers taking first uncertain steps over that threshold.

CHAPTER THREE

TOWARD A "LIVING" FUTURE

"The future isn't what it used to be."
—Yogi Berra

*"Our time is celebrating the balance, the reconciliation
between the man and the machine, between nature and
technology, and between past and future. That is the spirit
of now—of the end of the century."*
—Architect Renzo Piano

*"Now if you will only attend, Kitty, and not talk so much, I'll
tell you all about my ideas about Looking-Glass House.
First, there's the room you can see through the glass—that's
just the same as our drawing room, only the things go the
other way."*
—Lewis Carroll
*Through the
Looking Glass*

We could just dive in, pick a polarity and plunge over the
threshold, but it might serve us to look a bit before we leap. This
chapter touches briefly on a handful of theoretical topics that help
set the stage for the exploration before us. (Readers more interested
in practical application than in theory may wish to skim this chapter
for now.)

We will start by looking at some historical context. Then we
will look at what can be said at this point about the new sensibilities
being demanded of us. Finally, we will identify some of the potential traps, ways we can easily lose the path.

It is not necessary to fully agree with these notions to make
good use of the chapters ahead. I offer them as just one perspective.
To use this book profitably, the reader need only be willing to
entertain that new ways of thinking may be necessary and that
understanding polarities might help in finding them.

A Time of "Skin Shedding"

"[This is] a time of the parenthesis, a time between eras."
—John Naisbitt

Ideas about the future tend to take one of three forms. First there are "onward and upward" scenarios. In this view, the task is to work harder at what we are already doing. This view doesn't deny our problems, but it assumes that, given time, undiscovered technologies will emerge to solve them.

The second kind of scenario presents a polar view. This view assumes that in some major way we have gone astray. Images of destruction accompany it: a moral Armageddon; nuclear, environmental, or economic catastrophe. Such destruction may seem inevitable or simply what will necessarily follow if we do not radically and quickly change our ways.

Third there are more "evolutionary" scenarios. Evolutionary views also see fundamental change as essential, but less as response to some terrible wrong than because reality has gotten too big for past ways of thinking and acting. Such perspectives bridge the first two, including elements of each while stepping beyond either. I find this third perspective most helpful for making sense of what is happening on the planet.

A simple image helps frame this view of cultural change. Culture here resembles a snake that, in order to grow, periodically "sheds its skin." The "skin" here is the ideas by which we make sense of our experience and our conventions of behavior. As culture develops, reality periodically outgrows our explanations. We need a new conceptual "skin" in order to go on.

Frequent small "skin sheddings" occur, for example, with important new scientific breakthroughs. Less frequently, truly major ones transform history. I think of the time of the Renaissance as the last period of such all-embracing change. The death of the Middle Ages and the birth of the new "Age of Enlightenment" brought a fundamental reordering of human understanding.

Strong evidence suggests that we now live at a similar time of major "skin shedding." In a way quite parallel to late-medieval times, all around us old strategies—social, educational, political, economic—prove inadequate for the solutions we need. Indeed—and this is the hallmark of times of major "skin shedding"—as often as not, traditional ways of thinking even prove inadequate for framing the questions. History seems to say "You can't get there from here."

What does our current way of seeing things lack? What more does the future ask? A closer examination of where we have come from can help us get the needed perspective.

Each cultural "skin" is defined by a central truth that orders all other truth. I call this truth an era's "fundamental organizing image."

In the Middle Ages, the fundamental image pictured reality as an all-permeating battle between the forces of good and those of murky evil. These two great forces, equal in might, were seen as locked in a life-and-death struggle for both the individual's soul and the soul of culture.

The new image offered by the Renaissance was similarly polar, but now one pole dominated the other. Juxtapositions like objective and subjective, science and art, positivism and romanticism gave voice to this now less moral, more material reality.

The dominant pole, depicted most evocatively in the writings of people like Newton, Descartes, and Bacon, defined the universe as functioning like a great clockwork, a great logical machine. The complementary pole, secondary and separate, added decoration to this machine image. This new defining juxtaposition would prove immensely powerful, spawning monumental advances—multitudes of labor-saving inventions and technologies, democratic governance, scientific medicine, universal education.

But through the course of this century, this image too has come into question. It has come into question philosophically: How could a mere machine love, play, or create as we do? Even more pressing, it has come into question for its inability to address the critical needs of our time.

The "skin" of the snake of culture, it seems, has once again grown too small. We are now stretching it beyond what it can hold.

How is the old "skin" too small? The explanation, while challenging, is not complicated. If we look at the critical questions we face today, we discover that they are universally of a new type. This type, by definition, lies beyond the grasp of our old approach to conception. The new questions are *questions of life*, questions of exactly what a machine is not.

The issue of progress provides a ready illustration. Progress in our most recent world view was a fairly straightforward concept—it meant technical innovation and material growth. Quite appropriately, we were all for it. Today the issue is not so simple, a fact that if denied could very well lead to our destruction. In a world of very real limitations, bigger is obviously not necessarily better. And our increasing capacity to invent things that can cause irrevocable harm is sobering. If future progress is to be real progress, not a formula for planetary suicide, we must learn to understand and "measure" it from a radically new perspective: in terms of *quality of life* in the deepest and broadest sense.

In more circumscribed spheres—education, medicine, politics, business—the challenge is the same. The essential issues no longer primarily concern technical advancement, invention, competition, and expansion, but questions of "living" purpose in a "living" reality.[1] Mechanistic, individualistic thinking has served us well, but even when tempered with the most well-meaning romantic or humanistic sentiments, it remains inadequate for today's imperatives.

What does it mean to think in "living" terms? This, as I see it, reigns as the core conceptual question of our time. We've just begun to be able to address it. As yet there is much more unknown than known.

We can say one thing with some certainty. It will demand that we learn to bridge in our understanding. Previous central organizing images, at least those of more recent times, have been explicitly polar. The morally ordered universe of the Middle Ages found definition in great social and cosmological forces set in absolute opposition. The more materially ordered universe of the Age of Reason and Invention, while less combatively polemical, was even

---

[1] When I use the word "living" in this sense, I will place it in quotes. As we shall see later, I am referring to something more inclusive than what is usually meant by the word.

more definitely cleaved. The "separate worlds" reality of the Cartesian split relegated opposites to wholly different realms. Subjective stood clearly apart from objective, art from science, mind from body.

Such polar understanding, while quite adequate for its time, simply cannot suffice for addressing the more "living" questions that define today's critical challenges. To address life in living terms, our thinking must include all of who we are as life. Rather than setting scientific truth separate from spiritual truth, it must embrace the larger interrelated whole of truth. Rather than cleaving the health of the body from the health of the mind, it must address the larger health that mind and body together comprise. Rather than isolating my identity from yours, it must hold the larger identity we become through being unique together.

Where are we in the development of perspectives sufficient to the challenge? We appear very much like learned people in, say 1550, when the germinal inklings of our last major world view first stirred in the human soul. Eloquent arguments have sounded with increasing frequency throughout the last hundred years for the inadequacy of a purely mechanistic world view. The names are familiar and from every sphere: Thoreau, Einstein, Dewey, Whitehead, Russell, Freud, Jung. And new themes of possibility—and necessity—increasingly enter our awareness: needs for global consciousness, for new ways of understanding relationships of all sorts, for an essential kind of "remembering"—of nature, of our bodies, of each other, of the sacred. But in the task of making full sense of these changes and developing the perspectives and maturity needed to address them, we are barely at the threshold.

A New World View

"Man is entering upon a new stage in his evolutionary development."
—Jonas Salk

We can only begin to say what reality looks like when we begin to perceive in "living" terms. Yet it is important as preparation for our journey that we examine what, at this point, can be said.

Ideas that have succeeded in some major way at crossing our conceptual threshold during this century share at least three common characteristics. As we shall see, each is intrinsic to any act of bridging. Join the left and right hands of any polarity and one is immediately thrust into a reality with these characteristics. I present the three characteristics here bare-boned, leaving the chapters ahead to offer the needed flesh and spirit to bring them fully to life:

A "living" reality is relational, composed of interlocking whole systems.

In a mechanistic world view, reality appears reducible to separate analyzable parts: organs in the body, individuals in a community, nations on the planet. In a "living" reality, there is no such thing as an isolated part. From cells to societies to ecosystems, things enjoy existence only by virtue of their relationships in larger wholes.

A "living" reality is a "systems" reality. It is "ecological" in the fullest sense. Here the old dictum that the whole is always greater than the sum of its parts moves from being a philosophical condiment to an essential staple of the main course. The mind, in fact, never acts completely separate from the body, nor the body from the mind. And this me that possesses both body and mind exists only by virtue of its larger relationship in nature and with other bodies and minds.

Such is much more than a simplistic claim that "all is one." The notion adamantly bridges. There cannot be relationship without difference.

A "living" reality is evolutionary, with change an intrinsic ingredient.

In a mechanistic reality, things stay the same unless acted on by some kind of force: a bat hitting a ball, the action of a leader, willful choice, divine intervention. Things are how they are. Change presents the exception.

In a "living" reality, truth is as much a verb as a noun. Change is intrinsic. The earlier analogy of culture to a snake that grows by periodically shedding shows an example of this kind of evolutionary perspective. In the emerging picture, reality is dynamically "self-organizing."

Again, this is a bridging notion. Evolution in its full implication offers much more than a simple replacing of the static, push-pull reality of gears and levers with the free and everflowing reality of a river. In an evolutionary reality, form and freedom interpenetrate to create the dance we call life.

A "living" reality is "meta-determinant," uncertainty inherent in its workings.

Past conceptions of reality have been universally circumscribed by some final embracing determinism. Uncertainty has always been part of the fate of we mortals, ignorant and imperfect. But always, whether we defined it by the dictates of pantheons of gods or the laws of science, we perceived somewhere beyond us a final unchanging order, a definitive map for the workings of things.

The new questions challenge us to give up this security. Powerful new evidence suggests that there may be no once-and-for-all immaculate perception. Uncertainty may be a central theme not just in our personal stories, but in the story of existence as a whole.

We find some notion of the integral importance of uncertainty in almost all mature emergent thought. Its most familiar expression arises in Heisenberg's Uncertainty Principle, now a cornerstone of contemporary physics. This principle asserts that, regardless of the precision of our tools or the elegance of our techniques, we face a limit to what we can know. The ideas of quantum mechanics, presently our most powerful lenses into the inner workings of physical reality, reveal a world not of this here and that there, but of possibility and probability, a world where the future is neither predetermined nor predeterminable, but a unique expression of time and place.

A parallel new relationship to uncertainty lies at the heart of each of today's major social questions. Leaving behind gender roles requires embracing the already vulnerable meetings of intimacy with no final, external yardstick for our actions. Stepping politically beyond the need for evil empires means leaving behind the reassuring formula that ultimately we are good and others tainted.

Facing this fact of fundamental uncertainty is a prerequisite to planetary survival. Step one to avoiding destruction on a major scale requires finding the courage to acknowledge that the risks we face are real and to accept that neither the wonders of science nor God's benevolence will spare us from the imperative of a fundamentally new kind of human responsibility.

I like to put the challenge in a developmental metaphor. In the past we were like children, culture and cosmos our parents. Today's world demands that we make passage as a species into a new maturity. Safe images of ourselves as cultural children cease to serve us. This is so whatever the parental, all-protecting arms: those of technology, government, or an omnipresent conception of the divine.

Again, this is a bridging notion. While "living" truth is not predetermined, neither is it the opposite—something chaotic, purposeless. As we don't have a good bridging term, I've devised my own: "meta-determinant." Life's fabric is richly patterned, anything but random. But this fabric always requires a thread of uncertainty for its weaving.

All understandings that effectively traverse our conceptual threshold are in some way "relational, evolutionary, and meta-determinant." This is so whether the quandary propelling us toward that threshold poses a question of love, politics, religion, or economics.

Reality as Creation

"[We need] new and more comprehensive theories, which without contradiction will take care...of the diverse facts [within] our traditional incompatible doctrines."
—F.S.C. Northrop

A brief moment with one specific approach to more "living" understanding might help us get a better feel for the more conceptual side of what is being asked of us. The Creative Systems ideas presented in my earlier book, *The Creative Imperative*, illustrate one attempt at more integral conception. They also offer useful insights about the nature of polarities and what happens when polarities bridge. (We will return to these Creative Systems notions near the book's conclusion for a more detailed examination.)

To put together practical frameworks for times ahead, we must start by addressing the question of a new "fundamental organizing image." If reality is more than just a great machine, how might we better conceive of it? In *The Creative Imperative*, I propose that reality, rather than being mere machination, may be more essentially *creation*.

I use the word creation in its largest sense. Creation here refers not just to some event in our primordial past or to creativity in an artistic sense—playing the tuba or painting a picture—but to the whole of formative process. In a Creative Systems view, creation presents, to use Gregory Bateson's eloquent phrase, "the pattern which connects."

The idea is more easily communicated by example than by explanation. Let's take a moment to explore a realm of experience intimate to all of us: love. If we look at all closely at love, we see that neither of our common polar ways of thinking about how love works is adequate to its magic and passion. Love is obviously more than mechanical—"I do this to you and you do this to me" (the world view of science and analytic thought). It is "alive." Simultaneously, it is clearly more than simply fated—"It was meant to be" (as we like to see things from the more romantic or spiritual sides of ourselves). Such a view leaves out the very personal vulnerability and uncertainty central to love in real life.

So what is love? Can we move just a step closer in honoring the richness that it is about? For one thing, it is clearly a process. More specifically, it is a generative, *creative* process. When we meet, if that meeting is right and timely, something (we might call it a seed of possibility) is born between us. If we honor it, and take the risks it asks of us, it grows as a unique expression of who, together, we are creatively becoming. This growth takes us through some fairly predictable stages—a time of first infatuation, a time of struggle, a time of establishing roles, and so on. Gradually, if we succeed at meeting its many creative challenges, our being together takes on the qualities we call relationship, and love.

In a Creative Systems view of reality, a similar kind of generative dynamic is seen working beneath the surface in all the major rhythms of existence—in how we learn new tasks, in an individual's growth through his or her lifetime, in the evolution of cultures. All connections represent at least in some way creative connections, and all change in some way means creative change. Newton's picture of reality as gears and pulleys placed in motion by a separate divine architect is set aside and replaced by the more dynamically integral image of reality as infinitely interweaving patterns of ongoing creation.

Our three criteria for emergent conception are intimately imbedded in such a view. Creation is inherently *relational*—there cannot be creation without interconnection. Similarly it is *evolutionary*—creation is quite specifically the story of how things change. And it is *meta-determinant*—in creation, we can never fully predict what we will pull out of the hat from what we put in.

The nature of polarities offers strong evidence that generative dynamics of some sort are indeed at work in reality. If we listen carefully as we play with such wholly different pairings as matter and energy, work and play, art and science, we can hear a universal dialogue spoken. Polarities universally counterpoise something that feels more hard and defined—matter, work, science, the secular, fact—with something that feels softer, more ephemeral—energy, play, art, the sacred, the subjective.

Mythologists have a simple way of talking about these differences. They speak of the polar qualities that are harder, more form-defined, as "archetypally masculine." Their softer, less form-defined complements are said to be "archetypally feminine." The terminology can cause some initial confusion—archetypally masculine and archetypally feminine refer to qualities possessed by both men and women—but the concepts prove useful. What is important here is the obvious erotic connotations of the mythologist's language. The words imply that polarities interact in some "procreative" sense. By all evidence they do precisely that.

This notion that reality may function creatively offers possible answers for two critical questions about polarities. The first concerns the very existence of polarities: Why does this curious creature that we are seem so committed to thinking in either/or's when there is no reason to assume reality is anything but whole? One explanation: The creation of polarities is inherent to the workings of formative process.

"Living" reality is "procreative," an interwoven, ongoing, evolutionary dance between more form-defined, "archetypally masculine" elements and more germinally-defined, "archetypally feminine" elements. (Jeff Bickford and Lori Vadino, photo by Thomas Schworer.)

Look closely at any creative dynamic and one sees a similar unfolding pattern. Creation starts with unity, buds off new form—creating duality in the process—then with time reintegrates to a new, larger unity.

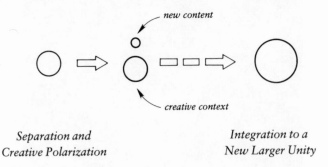

Separation and
Creative Polarization

Integration to a
New Larger Unity

FIG. 3-1: *Polarity as an Inherent Dynamic
in any Process of Creation*

The birth of a new idea illustrates. First it buds off from the "original unity" of past cultural assumptions. Over time, the new notion is variously ignored, deified, rejected, and struggled with. In the process it grows. Eventually, if it has value, it reconnects with the old unity. It becomes part of a new, now expanded cultural whole, part of a new "common sense."

Seen creatively, polarities are expressions of the tension necessary to bring the new into being. They juxtapose archetypal qualities because they represent, in myriad permutations, the evolving relationship between the "stuff" of new form and the more germinal reality of its creative context.

The second critical question concerns the fact of bridging: Why at this time in culture should we be seeing the interlinking of notions that before we've taken such care to keep separate? The answer that a Creative Systems perspective proposes is only a hypothesis, but a provocative one.

If we look at the course of any creative process, we see a specific point at which bridging becomes a central dynamic. Once the newly created object completes its tasks of budding off from its context and moving into the reality of forms, it begins to reengage the context that gave it birth, in the process both expanding that context and being challenged and expanded by it.

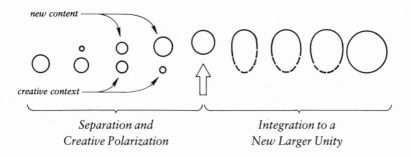

Separation and Creative Polarization   *Integration to a New Larger Unity*

FIG. 3-2: *Bridging as a Natural Point in Creative Process*

In our individual development, integral dynamics usually first appear around the time of the midlife transition. The journey of the first half of life focuses on achievement: as toddlers on learning to stand, speak, and delay gratification; later on separating from home and parents; and with time, on making our places in the world. Appropriately, as young adults we tend to define ourselves primarily in terms of what we have learned and become: Here is what I do, here is what I believe, here is where I live, and who I live with. In the second half of life we begin asking new kinds of questions. We can increasingly step back and look at the creations of our lives in their larger contexts. "So I'm a doctor—so what—what does that really mean to me, in terms of what really matters?" And new kinds of measures for truth come increasingly to replace achievement and knowledge. Questions of purpose and relationship—relationship to self, to others, to one's world—come increasingly to define value. To the degree we risk passage through this personal transformational doorway, truth in the second half of life grows into that more elusive and inclusive quantity we call wisdom.

Civilization may be at the threshold of a similar passage into creative maturity. As we shall see, the parallels with other creative processes are striking. At this point, this is just one possible thesis.

But given only a handful of words to describe what the future de-mands, words like perspective, balance, sustainability, and wisdom—the hallmarks of creative integration—would certainly be some of my first choices.

Traps and Fallacies

"You have to separate in order to unite, because uniting means two unique things that meet, not two fuzzy things that merge."
—Helen M. Luke

Besides guiding us in developing new ways of understanding, polarities can serve us in another way, by helping us separate the wheat from the chaff in our efforts. Since the challenges we con-front are new, a rather formidable amount of initial chaff should be expected. And we have certainly not been disappointed.

When we lose our way along the "journey" toward the kind of understanding the future demands, we tend to do it in one of three characteristic ways. The image of the conceptual threshold again proves helpful. We can bump into the right (more archetypally

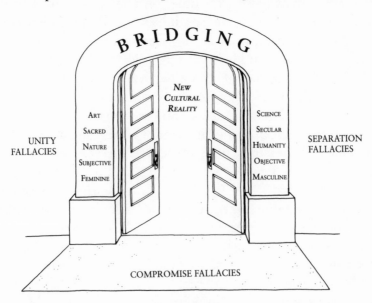

FIG. 3-3: *Traps*

masculine) side of the doorway, bump into the left (more archetypally feminine) side, or by confusing averaging with integration,
stub our toes on the doormat. I call more right-handed errors
separation fallacies, more left-handed errors *unity fallacies*, and errors that mistake splitting the difference with wholeness *compromise
fallacies*.

Each kind of fallacy leaves us equally short of true integral or
"third space" understanding, understanding that authentically
bridges, that in fact takes us over the conceptual threshold. Some
familiarity with the dynamics of each will serve us well as we ven-
ture forth.

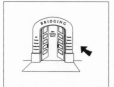

Separation fallacies are the most common in
usual thought. Indeed, from a fully "third space"
perspective, the entirety of our dominant world
view represents a separation fallacy. With separation fallacies we raise the "splitter's" hand in
victory and turn our back to the "lumper." Mind remains separate
from body, matter from energy, moral from immoral. East is East
and West is West and never the twain shall meet.

Along with this, in keeping with what happens when "twoness"
wins out over "oneness," we side with one half of the polar two.
Separation fallacies give ultimate truth to the more form-defined
side of life. They express simultaneously a bias toward the archetypally masculine's fondness for distinction and a preferential valu-
ing of the more manifest pole. Our modern defining of such things
as objective and subjective, humankind and nature, and masculine
and feminine as distinct has made not just a statement about difference, but as well about where "real" truth ultimately lies.

While separation fallacies are the most common in everyday thought, unity fallacies are most
apt to trap us when we consciously try to think in
integral ways. Unity fallacies confuse oneness
with wholeness.

The position of the doves in the political science class offers a
good example of a unity fallacy. The feeling state suggested openness and caring for others on the planet. It felt like wholeness. But
seen in the big picture, it was not. Like the hawks, the doves pro-

jected parts of themselves they didn't want to deal with onto others and in the process came to well-intentioned, but ultimately partial and ineffective conclusions.

When a purported "new world view" concept is in fact a "too easy answer," more often than not one will find some form of unity fallacy lurking. In the name of inclusiveness, unity fallacies quite specifically take sides, here with life's softer, more mysterious hand. When we fall for unity fallacies, in some small way, subtly or not so subtly, we confuse the oneness of the archetypally feminine with the more challenging reality of the creatively "living" whole.

Unity fallacies are most often one of two types. In the first we see polar identification with the "left hand" in opposition to the "right" (though often unconscious opposition). In the second, the fallacy comes less from opposition than simply from ignorance of the right hand's place and purpose.

A good place to see the first type of unity fallacy is situations where liberal, humanistic, idealistic, or philosophically romantic notions masquerade as new thought. "It is feelings that really express truth." "The task is to be always open and understanding." "It is the poets who know." Such left-handed assertions may provide a valuable counterbalance to dominant thought, but they are not at all new, simply the other side of the coin of the established perspective.

A common place to see the second kind of unity fallacy is in the popular equating of needed new perspectives with beliefs from earlier times in culture—with classical Eastern thought, Western Mysticism, tribal sensibilities. An important kernel of truth lies concealed in such equatings. In culture's early stages, wholeness, and within this the interweaving of opposites, were commonly seen as fundamental characteristics of reality. But images from early periods of culture have an inherent bias toward the archetypally feminine (and as we shall see, even when adjusted to compensate, lack characteristics critical to the mature integral perspectives our times demand).

Our analogy with individual development helps reveal how such notions stop short. Central to the dynamics of life's first half (indeed the first half of any formative process) is a certain amnesia for the developmental stages we have progressed beyond. Adolescents have a most difficult time making sense of the reality of children. And young adults find adolescence baffling even though, having just left it, they should be our greatest experts. In the second half of life, the basic structures of achievement established, these protective amnesias are no longer needed and gradually dissolve. Much of what we call wisdom is simply this process of creative "remembering." Our maturity offers a growing ability to see the larger process that our life has been about.

As we shall see, an analogous "remembering" appears as a pivotal part of new understanding. In the past we saw earlier cultural realities only "through a glass darkly" and either romanticized or demonized the faint images we could perceive. As these walls break down, we become capable of being at once more conscious about and more connected to the larger story of culture through time.

The important awareness here is that this dynamic is much more than *just* remembering. An elder and a child are related, but far from one and the same. As we reacknowledge the rich sensibilities of earlier times, we must not confuse the connectedness and oneness they so beautifully embody with the larger, more mature awarenesses that challenge us. In the difference between the elder and the child lies much of what will be most important if we are to survive and thrive in times ahead.

The key to avoiding unity fallacies lies in the recognition that "living" wholeness includes unity and duality as equal partners. They represent its left and right hands. A bias towards unity, whether in identification with the other side of the coin in the prevailing world view or with historical times when the unitary was naturally preeminent, means taking sides in the whole. Perspectives with such a bias, no matter how well articulated, leave us necessarily short of the mature, "third space" thinking our future demands.[2]

---

[2] It is important to acknowledge that ideas which stop short of being integral may nonetheless serve to help move us toward an integral reality. A good example is the dogma of radical environmentalism. Making nature divine and humanity evil provides ultimately a no better basis for good policy than its opposite. And yet, while people just begin to recognize the profound environmental dilemmas we face, this kind of polemic can at times serve a positive function in helping to galvanize awareness and action.

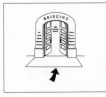

The compromise fallacy is not as sticky, but no less a trap. Such fallacies confuse integration with some additive middle ground. Rather than revealing the rich spectrum of colors that lies beyond black and white, they lead us to conclude that reality simply shows varying shades of grey.

We can use a simple example from organizational theory to contrast the compromise fallacy with its more specifically polar siblings. Asserting that organizations should always be hierarchically structured is a separation fallacy. Asserting the opposite, that hierarchies are bad, that decisions should always be made by consensus, brings a unity fallacy. A compromise fallacy would come up with some specific structure that combined hierarchy and consensus and then assert that this is how decisions should always be made. It misses that organizations are unique and evolve, that different contexts and times ask for dramatically different organizational approaches. The key to avoiding compromise fallacies lies in remembering that the task is not to split the difference between truth's two hands, but to live as the rich body of experience that joins them and animates them.

We now begin our journey across the conceptual threshold. Our guides for each chapter will be three key polarities chosen from one particular domain of personal and cultural life. Each chapter concludes with examples of polar fallacies commonly encountered in that domain.

CHAPTER FOUR

You and Me: Loving as Whole People

"If I am I because you are you, and if you are you be-cause I am I, then I am not I, and you are not you."
—Traditional Hassidic saying

"But once the realization is accepted that even between the closest human beings infinite distance continues to exist, a wonderful living side by side can grow up, if they succeed in loving the distance between them which makes it possible for each to see the other whole and against a wide sky."
—Rainer Maria Rilke

"Changes within and among families in the U.S. are striking at the heart of our notions about life and the way it functions."
—Arvonne S. Fraser

We begin our journey in the realm of relationship. No other area of change touches us more immediately or poignantly.

Profound changes are at work in every type of human relat-ing—in intimacy, in the structure of the family, in friendships, as well as in larger spheres of social identification—community, na-tion, biosphere. Some of these changes are exciting. Others feel at best unsettling and at worst deeply disturbing. They tear us one way and then another, leaving us confused and often afraid to reach out.

How do we make sense of these changes? Are they good or bad? And however we judge them, what implications do they bring for relationships in the future?

In seeking answers to such questions, I find the concept of bridging immensely helpful. It doesn't give final answers or make everything fine and comfortable, but it suggests ways to cope creatively with the changes we are seeing. It also suggests that there may be creative order in what may initially seem only chaos.

Many of our most central polarities define interpersonal relationships: you and me, male and female, friend and enemy, parent and child, teacher and student, doctor and patient. Major bridgings seem to be taking place within each of these polarities. Each is asking more of us. Sometimes by choice, but as often counter to our initial intentions, we find ourselves acting in ways that make the once absolute boundaries separating these polar worlds more permeable and dynamically alive.

What is happening? As I see things, we are being challenged to a new kind of human capacity in relationship. This is the ability for two people to relate not just as halves that together make completeness, but as unique whole beings. Put in "creative" terms, this is the ability of the individual to embody the creative whole.

If this view proves accurate, it has immense implications, both for the forms that relationships will take in the future and for the very nature of relationship as felt experience. We will need to understand all relationships in larger terms. And we will need to bring new skills and sensibilities to the tasks of relationship.

This chapter focuses on our most personal spheres of relationship, first on intimacy and then on friendship and community. The core question is: *What does it mean to love as whole people?*

Loved and Lover

"The desire and pursuit of the whole is called love."
—Plato

The last few decades have brought profound upheaval to the world of intimacy. The most basic questions are now up for grabs: What does it mean to say you love someone? What does it mean to be a man, to be a woman? What does commitment mean? What defines a family?

Such questions demand new answers. More than this, they demand a newly personal relationship to them as questions. In the past, these were primarily cultural issues, addressed by the church, the law, and social convention. Suddenly, love demands that we as individuals confront these questions and that we respond from the deepest, most personal levels of who we are.

A story further illustrates this present day challenge:

John and Lisa had been married for ten years in what they described as a storybook relationship. Then over the course of a year, to use their words, "everything started falling apart." They began to argue, usually over seemingly inconsequential things. Efforts to communicate made things worse instead of better.

They decided to try therapy. Their first session served as illustration that indeed they had become good at arguing about nothing in particular. Neither could speak more than a few sentences without getting some kind of "yes but" in return.

Then in the second session, in the middle of one of their spats, John stopped suddenly, took several deep breaths, and looked at Lisa.

"I think I know some of what's the matter," he said. "Before, you were the one who would always appreciate me, listen to my stories. You made me your hero, completed me, made me whole. I think we fight because this isn't right anymore."

I asked him to say more.

"We've had a very traditional marriage. If you want my image, it would be those two figures who stood atop our wedding cake. Lisa, in a very real way, has been my 'better half.' And I've been hers too. I don't think that was wrong, but somehow it's wrong now."

"I don't like admitting it," said Lisa, "but something in that rings true. Fighting has let us be more separate—but not really separate. We don't know how to love and be separate too."

John sat forward, his eyes questioning.

"We don't know how," he said, "and perhaps more, we're just scared to do it. I'm afraid if I'm more complete in myself, I'll lose you."

"I'm afraid of losing you, too," Lisa answered immediately. "I'm afraid of losing you...as much, I think, I'm afraid of finding myself."

"There's an interesting paradox," said John. "We came in wanting to be closer, and here we are talking about being more separate."

Lisa smiled. "And for the first time in a long while we are talking about love as if we really mean it."

John and Lisa's story is their own, yet it is one that we all share. John and Lisa found that for their love to continue to be love, they would need to understand love in a new way.

As a therapist, I frequently work with couples and families. In my training, I was taught that if a family was in pain, something was wrong, broken. My task was to help in fixing it. The best teachers went a bit further. Sometimes a family could experience pain because it was in transition. My task then was to help the family make that transition in a healthy way.

More and more, however, I encountered situations like that of John and Lisa where neither of these views seemed enough. A couple would come for help, confused and in pain. But nothing seemed "broken" in any traditional sense. And although their difficulties showed the hallmarks of transition, it was transition of a different sort than I'd been taught to deal with.

My feeling response to these couples surprised me most. I felt compassion for their confusion, but at the same time I felt admiration and even gratitude.

Over time, I realized that I did not respond as if something was wrong because fundamentally nothing was. The couple's pain and confusion came from their attempt to deal with an invisibly expanding cultural reality. The rules of intimacy were changing, and they were trying to find ways to cope with the consequences. However unwittingly they had taken the role, I was responding to them, appropriately, as pioneers.

I see such pioneers turning the first few pages in a new chapter in the story of love. The changes they risk are not at all easy. But these changes promise important new meaning and fulfillment, personally and within the bond of love.

We tend to think of love's dance as pretty much a constant in the human condition. Love is love. Yet, in fact, love by all evidence is—like every other aspect of human reality—evolutionary, mani-

The intimate bond has been a dynamic in which two people, as halves, together formed a creative whole. (Clark Gable and Vivien Leigh, "Gone With the Wind," Turner Entertainment Company.)

festing in unique and growing ways as an expression of our place in cultural time.

In most recent times, the intimate bond has been a dynamic in which two people as halves, man and woman, created a whole. Each person supplied one of the hands of truth; the ritual of matrimony joined these two hands.

My grandparents exemplified this kind of love. They met in grade school and were inseparable throughout their lives. When one died, the other died soon after. The primary "organism" of their existence was quite literally the whole created by the two of them together.

While this image once worked well, it appears to be simply not big enough for who we have become. For love to sustain itself, more is needed.

We do try mightily to make the old image work, but increasingly when one part of us attempts to make someone our other half, we can count on another part to undermine it. We create struggle, find ways to put the other off, and, in short, do anything to regain our embryonic yet critical connection with this next challenge in the evolution of love. At some level we know that however enticing love in the old sense might be, falling for it would be a mistake: It would make us less.

The idea of bonding as two halves is a hard security to surrender. However, we have no choice but to step beyond it. In the future, we will likely either learn to love in this new and larger way or be without love.

The challenge is a major bridging. Put simply, we are being asked to love as whole people—to love not as man and woman[1] in the sense of essentially separate species who fit together to form a single being, but to love each other as full beings. This process bridges masculine and feminine and, more fundamentally, it bridges between the loved and the lover in ourselves.[2]

Plato's dictum that love is the pursuit of the whole takes on a new completeness in meaning. Love has always been about finding

---

[1] For the sake of simplicity I will speak of intimate love between men and women. The observations are equally relevant to intimate love between men and between women.

[2] It is important to note that from an evolutionary perspective, two-halves-make-a-whole relating is not wrong, but simply no longer timely. Feeling the need to move beyond our brave knight and fair maiden mythology, it is tempting to reject it harshly, darken it with words like oppression or dependency. As I see things, doing this cheats us by making pathology where in fact we witness the wonder of creation in time.

In its timeliness, in fact, the romantic/heroic ideal was no less radical than the image that now presents itself. Implicit within it was the profound, and at that archetypal wholeness. The difference now is that the primary locus of this wholeness is shifting from the interpersonal to the intrapsychic. Increasingly, we can find wholeness with another only to the degree we can do so while staying whole in ourselves.

The question of what it means to love as whole people is not an easy one. Bridging here asks much more of us than we at first imagine.

There are many ways to miss the mark in our thinking. For example, we might think that being whole means being complete in oneself, or self-sufficient. In one sense it does mean this. But if being whole in love meant some final extrapolation of the rugged individualist, we wouldn't be talking about a new kind of love, but about the end of love. The wholeness we need to learn about demands more than the atomistic, individualistic wholeness of Newton's world—here is one apple, there is another. In creative wholeness, "living" wholeness, interconnectedness has as fundamental a role as distinction.

We might also confuse being whole in love with the feelings of collective caring that come with spiritual love. But spiritual love, even of a deep and mature sort, is not the same as personal love. Indeed, people strongly attracted to spiritual love often have quite low capacity for making authentic whole-person bonds.

Given that we are rank beginners at grasping what whole-person love means, what *can* we say about love in this new, larger sense?

When working with people exploring questions of whole-person intimacy, I often ask them what they find most helpful in learning to love in this larger way. While each person has his or her own language, three themes most stand out: the need for a new "measure" for love, the importance of rhythm, and the re-owning of projections.

---

time heretical, notion that love might be a thing of individual choice. The late medieval troubadours sang of romantic love, but as something idealized and unrequited. Mates were chosen by the family or by a village matchmaker. In an important sense the families or villages, rather than the couple, were the "bodies" that loved. The realization of love as romantic choice was a profound step forward in the creative empowerment of the individual. (See the concept of the Sphere of Personal Identification in *The Creative Imperative*.)

Most often emphasized is the need for a shift in referent, a shift in what we use to "measure" what is right and true in relationship. In the past, clear externals guided us—gender roles and culturally defined images decreed how we should act when we are "just friends," dating, or married. For whole-person relationships, these aren't enough.

Loving as wholes challenges us to make our referent in love that which is uniquely right and timely between two people. Framed creatively, our measure becomes the degree to which new life is brought into being, the degree that in our touching "one plus one" comes to equal more than two.

In a sense, the needed new referent is simpler than our old measure. It doesn't require detailed knowledge of intricate codes of behavior. Yet it asks much more of us. It asks a greatly expanded sensitivity to relationship as living process and in this to what makes relationship creatively vital. It asks that we learn to measure love directly rather than in terms of the symbols we attach to it.

In no sense does the use of a more fluid measure imply a lessening of the importance of commitment in relationship. Indeed, it demands a much greater sensitivity to commitment. Commitment is the "container" that holds the "life" of relationship. The change is that in whole-person relationship, commitment, rather than being predefined by culture, is made in a way that honors each relationship as a unique process.

An essential shift happened in John and Lisa's relationship when they decided to stop arguing about what the other should be and instead focus on what seemed to work. They played with the metaphor of an "aliveness thermometer" with a scale from one to a hundred. They watched to see when things grew more and less creatively alive and shared what they noticed.

They saw lots of surprises. Some things they had assumed were essential to their love turned out instead to get in its way. For example, they had always set everything aside to be together at dinner time. They discovered that two or three times a week this felt important. More than this became hassle and obligation. Other things they had not even noticed turned out to be essential—a moment for a quick kiss before they went off their separate ways, for example. They played together with what it would mean to shape their relationship uniquely as an expression of what felt alive and true between them.

This was a very new way of relating. Without the old guidelines, they often felt insecure. But they realized they were, in fact, following the path with greatest security. They were now using the real stuff as their guide. Instead of love's cultural packaging, they were using love itself.

As John and Lisa played with this new way of defining love, they realized they needed a new image for their marriage. When John had mentioned the couple on the wedding cake, both of them realized this image was now not enough. An image was needed that better reflected that their relationship was unique and that it was a process, something alive and growing.

They came up with the image of a small clay bowl in which lay some stones, a bit of earth, and a small tree. On first playing with it, they felt surprise—and concern—at how simple, and in a way embryonic, it seemed. But each felt deeply moved by the experience of it, both by how precious it felt to them and by how deeply they felt committed to it. They spent time exploring the question of what they would need to risk to keep it vital, and how, if at all, they might like it to grow and change with time. John and Lisa had found a new "measure" for what was right and true in their relationship.

The second commonly expressed theme stresses the importance of being conscious of rhythm in a relationship. Living relationship, like all creative process, breathes, moving between times of deep connection and times of separateness.

At the cultural level, an important change is happening with these essential rhythms. We did not need to pay them much concern in the past. If I married and carried out my gender expectations, the rhythms of when I worked, when I was at home, when I'd be together with my spouse, and even what we'd do when we were together were largely predetermined. This is no longer so. Whole-person relationships require a profound new sensitivity and ongoing consciousness to the dance between "oneness" and "twoness" that lies at the heart of love.

In working with couples, I often provide exercises to help them develop this consciousness. For example, I might have them take out paper and pen and write down the amount of time in the next week they would like to spend together and what they'd do. My interest lies in having them become conscious of the rhythms of relationship—when it feels good to be close, when space is needed. This deceptively simple exercise rarely fails to evoke important insights.

For John and Lisa it was particularly powerful. They realized several things. First, they saw how they'd never fully acknowledged the importance of separateness in intimacy. Parts of them really believed that if they loved someone, they would want to be with that person all the time. Acknowledging this shared myth and how far it lay from the truth brought a refreshing sense of freedom into their relationship.

With this acknowledgment came the awareness that real oneness and real twoness were each difficult. John and Lisa had tended, as most people do, to live from a safe middle ground. Each had fears, both of being really alone and of being really close. They saw that for their relationship to continue to be vital, they would need to be willing to take new risks in both directions.

Finally, they noticed an interesting polar pattern in who voiced the different parts of rhythm. Lisa tended to speak for oneness, frequently expressing the desire to be closer and to have more time together. John, by being too busy for this to happen, unconsciously acted out the voice of separateness. It was powerful for Lisa to realize that she didn't really want as much time together as she had imagined. In seeing how she often sabotaged closeness when she got it, she could begin to own her own need for distinction. It was equally powerful for John to take responsibility for how he had used his work to create separateness and for him to begin to take more initiative in making time to be close.

This example of polar roles nicely introduces the third commonly expressed theme: the re-owning of projections. Part and parcel of two-halves-make-a-whole relationships is the ascribing of some major part of oneself to the other person.

In our example, John made Lisa the "one who would always appreciate me," the part of him that received, cared, and nourished. In marrying her, he gave half of himself to her for safekeeping. Lisa returned the compliment, making John her "answer," the part of the whole she needed to feel complete. People comment that recognizing what has been "given over" to the other person provides one of the most powerful tools for finding wholeness in relationship.

I often use symbolic dialogues to help people re-own parts of themselves that they have "loaned out." Both Lisa and John made use of this kind of exploration in our work together.

In one session I asked Lisa for an image for the part she had given to John. "Well, it's that figure on the wedding cake," she said, "strong, kind, protecting, attentive."

"You know," she added, "I've tried hard to get him to be that for me. And at times he's done a pretty good job. But he's never really pulled it off. Now I see why. I was asking him to be something for me that another person cannot be."

I had Lisa place the image from the wedding cake in a chair in the room and begin to talk with it. Bit by bit, she began to own it as part of herself. At the same time, she saw that the person who she had thought she was—this person who looked to the attention of others, particularly men, to measure her self-worth—was, as well, only one part of her. She set up a second chair for this part. From her "third space" chair, she spoke to each of these parts about the more whole person she felt herself becoming. From here, she experienced herself as her own primary source of validation. She began to feel at once less dependent on John and more open to him as a person.

John did a similar three-chair conversation with the part of himself that he had given to Lisa and the part he had consequently become. He discovered in his projected "feminine" aspect a part with a keen sensitivity to feelings and things in the environment. At the same time, he found new freedom in being able to relinquish the role of the responsible one. The new completeness he discovered through these conversations brought a new appreciation both for Lisa and for himself.[3]

---

[3] I don't wish to imply that the projections of intimacy are simply a giving of the feminine to the woman and the masculine to the man. This is the most common central dynamic, but what happens is always more subtle, multilayered, and individual than this alone.

Whole-person relationship asks of us a new maturity in love. The demands are paradoxical. It asks that we accept, to use Lily Tomlin's delightful phrase, that "we are all in this alone"—that there is no other who will make us happy forever after simply by his or her presence. Yet it also invites a profound new capacity for closeness. For the first time, we are learning what it means to fully love another.

Masculine and Feminine

"Women have strengths that have no name."
—Betty Friedan

If men and women are not to be viewed as separate species, each the "opposite sex" to the other, how do we best understand their differences? This is an immensely important question for how we think of ourselves. And its answer bears critical implications for what love will look like in the future.

Finding a "third space" here is tricky. We find it difficult to step beyond arguing either that men and women are essentially the same or that they are essentially different. Yet neither view wholly satisfies.

In the past, there wasn't an issue. Men were men, and women were women, and that was that. In contrast, today we frequently hear it proposed that few, if any, inherent differences exist between men and women, that the dissimilarities we see are simply products of conditioning. But while unisex perspectives work well to get us beyond sex role stereotypes—which now clearly limit us—they seem not enough. Spend much time with them and they can't help but leave one a bit cold, even a little frightened that one might wish for this sameness.

We need something more if we are to learn to appreciate fully ourselves and each other. We need ways of thinking that let us affirm both individual uniqueness and the essential gift of gender, dynamic ways of bridging the old absolutes of masculine and feminine.

This issue of how we are the same and how we are different is of much more than just academic importance. It defines the most pivotal question concerning love in the future: What will make love work?

The "glue" that previously determined commitment in relationship was precisely the two-halves-make-a-whole dynamic that we are leaving behind. This central force bound both the pragmatics and passions of love. Our ability to add reliably to each others' lives relied on the inherent complementarity of interlocking sex roles. And the experience we most associate with love—the magnetism of romance—arose as a direct function of our polar halves and the electricity that inextricably links them.

If men can embody the feminine and women the masculine, and if each can perform most of the tasks that used to lie in the other's province, where lies sufficient motivation for any depth of bonding? Clearly there is still sex, but for the task of committed relationship our erotic touchings are rarely enough. As we come to the place of greatest potential for fully personal intimate love, are we also losing any real reason to risk it?

My hunch is that love will survive, but it will certainly ask more of us than in the past. Our growing capacity to approach relationship as process, as a gradual exploring of what is uniquely right for two whole people, should play an important role in making this possible. Equally important, I suspect, will be a new, more vital and mature whole-person relationship to gender.

How might we approach the question of gender more integrally? I find a simple awareness useful for getting started. Gender, as we commonly use the term, refers not just to one thing, but to at least three related but separate variables: biological gender, gender role, and gender archetype. Understanding the relationships between these variables—how they influence one another, and particularly how these influences evolve through time—can take us several important steps down the path toward the thinking we seek.

Biological gender is pretty clear cut. With rare exception, once we get past paramecia and the like, nature counts in two's. We get either two X chromosomes or an X and a Y, and with them a recognizable package of plumbing and padding.

Gender roles present the particular attitudes and actions that a specific culture at a certain time defines as right and appropriate for male or female behavior. Patterns are recognizable between cultures, but significant variations—even flip-flops—occur between what is considered masculine in one culture and feminine in another.

The third concept, gender archetype, I introduced earlier in talking about the "softer" and "harder" sides of things. We all have certain polar qualities simply as a function of being human and alive. Because men and women tend to embody greater and lesser amounts of these qualities, we tend to think of them in gender terms. Some of the more familiar "masculine/feminine" polarities are reflected in juxtapositions such as expressing and receiving, doing and being, and thinking and feeling. Framed in terms of creation, the archetypally feminine is that half of us which responds most to the fragile beginnings of things and to context. The archetypally masculine is that part concerned more with creation as manifestation, with content, action, and structure. In terms of polarity, the feminine speaks more the language of oneness, the masculine that of distinction.

Immense variation occurs in the balance of these qualities in different people. Archetypally masculine qualities may predominate in a woman, archetypally feminine in a man. And there are normative differences. Overall, there seems to be about a 60/40 balance relative to gender.[4]

Gender archetype is a good place to start in addressing new relationship and the challenges of gender, for here the primary change process is most clearly framed. Being whole in relationship means learning to live and love in such a way that each person embodies the archetypal entirety. It means that a woman must own the parts in her that are more archetypally masculine equally with the feminine—a man the reverse.

---

[4] The physical evidence suggests that this balance reflects more than just conditioning. Even when men and women engage in similar activities, women's tissues tend to remain softer to the touch, and men's remain more solid. With this, we find important differences in where men and women carry both their physical and emotional "weight" (both their physical mass and where they are most "present" in their bodies). Men tend to carry themselves higher, more in the chest and arms; women, on the average, carry themselves several inches lower, more in the belly and pelvis, closer to the earth.

What implications arise from this? For one thing, it makes gender roles, in any absolute sense, obsolete. Gender roles have served a specific and important purpose. They've given us our means for creating predictable two-halves-make-a-whole identities. Gender-role signals caricature archetypal qualities. The cut of men's suits gives the image of shoulders that look broader and stronger than they are; dresses emphasize connection downward, and such things as lace, bows, and soft colors exaggerate women's natural receptive signals. By taking subtle normative differences in archetypal balance and depicting them as qualitative distinction, gender roles tell us which parts of ourselves to claim and which to project.

In a whole-person reality, this creative purpose ceases to exist. In the future we should find ourselves recognizing what, in fact, has always been the case—that male and female attitudes describe not two separate domains, but interplaying realms of choice within a continuum of potential ways of being.

Does this then mean that at least in terms of attitudes and behavior, men and women are essentially the same? Certainly it suggests that we must step beyond thinking in terms of categories and perceive instead in terms of tendencies. It also suggests that if we want to talk about tendencies, we need to do so with a keen appreciation for the immensity of individual variation. For most characteristics where we see normative differences, the variation within each gender is significantly greater than the average difference between them.

But we remain a step short of a fully integral perspective. An image of gender as a continuum of qualities helps us step beyond absolutes, but such an image leaves us dangerously close to what I earlier called a compromise fallacy. It is not fully this. A pure compromise fallacy equates equality with unisex equivalence. But it leaves us still short of the fully living, "third space" perspective we seek. With increasing frequency, I hear people express that although we need to leave behind gender stereotypes, we also need to find ways to affirm the essential gift of gender.

What is the missing piece? Thus far we've set aside our first gender variable, the body. And while relegating mind and body to separate realities has been acceptable in the past, as we shall see in future chapters, it won't do for times ahead.

When we include both mind and body in questions of gender, the picture becomes much more dynamic and interesting. From the perspective of the mind, male/female differences appear quantitative, if they exist at all. But from the perspective of the body, differences are decidedly qualitative. *Vive la difference!*

The "third space" challenge is to embrace the greater "living" whole of these mutually exclusive realities. We are much more similar than we've ever imagined. Yet, when we take off our polarized spectacles, one of the things that seems most obvious and important is that, as men and women, we will always remain special gifts and mysteries to one other.

The implications for relationship? In the future we will have to do without our old reflex magnetisms. But we will likely find ourselves increasingly sensitive to the differences we do find and to the particular sorts of power and beauty that being a woman or being a man can offer. We will have greater appreciation of individual differences. At the same time we will more deeply cherish the special nuances that gender brings to experience.

Self and Other

"In the deepest sense we all dream not out of ourselves,
but out of what lies between us and the other."
                                            —C. G. Jung

Two other kinds of relationships have particularly intimate places in our lives: friendship and community.

Actually, we've already made a start with friendship. Whole-person intimacy involves a dual bridging. Along with Masculine and Feminine, it bridges Self and Other. To be intimate as wholes also requires discovering the meaning of whole friendship.

At first glance, friendship doesn't seem to have much to do with polarities. Particular friendships can have polar dynamics, such as a Don Quixote and Sancho Panza, or a Laurel and Hardy. But mostly friends are just people who like each other, right?

Not quite. In fact, polarity plays as much a part of friendship as it does of intimacy. And our ability to be larger than these polarities will be equally important for the tasks of life ahead.

We easily miss the polar dynamic for a fairly simple reason. The polarity lies someplace else—outside the overt relationship. We get a strong hint about the dynamic in a common phrase defining friendship: A friend is someone who is "on our side." Traditionally, friendship has been based on a hidden polarity—our side and theirs.

The other half of this dynamic is a tacit agreement to play "answer" for one another by acting out the myth that as friends our realities are essentially the same. Traditional friendship, no less than traditional intimacy, has been a two-halves-make-a-whole dynamic.

More and more frequently in my daily life I'm struck by how friendships with a hidden two-halves-make-a-whole dynamic simply no longer satisfy. In my weaker moments I may want someone to be "on my side." But if someone falls for the invitation, I resent our collusion. Though it makes life less safe and predictable, I ultimately want friends who have the courage and capacity to be whole people with me. And I want to offer this in return. Increasingly, I find both colleagues and clients voicing similar sentiments.

Whole-person friendship is not easy. But, again, it is not really a question of choice. This simply is what friendship, as something alive and creative, is becoming. Two-halves-make-a-whole friendship, like role-defined intimacy, is becoming vestigial. Just as in intimate bondings, in friendship we are being asked to engage in relationship with a new maturity and to learn skills and sensibilities new to us as a species.

These new skills and sensibilities are not qualitatively different from those basic to whole-person love. We need to replace allegiance as the basis of friendship with a more living, dynamic referent, with a sensitivity to each relationship's unique life as a creative process. We need to be newly sensitive to the rhythms of relationship, to their necessary inhalations and exhalations, ebbs and flows. And we need to remain ever conscious of our projections, of the ways we can collude to protect ourselves from how big life asks us to be.

These kinds of skills will be critical in the future. As with intimacy, we are losing much that in the past made friendships work. Good friendships have become rare in our time. In the future, more and more, fulfilling friendships will require conscious commitment and new, more sophisticated sensibilities.

Close to this question of friendship lies the issue of community. Sharing in community, like friendship, used to be pretty much a given. We grew up in neighborhoods and lived in close, extended families. Today few people retain strong group bonds.

People increasingly express a desire for community in their lives. It seems to be a critical future need. But as with new intimacy and new friendship, the task is much greater than simply resurrecting familiar forms. The kind of community the future asks of us differs in essential ways from what we knew in the past.

The foundations of community historically rested on such things as blood ties and shared dogmas. Imbedded in this two-halves-make-a-whole dynamic has always been some notion, subtle or not, of a "chosen people," of an "our side" and a "theirs."

Old images of community are not big enough for who we have become. Because this is generally not recognized, modern attempts at "intentional" community—from simple shared ownership of land or dwellings to fuller communal experiments—have, more often than not, gone sour. Either the experiment was short-lived, the ideal and people's need for private lives coming into conflict, or it endured, but precisely because it appealed to regressive needs (often, as at Jonestown, with disastrous results).

Just as two-halves-make-a-whole love and friendship no longer serve, neither does community as we have known it. The challenge here is parallel: to meet and grow together as whole people. And again, the first step is to acknowledge that we are beginners at this.

At the Institute for Creative Development, questions of whole-person community are an ever-present part of our interactions. Such questions challenge not just because it is nice to get along, but because if we are not together in big enough ways, we will fail to see and deal with the issues we come together to confront.

Several months ago I walked in as the core think tank group prepared to convene. People were making tea, starting a fire in the fireplace, and settling into the room. As I stood by the door, I was struck by the immense depth of caring between these people. Tears came to my eyes.

In a certain way the strength of the bonds I felt in the room took me by surprise. It's not that I hadn't noticed before, or that I hadn't acknowledged that our bonds were important. But we'd never done much consciously to build our sense of group. Our commitment was simply to meet and to confront as courageously as we could the questions in the world that mattered most to us. I realized as I stood there that we could not have designed a better "technique" for becoming authentically close.

The question at the heart of new community is both simple and profound: What does it mean to be a community of unique individuals? What does it mean for bonds to grow, not through the collusion of shared belief, but through the gradual discovery of how in our connections we can make each other, and life as a whole, creatively more?

The challenge of whole-person relating—in love, in friendship, in community—is at once exciting and humbling. We couldn't ask for more than the richness that this more mature bonding makes possible. And taking on that challenge means being continually reminded of how young we are in the task of making real this next chapter in the story of human relationship.

Traps

Separation Fallacies:	I do my thing—you do yours; girls are girls and boys are boys (and boys are better); there are friends and there are enemies.
Unity Fallacies:	Love is being one together; girls are girls and boys are boys (and girls are better); all you need is love.
Compromise Fallacies:	Love means always meeting the other half way; the unisex ideal.

Bridgings

Love is creative and rhythmic—a dance between the singular wholeness of our meeting and the separate wholenesses that we each are unto ourselves.

The task of gender completeness for a man is to be whole as a man; for a woman to be whole as a woman.

A friend is not just someone "on my side," but someone who, by his or her influence, makes my life more.

CHAPTER FIVE

US AND THEM: THE GLOBAL CHALLENGE

"It may seem melodramatic to say that the United States and Russia represent Good and Evil. But if we think of it that way, it helps to clarify our perspective on the world struggle."
—Richard Nixon

"The love of country has succeeded at bridging people at the national level. The great new historical challenge is the development of love among all of the earth's inhabitants, and for the earth itself."
—Sigmund Freud, in an exchange of letters with Albert Einstein

"We have met the enemy, and he is us."
—Pogo (Walt Kelly)

We shift our attention now to a sphere that might initially seem as far from our first focus as we could get. From the personal and intimate we turn to the political, to questions of relationship at the scale of nation, region, and planet.

A most amazing drama is presently unfolding on the world stage. Parts of the drama inspire, suggesting that one of humanity's most fond hopes and dreams could, with time, come to pass. Other parts frighten so absolutely that we can hardly open our eyes to their implications.

The reflex animosities that drove the Cold War show signs of breaking down. We wonder: Could we learn to live in peace? This time, instead of replacing familiar hatreds with new ones, can we learn to live with some semblance of mutual caring and cooperation?

At once, we face that the nuclear genie's escape from its bottle has irrevocably altered the human story. Animosities of any degree place us in profound peril. Peace has shifted from the realm of ideals and possibilities to that of an imperative. Either we learn to relate with others on the planet in new ways, and do so quickly, or we will not be here to relate.

Although love and world politics may seem far removed, the challenges at these extremes of relationship are kindred. Each sphere asks us to bridge, to find new maturity and wholeness in our relating. Love demands that as individuals we learn to relate as wholes; the future well-being of the planet demands a parallel capacity for wholeness and maturity in our cultural relatings.

Nothing could be more important than exploring what this means. In this chapter we take a few steps together over the threshold into this larger understanding. The core question asks: *What does it mean to relate culturally as wholes?* We will briefly explore three bridgings—Ally and Adversary, War and Peace, and the political Left and Right—that relate to this critical capacity.

Ally and Adversary

"If we could read the secret history of our enemies, we should find in each man's life sorrow and suffering enough to disarm our hostilities."
—Henry Wadsworth Longfellow

A brief story sets the stage:

I had a high draft lottery number. My friend Jim did not. I stopped by as he was packing his things to report for duty. Tears were in our eyes as we hugged good-bye.

Jim came back early from Vietnam. He had experienced a psychotic break. After some time in a hospital there, he was sent home.

Shortly after his return, I went to visit him . He tried to seem like his old self, but it was an act. He was tense, easily distracted, taken at odd moments by emotions unrelated to what was being said.

We talked at great length. At times he spoke with surprising clarity and perspective about the war. At others he would be tossed this way and that, by images of the bloodshed, by feelings of shame at having "lost it."

At one point, I asked him what memory he most associated with "losing it."

"I hadn't been in Vietnam more than a week," he said. "We were on patrol and started taking some fire. I'd never shot at a person before, for real. I aimed and got ready to return the fire. But what I saw in my sights wasn't a 'gook' or a 'Charlie,' it was a human being. I tried, but there was no way I could pull the trigger. I froze, I couldn't move…. Two of my buddies died in that exchange."

He met my eyes, and I felt the chill of that moment between us. Then, after a long moment of silence, we went on talking.

"Why do you think you couldn't pull the trigger?" I asked.

"I don't really know," he said. "Afterward I kept remembering Kim, the Chinese kid who lived down the block when I was growing up. I've always been fascinated by people from other cultures, I guess. Somehow I couldn't make the person in my gunsights the enemy, at least not enough to kill him.

"After watching my buddies die," he said, "I felt terrible guilt. I resolved that I would not freeze again. The next time I didn't. I pulled the trigger and watched the bullet blow a man's head off. The next day, I cracked up."

Human beings have never killed other human beings. They've killed japs, nazis, dinks, pagans. Look beyond the particular names and places and we see that when we have fought, we have not so much fought other people as we have fought symbols.

A remarkable consistency permeates this symbolism. Our enemies appear inhuman and greedy, immoral and sadistic. We see them as incarnations of the devil.

Why this symbolism? And why such extremes? Is it just that distortion is needed for carrying out the unpleasant but necessary task of protecting our borders from those less peaceloving than ourselves?

Although this may be part of it, the dynamic is clearly larger. A quick look at history reveals that these distortions are hardly one-way. In any conflict, each side sees itself as pure and the other as soiled.

All wars are "just" wars. For each nation that sees itself as a force for freedom and justice, another sees that same nation as a force for their antithesis. Every war is in the end, and simultaneously in each direction, a holy war, right to left and left to right, a battle between the forces of the divine and those of darkness.

The best explanation for why we have painted our cultural world in such stark black and white suggests that this has been necessary for social identity. Just as before in personal friendship we've needed an "other side" in order to define our wholeness together, so culturally we've needed a clearly delineated "other" to define the wholeness of our social bonds.

Beneath the noise and clamor of ally and adversary as clashing opposites, lies a mutual dependency. It appears that just as we have needed our friends, so we have needed our enemies. The blind absolutism of our enmities gives us away, revealing the unconscious dance of collaboration. Just as love and friendship have operated as two-halves-make-a-whole dynamics, so have our connections to those on the other side of the dark chasm of cultural dis-identification.

This is not to say that history has had no Hitlers. I do not suggest that we succumb to the trap of making politics nothing but psychology (an easy unity fallacy). Our images of the enemy have not all been projection—or perhaps more accurately, history has occasionally given us figures that required little stretching on the part of our projections. As is popularly acknowledged, even paranoids have real enemies. But it is increasingly clear that in the big picture it is not sufficient to look, as has been our wont, on the characteristics we ascribe to our enemies as objective facts of the external world.

A look at the rogue's gallery of twentieth century "enemies of democracy" reveals these polar dynamics. If it were indeed the case that the world is composed of "good people" and "evil people," then we should expect that our enmities would stay relatively stable through time. But in fact, the group that holds our dark images shifts with remarkable rapidity. First the Chinese were good, then they were evil, then good (though now again not so good). The

Soviets were good, then bad (though now starting to be okay at times); the Japanese were bad, then good (though now that they are outdoing the West economically, maybe not as good as we thought). How willingly our memory steps aside in service of our need for an "evil other."

What do we give away in this particular two-halves-make-a-whole dynamic? What do we hand to the other for safekeeping? Carl Jung had a good word for it—our "shadow." We give to the other all the feelings and tendencies inconsistent with our self-images as "good" people. By giving our rejected qualities to another, we can affirm our polar self-concept as the "chosen ones," the children of the light.[1]

Upon recognizing our projections, we are easily self-critical. However, I see our past projections not as bad but as part of a dynamic that once had purpose, but that now no longer serves. In its time, the reflex to project fulfilled important needs. It helped us to bond. And it helped us to keep parts of ourselves that as social wholes we were not developmentally "big" enough to manage at a safe arm's length. Bridging good and evil culturally is a large order, something that previously lay simply beyond our reach.

But this is changing. People are beginning to see through their consensual paranoias.

Several factors seem to contribute to such a larger view becoming possible. The simple fact of our increasingly global world offers a major one. On a daily basis, we meet our potential "others" face to face and heart to heart. The more this happens, the harder it becomes to make our projections stick. Jim and his childhood friend illustrate this.

More deeply, we experience our growing capacity, as individuals and societies, to embody that creative whole. Hard as we might

---

[1] Such shadow projections include both "right-handed" and "left-handed" elements. Enemy images express the shadow elements of the archetypally masculine in being characteristically large, looming, and tyrannical. At the same time, in being characteristically dark, seductive, and devious, they express shadow elements of the archetypally feminine.

The projection of our cultural "shadows" onto other peoples not only fails to serve the tasks of identity, with modern arsenals, it becomes a formula for world destruction. (TOP—Sergei Elkin, Voronezh, U.S.S.R.; BOTTOM—David Miller, *San Francisco Examiner.* Both from the U.S.S.R.-U.S.A. Cartoon Exchange.)

try, we increasingly find it less than satisfying to project our cultural demons. At some level we know how much less we are being than what is possible—and necessary. Rather than swelling our chests with pride, blind nationalism, when confronted within, increasingly makes us feel unsettled and small. This is gradually becoming so for both the common person and for the political leader. In a Kremlin speech in May 1988, we hear Mikhail Gorbachev declaring that "habitual stereotypes stemming from enemy images have been broken loose."

What does it mean to have whole-person—now "whole system"—relationships between groups on the planet, between our planet's various cultural "bodies?" Recognizing that the old mythos of good peoples and bad peoples must be left behind doesn't get us over the conceptual threshold. It just acknowledges the threshold's presence.

As a start we can say something about what whole-system relating is not. As with new relationships between friends and lovers, wholeness here is not the simple concept that it might appear to be. It doesn't at all suggest that we should ignore difference, that we should replace this stark black and white with images of sameness. Some relationships on the global scene are safe; others require real caution. And even where relationship is safe, a world without the rich tapestry of human difference would be an empty place indeed.

The task is to engage global relations fully as "relationship," not as the knee-jerk push and pull of mythic parts, but as the creative meeting of living wholes. This means being able to appreciate our common humanity. It also means appreciating the irreplaceable gifts of unique traditions and heritages. It means being willing to listen, to hear in the voice of the other our shared purpose. And it means remaining willing to stand firm when the quarrel is real. It means joining together in the profound task of realizing vital planetary "community."

War and Peace

"Onward Christian soldiers, marching as to war."
—Traditional Hymn

The need to bridge Ally and Adversary won't arouse much disagreement. But to bridge Us and Them in a way that can achieve the kind of peace the future demands requires a further bridging, the suggestion of which easily brings confusion, even animosity. This further bridging spans War and Peace as we have conventionally conceived them.

"Surely this polarity is clear cut," we hear ourselves say. "War is bad; peace is good." But again, things are not so simple. The kind of peace needed for the future differs fundamentally from our popular notions about peace. Indeed I would suggest that common ideas about peace contribute to making peace in this larger sense unreachable. The peace we must seek is a much more dynamic phenomenon.

I might share some of the story of how my own views about war and peace have evolved in recent years. I've found myself forced to reexamine ideas that before seemed self-evident. Views that I'd taken to be "enlightened" have shown themselves not only to involve fairly obvious projections, but to have the potential to work exactly counter to what I would want to achieve.

During Vietnam times, I was strongly opposed to the war. I opposed that particular war, but more than this, without giving it much thought, I was "anti-war." I was "on the side" of peace. During this same period, I found myself deeply drawn to exploring my Irish roots. I read Celtic mythology and learned to play Celtic music. One day in my readings I came across a description of Celtic warfare. It told of warriors going into battle naked, their bodies painted in intricate ritual designs; poets on the hilltops, telling the story of the unfolding drama below; not just men, but often women as well, taking part in the fray. I could not help but be taken by the mythic potency of the images. This was war, war of a most unabashed sort. Yet somehow I could not bring myself to condemn it.

There was something deeply powerful in it, even beautiful—somehow essential to life.

I realized then that to know myself I would need to come to grips with the part of me that could kill and acknowledge it not as evil—a part to apologize for or to try to eradicate—but as a fundamental voice in my being. I saw that to be whole, I would need to understand not just war's savagery, but its beauty as well.

And I realized something more: that it would be possible to understand peace and effectively work toward it only to the degree I could do this.

Throughout history we have deified our great warriors: Achilles and Agamemnon, Arthur and the Knights of the Round Table, Napoleon, Washington. I had to ask myself: Is this because we humans are basically vicious, that we have within us some fundamental malevolence?

Once more, truth asked me to be bigger than I had bargained for. War on any major scale is no longer consistent with survival. And a good argument can be made that war in any form, killing others as a way of dealing with conflict, is now an outmoded sentiment. But I realized when I reached deeply in myself that making war and warriors intrinsically bad is not only partial, it is in its own way violent. It cuts off something sacred. I saw that we remember our great warriors as heroes for a very good reason: They have given expression to a most important and vital part of ourselves.

Veterans, while asserting that "war is hell," often nostalgically share stories of the combat years. Many men regard their moments in combat as the times in their lives when they felt most alive. A parallel I've heard several times compares the experience of battle for a man with childbirth for a woman. Each involves pain, yet is imbued with a special, primal beauty.

In these times when peace presents such an obvious imperative, why am I going out of my way to justify war? I do so for several reasons.

I do it from a basic truth that every really effective therapist knows. Real change rarely happens from a posture of self-condemnation—"I have been bad, and now I am going to be good." Instead of growth, one gets false virtue, repression, and ultimately a prolongation of the inner struggle. Real growth happens from a para-doxical place of at once awareness and self-acceptance. It happens when a person, in his or her unique way, can say: "How I have been, virtuous or not, has worked. It has filled important needs. And now I am ready to move on."

I do so as well out of a deep love for the whole and out of a wariness of imposters as we face the critical challenges of peace. "Nice" people who side with peace and see the devil in the face of politicians, the Pentagon, or masculine aggressiveness are no less projecting their shadows, no less denying responsibility in the whole, than those who place the demonic in an external enemy. They no less project their demons, and they are ultimately no more trust-worthy with the reins of power.

The challenge requires that we conceive of peace in qualita-tively larger terms, not as the opposite of war but in a way that embodies the larger whole of the traditional war/peace duality. What does this mean? Again, recognizing the polarity only gets us to the threshold, not over it.

At the heart of the challenge is a recognition central to all kinds of relatings, personal relatings as much as relatings between coun-tries—conflict is equally as important as equanimity in real peace. We too easily make discord a problem, seeing it as the opposite of peace. But in the big picture, peace and conflict stand as anything but opposites. The Greek Philosopher Heraclitus said it centuries ago: "Out of discord comes the fairest harmony."

Conflict and equanimity present the right and left hands of living peace. Peace without room for conflict offers not peace at all, but deadness, suffocation, and tyranny. The effective pursuit of peace in an integral sense requires that a person be not only toler-ant of conflict, but understand its critical role in any creative process. If we reject our inner warrior, we will find ourselves facing its dis-torted image in our efforts at peace. In the name of peace, we will, in fact, wage righteous war.

A recent experience reminded me of conflict's essential role in real peace:

I got a telephone call from two people, Anne and Melinda, whom I had met at conferences earlier in the year. I had a lot of respect for each of them. Both were energetic and deeply committed to social issues.

But I was surprised that they would know each other. They were about as different from one another as two people could be: one a fundamentalist Christian, the other a self-described "New Ager."

On meeting they had somehow hit it off and, because they shared concerns about world hunger, had decided on a whim to teach a class together.

They asked if I would consult with them in designing the course. Since I wanted to get to know each of them better, I said I'd be glad to. I sensed some tension in their asking, but didn't think much of it.

When we got together, I immediately felt something was amiss. I asked them if they knew what was going on.

Anne said she did and that it was a big part of why they wanted the consultation. Shortly after committing themselves to do the class, they began to discover just how great their differences were. Though it was too late to do it gracefully, they were considering withdrawing the class.

They had begun to sense how polar many of their views were. And each being a "good" person, they were walking on eggshells to keep these potential conflicts from turning into open warfare.

They asked for my reflections. I shared my impression that if they really wanted to do the class—at least if they wanted it to be at all alive—they would need to take more risks with each other. Most specifically, it was clear that they had some big differences in belief, in general and in relation to the topic at hand, and that they needed to get them out on the table.

They agreed to give it a try. We started in, at first with kid gloves, but soon made good headway.

I eventually asked if each would be willing to share her greatest fear, her "paranoid fantasy" about the other's beliefs. With hesitation they said they would try.

"Melinda," Anne started, both fear and anger obvious in her voice, "I think I can respect the differences in most of our beliefs. But I'm afraid you fundamentalists will get us all killed. I've heard about the Armageddon scenario, people who believe that nuclear war is prophesied, supposed to happen to rid the earth of those who are not true believers. That scares the daylights out of me. Is it true that you people believe that? And how can that fit with all the energy you put into world hunger?"

Melinda sat uncomfortably and was quiet for some time before speaking. "Some fundamentalists do believe that," she said. "It doesn't exactly fit for me. Honestly, I don't know where I am with it. I understand how you could be concerned. In terms of the class, all I can say is that the hungry of the world are God's children and I am committed to helping them."

I suggested we turn the tables and have Melinda share her greatest fear. "It's interesting," said Melinda, "mine, like Anne's, has less to do with religion per se than with questions of how to achieve peace." Again there was tension, some anger. "I'm afraid that beneath the surface Anne is really anti-American. Communists are atheists. I don't think she understands that. My 'paranoid fantasy' is that Anne would just as soon have them run us over." She sat back in her chair, surprised at how much she had said.

Anne, like Melinda, took time to reflect, and not altogether comfortably. "I can understand some of your concerns," she said. "I don't see communism as the kind of threat you do. There is a lot I don't like about American life—its materialism, the huge discrepancies in wealth. The only thing I can say is that while I'm not that gung-ho about the American Dream, this is where I'm choosing to live, and I wouldn't be any happier about Russia invading the U.S. than I would about the U.S. invading Russia. Like you not being sure about the Armageddon stuff, I go back and forth about how wary we should be of the Soviets. Sometimes I feel like, hey, we are all just people. Other times it's clear things aren't quite that simple."

We talked this way for over an hour. The agreed task was to try neither to "win" the argument, nor to find agreement, but simply to ask questions and give responses so the real differences might be aired. I enjoyed watching the feelings unfold.

I could sense that some of their initial interest in each other was returning, but their positions were so profoundly disparate it seemed unlikely they would still want to do the class or be able to. Just to be sure, I asked them.

There was a long pause. Then a hesitant smile crept onto each face. "I'd like to try it," said Melinda. "We aren't going to have a lot of answers for them, but there sure won't be any shortage of far-flung opinions."

"I would too," said Anne. "I don't know how it will be for the students, but I'd learn a whole lot. I think the trick will be if we can stay willing to really share our differences. Melinda and I both want to end world hunger. So our goal is the same. The kinds of questions we want to address don't have textbook answers. We probably couldn't give the kids any greater gift than to let them see our differences and let them struggle with us to find solutions."

The class, as you might guess, was a great success.

Being with Melinda and Anne helped me see once again how peace and conflict ultimately work not as opposites, but as partners in the quest to live life with full integrity.

Once we accept that conflict has a place, we can leave behind the diverting drama of war set against peace and confront the real issues. A major question concerns what we are to do with the needs war has fulfilled now that war on any major scale has become incompatible with survival.

In our past war has had four primary functions. First, as we examined earlier in addressing our images of enmity, war has defined social identity. We have used it to delineate self and not-self in the social sphere.

This function should gradually become a thing of the past, though we must work actively to bring this about. With our increasingly global world and our growing capacity to embody the creative whole, seeking out "evil others" should become less and less satisfying as a means for affirming our sense of social self.

To manifest these changes, we will need not only to transcend our personal projections, but also to take strong stands for integral social policy. In the past, the most sure-fire way for a leader to garner allegiance was to create a common enemy. (Witness, for example, the rallying behind Margaret Thatcher that took place following the Falklands War.) We must refuse to fall for this kind of easy grace. Our standard for good leadership must be the ability to keep a "third space" perspective in the face of enticing polarities.

A second function served by war has been a ritualistic one. War has served as a symbolic stage upon which we've battled with the chthonic underworld of existence and acted out our need for dominion over darkness and death.[2]

This function should also grow vestigial. As we shall explore later in some detail, further chasms we are bridging lie between past concepts of both good and evil, and life and death; with integration, dark and light themselves cease being at war. In the future, we should find an ever decreasing need to ritually act out these primal relationships on the symbolic stage of social relations.

A third function has been territorial expansion. We easily deny our part in this. It is our enemies who have been the aggressors, we say; our weapons have been only for defense. History, however, belies almost all such blanket claims to innocence.

At one level, we must learn to say "no" to this face of the warrior. We have run out of room for such expansion. But the task, I would suggest, is not at all to discard this part of ourselves. We wouldn't want to throw it out, and couldn't if we did want to.

Henry James talked about "moral equivalents of war." Such are all about us—issues of environmental degradation; poverty; the need for new levels of integrity and new ideas in education, medicine, business, and government. Rather than to diminish the expansive warrior within us, the task is to bring those immense energies to bear at the critical new frontiers of human value and purpose.

The fourth function fulfilled by war has been defense of boundaries. We have fought to protect home and hearth from invasion. Because of this function, armies will always have a place:

---

[2] This need is dual and contradictory: at once to define separateness from death and mystery, and to reaffirm our ties with these primal powers.

In early cultural stages, the need for connection predominates over that for distinction. It is not uncommon in tribal warfare for conflict to proceed only until first blood is drawn, or the first of the adversary killed. This is enough to reestablish the primordial bond—with death, mystery, generativity, ancestry. Warfare often ties directly to rites of fertility.

Later in culture, distinction steps forefront. The medieval Christians, in their righteous annihilation of the "heathen hordes," were setting themselves with moral absoluteness above the "darkness and chaos" of the pagan world and, simultaneously, with similar absoluteness, above death.

However wise we become as a species, times will arise when we must protect ourselves. But to the degree we can own our cultural projections, we should get better and better at resolving conflict in ways that stop short of bloodshed.

These changes in our relationship to the past functions of war suggest that the ancient dream of world peace could indeed be realized—at least if we reframe peace in integral terms, as an ongoing creative process that includes conflict, rather than as an endpoint of blissful equanimity. As I see things, it *is* a real possibility.

Left and Right

"Truth cannot be expressed in an ideology, for truth is that which overlights the conflict of opposed ideologies."
—William Irwin Thompson

One of the most fascinating bridgings in the public arena occurs between left and right in the political spectrum. This bridging brings implications both globally—between the prevailing ideologies of capitalism and communism—and within traditional party rivalries.

Globally, major cracks are growing more and more evident in the absolutist edifices of the dominant ideological stories. Pure communist and socialist ideals are coming increasingly into question. More and more, collective ownership, at least as traditionally conceived, proves itself simply unworkable. Centrally planned economies require massive bureaucracies, imbuing them ultimately with a fatal inertia. And while the notion that collective spirit can serve as fuel for an economy may not be wholly wrong, those who have used collective forms increasingly recognize how competition can work wonders for igniting that fuel.

Since capitalism is a bit closer to home, we cannot see its shortcomings as easily. On witnessing the current tremors in world communism, it is hard for us not to raise our hands in victory, proclaim ours the right and true system. But, in fact, capitalism in any pure form remains equally partial. Its major flaws relate to the fact that its big rewards lie in short-term material gain and individual advantage. It offers little incentive for not riding the horse of profit full gallop, then simply discarding it when it tires. For the industrial revolution, this view did not work badly. For the future, unchecked, it becomes a bomb with the fuse lit. The critical economic questions ahead concern not just wealth, but quality of life, and not just quality of life for today, but for our children and our children's children. In the big picture, capitalism's flaws reveal themselves as no less potentially fatal.

In the future, we should find ourselves experimenting increasingly with new, more dynamic forms—approaches that in various ways join these hands of economic determination. We see the beginnings of this with the growing insertion of free market incentives into formerly collectivist structures. Pure communist and socialist economies are fast disappearing from the planet.

On the other side, we should find ourselves looking closely at how we can more directly address questions of the common good within free market structures while continuing to value individuality and competition. This need not come from a sudden bout of altruism, though the dynamics of bridging should give altruism a better name than it now enjoys. The growing visibility of social dynamics that impact us all—overpopulation, environmental destruction, escalating crime rates—should make it increasingly obvious that questions of the common good are ultimately inseparable from those of individual well-being.

Along with this global bridging, we should see a similar bridging within countries between the traditional ideologies of political parties. The back-and-forth warfare of partisan politics serves increasingly only to mire our good intentions in bureaucratic gridlock. Left opposed to right is simply not big enough to hold the new questions.

More and more, we should see leaders setting aside party ideologies to propose programs inconceivable from either side alone and inconceivable even through compromise. The story that opened this book illustrates movement toward such a "third space" posture with regard to traditional right/left positions on defense. Questions of global safety will require an ability to recognize commonality and common benefit, a strength in the doves' "softer" views.

Simultaneously, they will require a willingness to acknowledge differences where they exist and make needed boundaries, a strength of the hawks' more "hard-nosed" position. Even larger than the two positions combined, they will require an ability to see global relations as dynamic living processes—something possible only from a mature whole-systems perspective. The best defense in the future will be a world in which all peoples feel safe. Making this real will require the ability to conceive in terms of subtle interplays of cooperative and competitive relationships, and in terms of interactions between peoples who, by virtue of both unique traditions and places in the evolution of culture, may see the world through markedly different eyes.

Similar kinds of bridgings will be needed for all major future governmental tasks within countries, and little by little such positions are being expressed. Policy regarding the disparate conditions of our country's "haves" and "have-nots" offers a further example. From the left, we see a begrudging but growing acknowledgment that programs based solely on a Robin Hood philosophy—take from the rich and give to the poor—often do little good. If not carefully conceived, they create dependency, taking power away from precisely the hands they were meant to help. From the right, we see the beginnings of a parallel tempering of the traditional view that major discrepancies in wealth are just a part of life in a competitive world. As social ills such as crime, child abuse, and drug addiction grow ever more rampant, we hear acknowledgment even from hard-bitten conservatives that poverty makes us all poor.

In chapters ahead we will examine a wide array of major future social challenges: issues of the environment, ethics, education, labor relations, health care, and more. In every case we will find traditionally liberal and traditionally conservative viewpoints inadequate either for providing the needed solutions or for even fully framing what needs to be asked. Decisions in times ahead will require an increasing ability to think in terms of the whole living picture. This means coming to understand the larger process that left and right together comprise within each of the spheres within spheres of action that define our lives.

Traps

Separation Fallacies:	There are allies, and there are enemies. The way to peace is a strong army and the willingness to use it. Freedom lies in individualism, competition, and a free market.
Unity Fallacy:	We are all one people. The way to peace is simply to love. Freedom lies in government guaranties of equality and prosperity.
Compromise Fallacy:	The way to peace is to always seek a middle ground.

Bridgings

The task is to find identity in, at once, the power of our common humanity and the beauty of our uniqueness.

If embraced fully, equanimity and conflict are not opposites, but the left and right hands of a fully dynamic and generative peace.

The mature realization of the ideals of the political right lies in their creative marriage with the sensibilities of the left— and equally the reverse.

CHAPTER SIX

LEADER AND FOLLOWER: AUTHORITY, FREEDOM, AND EMPOWERMENT

"The old ideas and assumptions that made our institutions legitimate are being eroded. They are slipping away in the face of a changing reality, being replaced by different ideas, as yet ill-formed, contradictory, unsettling."
—George Cabot Lodge

"You must never give to another human being...your ultimate manifestation of consciousness, which is your ability to make decisions for yourself.... Understand this: no man has power except the power his followers give him."
—J. Krishnamurti

"In a master-slave relationship, the master is as bound as the slave."
—G.W.F. Hegel

So far, we have explored relationships between individuals or groups—intimates, friends, political parties, or nations—of relatively equal status. The polar dynamics have been for the most part "horizontal." Here we examine polarities where a major portion of the felt dynamic is "vertical," polarities that order relationships such as that between teacher and student, management and worker, president and populace, or parent and child—relationships in which questions of leadership, control, or hierarchy play a major role.

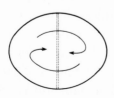 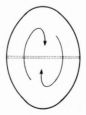

FIG. 6-1: *Horizontal and Vertical Bridgings*

We must learn to bridge the either/or's that are more vertically ordered just as surely as their more horizontal counterparts. The future will require a more dynamic understanding of both the nature of authority and the purpose and function of organizational structure.

Our times cry out for good leadership—periods of rapid change demand creative, alert, and firm decision-making. But a look around reveals that authority is in as much flux as everything else. Ways of leading that previously served us have ceased to be effective. And our faith in authority of all kinds has diminished.

Kids, it is frequently observed, are less respectful of their parents and of the institutions of culture today. The oratory of modern political leaders as often evokes weary apathy or sarcasm as the hoped-for zeal and allegiance. The honor once automatically accorded such figures as lawyers, teachers, doctors, judges, and ministers has been replaced with, at best, an unwillingness to offer one's trust so quickly and, at worst, outright cynicism. Public education and related social institutions, at one time revered with motherhood and apple pie, come under mounting scrutiny.

We might easily conclude that we are in real trouble. More than one theorist has warned that we are seeing an erosion of order frighteningly similar to that which presaged the fall of Rome.

Multiple dynamics are obviously at work here, but as I see things, the significance of these changes is ultimately more positive, or at least potentially positive. Good evidence suggests we are witnessing a fundamental redefinition of authority. The new questions require both a larger understanding of the nature of authority and new, more dynamic decision-making approaches. The needed bridgings go each way. To be effective, leadership must come to have a new and larger meaning. Along with this, the common person must come to assume a new kind of responsibility and mature power.

The core question is: *For times ahead, how do we best frame concepts of leadership and authority?* To address it, we will explore some of the potential territory beyond three kinds of polar dynamics. With Expert and Ignorant we will look at next steps in the evolution of dyadic authority relationships—doctor and patient, teacher and student, parent and child. Management and Worker will turn our attention to questions of organizational leadership. In Government and Governed we will look briefly at questions of governmental authority, with a particular focus on global determination.

Expert and Ignorant

"We get the leaders we deserve."
—Thomas Jefferson

Jefferson's words touch at two levels of meaning. Most simply, they suggest that we end up with the kind of leadership we are willing to work for. More deeply, they hint at the important sense in which leadership means not just leaders leading and followers following, but a systems dynamic in which leader and follower function together as co-generative elements in a larger creative story.

In looking at emergent challenges in the realms of intimacy and politics, I suggested that the essential, and decidedly tricky, task was to begin to move from two-halves-make-a-whole to whole-person/whole-system relating. For relationships in which the primary polarity is more vertical, the task appears to be analogous.

In the past, we have viewed expert and ignorant in whatever sphere—teacher and student, priest and supplicant, coach and athlete, parent and child—as discrete entities with a specific causal relationship. Experts were active and powerful—their task to lead; their polar complements, non-experts, filled a passive role—their task to follow.

I would suggest that the truth has always been larger and more interesting than this. But we couldn't know it, for it would have made reality too big, greater than our capacity to handle it.

This is changing. Present times challenge us to see and take ownership in the larger process of authority. And as with more horizontal polar relationships, we are beginning to respond to that challenge.

An experience early in my medical training set in high relief some of the hidden dynamics of authority and helped illuminate where we need to go:

The task of medical education as traditionally defined is to help doctors learn to diagnose and treat illness. Only a few weeks into medical school, I realized that these were not at all the only things we would be "taught." The further teachings came less overtly, more subliminally. But the emotional charge that accompanied them made it clear they were in no sense of secondary importance. I found myself fascinated with trying to understand just what was being "taught."

Although most of this second kind of teaching happened invisibly, through attitude or tone of voice, some came more directly. I remember well the controversy about wearing white coats that took place in my first year. White coats had been an assumed part of the ritual garb of the profession. Now some people said that they might not always be necessary. Many responded to this questioning almost as religious heresy.

At the time, I happened to be reading about rites of passage in primitive tribes. The parallels between these rites and this second kind of learning became immediately apparent. Along with learning skills, we were being inculcated into an order— given the ritual garb and taught the behaviors that denoted a specific role and status in the mythic whole of society.

As the year progressed, I watched the workings of this ritual process with growing curiosity, fascinated particularly with how it all took place completely beneath the surface of conscious explanation. We underwent rites of denial and asceticism (forty-eight hour stints in the Emergency Room without sleep—pity the poor patients), tests of courage (rounds with the chief of staff at the patients' bedsides where wrong answers could bring abject humiliation), and, over time, the subliminal communication of ever greater subtleties in ritual behavior and adornment (just the right way to carry one's stethoscope, proper tone of voice for talking to a patient, right pace and posture when walking about the wards).

The significance of all this took on a new dimension when in my second year I briefly became sick and found myself on the other end of the equation. Now a patient, I was profoundly struck by how much this, too, was a role. Not that I wasn't sick, but clearly here I had moved into a ritual identity as much as I had when I donned that white coat.

At first my symptoms weren't too bad, and I went about life as usual. Then they got worse. I found myself asking from some corner of my psyche if I really felt sick enough to be sick. When it was obvious that I did, indeed didn't have an option to be much else, I watched as in a curious sense I "chose" to be a patient. I saw I knew a whole array of appropriate patient behaviors and took them on one by one.

The hospital knew these behaviors as well and helped me to settle into my new role. My clothes were taken away. I was dressed in the traditional rumpled hospital gown with its unique capacity to reveal body parts that in proper society would be the last we might make public—and which in animal societies signal submission. And I was instructed that if I wished to go to the bathroom, which I felt fully capable of doing, I should ask permission.

I remember sharing my observations on "patient as mythological character" with a fellow medical student who came to visit. She related to me something she had just read about the ritualized behavior of the sick in a particular tribe in New Guinea. When people became ill, they went to their huts, covered themselves with ash and dirt, and even changed their voices, responding to questions in a trembling falsetto.

I saw that in a similar way, on entering the hospital, I took on a very specific social identity. I was to be weak and helpless and to look outside myself to the external expert for any answers. I was to be literally the "patient" one.

My medical education was teaching me the other side of this mythological relationship. I was learning the postures and intonations of the one who sees and does, the sacred keeper of the truth.

Seeing the doctor/patient relationship in this light evoked several responses in me. It brought a sense of awe that the human creature could evolve such intricacies of behavior. And it brought a deepened commitment to a next step in our evolution and a new sensitivity to what that might entail.

A common first reaction on seeing the mythic ingredient in traditional authority is distaste. We interpret the symbolic trappings as simply expressions of the authority's need for god-like status. But if we stop with this first response, we shortchange ourselves.

The symbolization of authority has, in fact, served us in essential ways. The two-halves-make-a-whole nature of the leader/follower relationship has been critical to successfully carrying out the tasks of such relationships.

The doctor/patient relationship makes a good example. Until very recently, neither doctor nor patient could have tolerated the immense uncertainty inherent in the healing endeavor without the protecting belief structure of this symbolism. More than this, actual healing took place by virtue of its power. Today we use words like "suggestion" or "placebo effect." In the past, this power manifested through incantations, rituals, and potions. We are only beginning to recognize the extent to which healing takes place through a symbolic linking with authority.

And, just as two-halves-make-a-whole relationships in intimacy and friendship are ceasing to be enough, so we find emergent reality demanding that we relate in larger ways within traditionally hierarchical relationships. The challenge is analogous: to meet as wholes.

We are just beginning to glimpse the meaning of authority in this larger, more creative sense. At the simplest level, it means that as "leaders" we must learn to catalyze and enable as well as direct. We must understand that good leadership involves following as much as leading—learning from and being directed by the larger truth of relationship as a creative process. As "followers" it means owning the strength and significance of our place in that relationship. We must learn to be conscious, empowered co-participants in the creative realization of "authority."

I use the term "integral leadership" to speak of the whole-person kind of authority our times demand. As with other integral concepts, it is a subtle, multifaceted notion—one-liners will not sufficiently define it. In working with groups of professionals, I frequently make integral leadership the central theme. I start by challenging the group with the idea that we have no choice but to learn to lead—to manage, to teach, to heal—in larger ways than we have known before. Then, to bring a sense of what we are dealing with into the room, I have people share personal awarenesses and experiences that they sense may relate to such new authority. Remarkably consistent themes emerge across domains and professions. A few snippets, starting with comments from physicians, follow:

"A major change for me has been getting better at listening. I have to admit I started doing it first because my practice wasn't doing that well, and you hear so many complaints about doctors not caring. I find myself forever amazed by and grateful for what this simple change gave me. In what people say about their illnesses, I'm hearing things that completely passed me by before. I'm just learning a lot about life, too."

"I've been working on how best to present options to patients. The right thing is often really different with different patients. I want each person to know that the final choice in what happens to them is theirs. At the same time it is important that I share what I think the best option or options may be—that is part of what I'm being paid for. It is easy to err on either side—being too much the authority or holding back."

"I think I'm seeing more clearly just what my part is in healing. I used to put it all on my shoulders, expect myself to understand and do it all—in effect be God. You know, what we doctors do is really pretty small—we sew up cuts, offer pills that do this and that, we care. Most of what happens in healing is a mystery. It's sort of paradoxical, but admitting the limitations of what I do is making me a much better physician."

Teachers have similar reflections:

"The big one for me has been working at letting myself be affected by my students. I think in the end I have robbed both myself and the student if I don't find at least some way for each student to be my teacher."

"I've always said I wanted students who aren't afraid to ask questions and get a little messy trying to deal with them. I'm finally realizing if that is going to happen, I've got to be willing to get messy myself. I'm working at being better at not knowing, at diving into the questions with them, at letting myself feel confusion, curiosity, wonder."

"I'm exploring being more versatile and flexible in how I teach. Sometimes standing up there and being the teacher works just fine. But as often, the most powerful thing is to just get out of the way. To teach effectively, I need to be willing to wear all kinds of garb, be part grand inquisitor, part muse, part cheerleader, part village idiot, part marine corps drill sergeant. Different kids and different moments need such different things."

And the comments of parents reveal similar themes:

"I'm learning at new levels what it means to appreciate my daughter for just who she is. Before I had her, someone gave me Kahlil Gibran's quote about our children not being ours, but just ours to care for...something like that. It is so easy to raise our kids as extensions of ourselves. We forget how they are each unique souls. We so rob ourselves and them whenever that happens."

"I'm working at being more comfortable with not knowing. Oh, for the times when there were simple answers to children's questions. Actually I'm glad I'm alive now, but it sure isn't easy. It is so important to find the right balance, to give enough structure so there is security, yet to be willing to admit how uncertain things often are for all of us."

"My kid startles me with how much he understands. That doesn't mean there aren't times when I need to be stern. But I really have to be open to learning from him. I'm getting better at it. There are ways in which he is ahead of me on this 'whole-person relationship' stuff. At the very least, we are clearly in it together."

As with all bridgings, questions of new leadership involve gaping traps for the unwary. Most importantly, integral leadership in no way means simply falling off the other end of the teeter-totter and negating the importance of leadership and expertise. (Time spent with children raised on the belief that liberated child rearing means never saying "no" cures this common unity fallacy.) Rather it means utilizing fully and consciously the rich complementarity of creative elements that together make up the workings of authority. True bridging in fact potentiates the power of good leadership.

Leading from a more integral place is not something one can just choose to do. One can grow more sensitive to what is involved, but ultimately it is predicated on finding a newly integral relationship to authority in oneself. This is not easy business. It asks a major kind of growing up.

With personal passage at midlife, we let go of parents as the ones with the answers. Integral leadership requires a parallel passage in our inner relationship to cultural authority. "Experts" in the past, besides being people with knowledge, served the role of

emissaries for our sacred and secular images of an external absolute. They allowed us, whether our role was as Expert or Ignorant,
a symbolic bonding with surety. As emergent reality takes us beyond final truths, this symbolic function grows obsolete. It no longer
serves the well-being of either those who seek images of the omniscient or those who have become accustomed to assuming them.

As a psychiatrist, one of the most significant roles I play is that
of the "great final disappointment." Most people who come to see
me hope on some level that I can give them the answer that will
make all safe and pleasurable. At this I fail. Learning the art of
"failing" in this way will be an increasingly important part of the
role of all kinds of "experts."

Authority, in the new sense being demanded of us, entails critical changes from each side. We must learn to "lead" in ways that
honor uncertainty, process, and our integral place in the creative
whole of what we do. Equally we must learn to "follow" in ways
that honor the authority of our uniqueness and our place as co-
participants in that whole. Our success in addressing the future's
critical questions will be a direct function of our ability to embody,
from both "above" and "below," this more integral and creative
relationship to authority.

Management and Worker

*"Labor relations is almost an obsolete term. [Both labor
and management are sensing] a strong need to move
from an adversarial to a cooperative model."*
—Marina Whitman

We shift our focus slightly now from more dyadic relationships
to questions of authority and leadership in the organizational setting. Again, a story sets the stage:

In 1985, Springfield Remanufacturing Company of Springfield, Missouri, a company noted for keeping people on the
payroll even in hard times, signed a $75 million contract with
General Motors to remanufacture diesel engines. In 1987, after
Springfield had turned over the majority of its production to this
effort, GM drastically cut the order.

Jack Stack, Springfield's CEO, could see no other way out of the situation than to lay off 100 employees. He agonized endlessly over the decision, blaming himself, seeing the faces of people he would have to lay off in his dreams. For 19 years he'd found ways to avoid this happening, but now there seemed no other choice.

As crunch time neared, it occurred to him that he was trying to make a decision that perhaps wasn't appropriately his to make. He called his 350 employees together, old-fashioned town-meeting style, and painted the grim situation. They could try to keep everyone on. But if they did, they would need to generate 50,000 hours of new work, and even then there were no guarantees. They could end up folding, putting everyone out of work.

Almost unanimously the workers said go for it. It was a terribly difficult year. Nobody made as much as in the past, but rather than laying anybody off, they actually brought on new workers.

Jack Stack commented afterward, "The neat thing was to realize that I couldn't make the decision myself. It was not a manager's decision but a people's decision. It was their future and their company." If he had made the decision to lay people off, there is a good chance that, with the resulting demoralization, the company would have gone under. If he personally had made the choice not to, it is unlikely the needed energy and commitment could have been generated. With his sensitivity to the most creatively appropriate locus of choice, the result was a company revitalized from within.[1]

Jack Stack's handling of this crisis would have been unorthodox ten years ago, nearly inconceivable twenty-five years ago. Today, while still unusual, the setting is rare where it would be dismissed out-of-hand. The same kinds of bridgings that are reordering dyadic authority relationships are transforming decision-making processes within organizations. And the implications are similarly profound.

Not long ago I talked with a neighbor who worked for many years as an executive with Bell Telephone. He described how dramatically the work environment has changed in recent times.

---

[1] Originally reported in *INC*, January 1988.

"Management just doesn't mean the same thing that it did twenty, or even ten, years ago," he said. "We need different kinds of people with different kinds of skills and a whole redefinition of the work setting.

"And it's not just that the demands of the workplace are changing; what people want and need is changing," he said. "It used to be that the way to attract the best employees was to guarantee job security: a clear path up the ladder of success and the promise of a gold watch after forty years. The best people these days want more than this. Workers want more say-so in how things happen. And both managers and workers want to feel that their efforts contribute in some larger sense, that they do more than just put bread on the table.

"Before, attitudes like that would have been a problem," he said, "but now it's quite the opposite. With change so rapid today, we need managers and workers who enjoy challenge and innovation and who are willing to take initiative. People's new wants fit right in with what we need. The corporate environment has to be much more flexible and responsive than it has been in the past. But the changes aren't easy. We are having to rethink our ideas about right management and corporate organization from the ground up."

Just as our times demand new concepts of authority, they also demand radically new concepts of organization. Today's institutions require, for both efficiency and employee satisfaction, a dynamic flexibility in their organization that was not only not needed, but which often would have been a liability in the "Age of Industry."

Over the last fifteen years, numerous books have appeared proposing theories and techniques of "new management." Most of these suggestions in some way bridge between the traditional institutional "above" and "below" and move us toward a more dynamic and systemic view of organization.

Focusing on the "above," we repeatedly hear the importance of hands-on, involved leadership. Peters and Waterman, in their highly popular *In Search of Excellence*, talk of the value of executives getting out of their shielded offices and into the daily hubbub, what they call "management by wandering around." We hear of the value of reducing the tiers of middle management, "flattening the hierarchy" to maximize human communication. And we hear of organizations having their managers periodically assume the various jobs under them so they will know first-hand the territory they are managing.

Focusing on the "below," we hear of the value of ongoing worker involvement in decision-making, both the motivational rewards to be reaped and the importance of such involvement for organizational responsiveness and innovation. Rosabeth Moss Kanter in *The Change Masters* calls this "energizing the grass roots." She emphasizes how the people closest to the work are often the best ones to see problems and offer new solutions. We see a growing number of experiments designed to formalize this empowerment of the "below," such as using small, relatively autonomous working groups to replace traditional hierarchies and instigating partial or complete worker ownership. Increasingly, the organizations that prosper make the well-being and creative authority of all the people who work in them high priorities.

We again must be careful of our by-now-familiar traps. In bridging the organizational "above" and "below," a couple of common unity fallacies can snare us.

In the name of integral organization we can simply turn the patriarchal pyramid on its head, take the side of the "below." A call of "power to the people" can, in certain situations, help catalyze change. But when held to as final truth, it most often just replaces one oppressive hierarchy with another.

Or we can try to get rid of the pyramid and make all decisions by consensus. As anyone who has fallen at all deeply for the illusory beauty of the conceptual siren of consensus has learned, this too lies far from "the answer." In the right situations, consensus decision-making can be richly empowering. In the wrong ones, if it is not simply a mask for its own kind of tyranny, it is at the very least impossibly unwieldy and inefficient. Springfield Remanufacturing succeeded not because everyone should get involved in all decisions, but because everyone needed to be involved in that one particular decision.

Compromise fallacies can also detour us. There are two common variations. First, one can imagine one is dealing with integral

Management and Worker stratifies both organizations and culture as a whole. This symbolically evocative photo was shot during excavation for the Seattle bus tunnel. ("Upstairs Downstairs," Robert DeGuilio/ *Seattle Post-Intelligencer.*)

organizational structure when in fact one simply has a more balanced division of power in the battle between "above" and "below." A common example occurs when labor unions and management, while clearly still adversaries, reach a kind of peaceful coexistence. It is easy to get stuck here, but it is important to move on. The words of economist Marina Whitman at the beginning of this section point nicely toward the emerging reality for management and labor. Increasingly we should find shared purpose standing ahead of old polar allegiances, with the recognition of this shared purpose serving as the basis for new organizational approaches.

The second common variation on the compromise fallacy happens when an organization or theorist finds a more integral approach that works in one situation, then applies it like a blueprint to all others: "The formula is ten-person working groups that get together twice a week to brainstorm." Here the dynamic nature of integral reality is being missed. The most creatively vital organizational forms may be markedly different for two different kinds of organizations and different as well for different stages in any one organization's growth. Moreover, two organizations, similar except that key people display different personality styles, may need to evolve in very different ways.

I learned some of the lessons of integral organizational change the hard way during the last year of my psychiatry training. The story is worth sharing.

I was assigned to an antiquated, backwards inpatient unit—not a pleasant place. Staff morale was terribly low, and for the patients, the area was not much more than a holding pen. I realized I wasn't going to keep my own sanity there if I couldn't do something to improve conditions. So I set about trying to figure out what might help.

First, I noticed that very little contact occurred between psychiatrists and staff, and what communication there was went only one way. The psychiatrists would meet with staff at rounds once a week and hand out treatment plans. That was about it.

Second, I noticed that it was the staff who really knew the patients best, and, though it was not acknowledged, made most of the decisions and did the much greater part of the therapy. The doctors had, at best, 15 minutes a week with each patient. The staff worked there all day. Their training was generally minimal, but many had worked on the ward for ten or twenty years, and others frequently had street smarts that made the simple things they did very effective.

Finally, I saw that an inordinate amount of the staff's time was spent grumbling about the psychiatrists' decisions and complaining to each other about how little say they had in what was done.

The solution seemed obvious. The staff made most of the real decisions anyway. Make that authority overt.

I made my proposal to the chief psychiatrist. It was hardly radical really. We would use treatment teams with staff having ongoing involvement in the decision-making process. I expected to be stonewalled. He was skeptical, but gave his go-ahead.

The surprise for me, the idealist, came when I announced the "great news" to the staff—what they had been saying they wanted could now come true. To my amazement, the response was at best reserved. Some denied that they had ever wanted things to be different. Others, while not opposing the idea, did things to undermine any real change.

I had entirely missed the symbolically collaborative nature of the relationship between psychiatrist and staff. I had looked on the staff as simply oppressed by "the system," assuming that what was needed was just to give them their rightful power. I had missed the hidden polar story, the sense in which what looked like conflict was as much collusion. Together the psychiatrists and staff had formed a creative unit. The psychiatrists carried the responsibility, but little real effect. The staff had considerable effect, but needed to take almost no responsibility. I was asking not just a simple change in behavior, but a major expansion in capacity, a significant new step in maturity on everyone's part.

Realizing that in my naivete I'd seen only the smallest part of what was going on, I took four quick steps backward and moved much more slowly, and with more humility. With time, we did set up treatment teams. It was just a beginning—many who were most powerful on the ward continued not to own that authority—but it meant a start.

Government and Governed

*"[O]ne of the great needs of our time is to develop means
for the mastery of complexity and uncertainty, which
will dominate governance for decades to come."*
—Alexander King
President, Club of Rome

Like dyadic and organizational authority relationships, government too is a systems dynamic. The awareness is critical, and one we easily miss. We think of an Alexander the Great, a George Washington, a Winston Churchill as simply great people. History changed because of the force of their personalities.

In fact, while personality plays a part, the mythic place a person as leader holds in the creative whole of culture always carries at least equal significance. In the act of assuming leadership, one takes on a deific role, embodying for the culture what a parent symbolizes for a child. One becomes the projection point for the society's capacity for determination, the symbolic "head" to the "body politic."

Throughout history, these projection dynamics have evolved in specific ways. Early civilizations regarded leaders as embodiments of the divine. To the ancient Egyptian, for example, the Pharaoh was a direct incarnation of the sun god Ra. By the time of kingly rule, the position of leader had evolved to something between that of god and mere mortal. Kings had Divine Right and often divine capacities (for example, the anointed rulers of France and England were believed to have the ability to heal certain illnesses simply by a gesture, the "Royal Touch"), but were not themselves regarded as divine.

Part of the mythology of modern times is that such superstitious notions of authority represent things of the past. Democracy is an objective process. Our leaders are simply elected representatives.

By all evidence, however, our concept of government by the people is much more a poetic notion of potential than anything thus far manifest. What we have had in modern times is most accurately government by institution. We elect a leader and then surrender our ascendant power to the parental image of his or her office. The relationship between president or prime minister and populace *is* of a new sort, but it is still fundamentally polar—"parental." This appears most obviously with strongly mythologized leaders such as a Washington or a Lincoln, but the dynamic has been ever-present.

And now? If the concept of bridging is accurate, real government by the people may be emerging as an authentic possibility. Recent rumblings in our relationship with governmental authority support the idea that we may indeed stand at the threshold of this most important evolutionary step.

The last American president to evoke a mythic response on a universal scale was John Kennedy. Others since have done so for certain segments of the population, but in general, presidents in the last two decades seemed all too human.[2] One might argue that the reason lies in the inadequacy of those who have run for the office, but such cynicism ignores a subtle but significant shift in attitude that has marked the past twenty years. Although we remain far from invulnerable to the seduction of easy answers, we do seem increasingly reluctant to make the person of the leader that answer. We bemoan the fact that no one seems able again to invoke images of Camelot, but at the same time we seem more and more dubious of any pretendings toward such an exalted role.

If we are indeed growing up in our relationship to political authority, what does this imply? What does a whole-person relationship to governmental determination mean in terms of policy? Again, we are just getting first glimpses, but we can say several things with some certainty.

First, it should mean that in the future we will view elected leaders more and more as simple mortals with a tough job. By freeing government from the considerable demands of symbolic fanfare, we open the possibility of more effective governance. At the same time, by giving people a clearer view of what government

---

[2] Ronald Reagan was an immensely popular president, and much of that popularity came from his fatherly image. But surveys show that while people liked Reagan and felt comforted by his fatherly assurances that all was well with America, they saw him as neither well-informed, nor particularly wise.

actually does, it should help set the stage for greater popular involvement in governance.

The second piece relates to the first. As we experience a more whole-person/whole-system relationship to governmental authority, we should find ourselves wanting a more involved and ongoing role in the process of governmental decision-making. Some evidence for the beginnings of this appear in the growing use of the initiative process. A desire for greater ongoing popular input combined with such things as new communication technologies could result in some exciting experiments in more participatory democracy.

A third piece concerns the question of governmental "structure" in the future. As with other kinds of organization, we should find ourselves leaving behind the images of our recent Age of Institution and moving in the direction of more flexible, dynamic conceptions. This need becomes more and more apparent as institutional structures grow increasingly unwieldy. The dilemma was succinctly voiced on a bumper sticker—"Bureaucracy: A system for converting energy into solid waste."

The importance of a next step in the evolution of governmental structure comes into particularly sharp focus when we turn to issues of global determination. We increasingly confront questions that can only be addressed at a planetary level. Just how can we deal with these issues? Is the task to establish global institutional government, to work toward electing a "President" and governing body for the planet as a whole?

If it is, we face major difficulties. It looks unlikely that traditional democratic forms could be made workable at this scale. The inherent inertia of institutional bureaucracy, combined with the fact that at a global level we are all minorities, would bring such an attempt to a grinding standstill. One could well argue that the only traditional governmental form workable at this scale would be a dictatorship, something which I suspect at this point in cultural evolution we could not tolerate.

Notions of integral leadership and new organizational structure suggest further possibilities. If the concept of bridging is accurate, we should find ourselves addressing questions of global determination in increasingly dynamic and systemic terms. This means viewing government less as a pyramid-like structure than as the creative interplay of a variety of multicentric, multilevel determination processes.

Governance in this larger sense asks new levels of awareness. It requires an ongoing sensitivity to the multiple evolving spheres of determination that make up governance—person, to neighborhood, to city, to region, to nation, to planet. It requires an appreciation of the great variety of forms right determination can take—as a function of a sphere's scale, where it is in its evolution, and who comprises it. And it requires an ability to think in fully global, whole-systems terms about the place and purpose of governance.

The ability to think from a larger perspective makes greater subtlety possible in the selection of governmental forms. As well, it makes possible the creation of new, more dynamic forms. Both will be necessary if we are to be effective creative managers at a global scale.

This more systemic picture presents an easily unsettling question: Who is in charge here? The important recognition is that in a fundamental sense, no "one" has ever been in charge. The illusion of the omniscient power of designated leaders has served a valuable function, but the workings of culture are far more complex than could ever be determined by anyone's purposeful design. The challenge of new governance is not so much to give up control as we've known it, as to accept responsibility in a world that has always been bigger than our ideas about control.

Traps

Separation Fallacies: Experts have the answers. The job of leaders is to lead. Organizational structures should be centralized and decisions made from the top down.

Unity Fallacies: The common person knows best. The job of leaders is to get out of the way. Organizational structures should be decentralized and decision-making done by consensus.

Compromise Fallacies: We each give our opinion, then split the difference. The goal is an equitable balance of power between management and those being managed.

Bridgings

The challenge in dyadic authority relationships is to relate as whole people with creatively complementary roles to play in the full manifestation of authority.

The challenge organizationally is to embrace one's organization as a creative dynamic, an interplay of unique and evolving individuals set in the context of an equally dynamic and evolving environment.

The challenge governmentally is to make manifest true "government by the people." The tasks include accepting ongoing responsibility in authority, establishing structures that will support such ongoing responsibility, and learning to approach governance as a process involving the interplay of multiple layers and levels of determination that often cannot be logically reconciled.

CHAPTER SEVEN

FACT AND FANCY: TRUTH IN AN INTEGRAL REALITY

"Our lives are suspended like a planet in a gimbals of duality, half sunlight, half shadow."
—Timothy Ferris

"It is my deep conviction that only by understanding the world in all its aspects—reductionist and holist, mathematical and poetical, through force fields and particles—will we come to understand ourselves and the meaning behind this universe, our home."
—Physicist Paul Davies

"Rigor alone is paralytic death; imagination alone is insanity."
—Gregory Bateson

"Try to remember when life was so tender that dreams were kept beside the pillow."
—The Fantastics

Bridging helps us redefine interpersonal relationships—between intimates and friends, within organizations and political structures. What about relationship in a more elemental sense, relationship to ourselves and relationship to reality as a whole? Can it also help us here?

Such questions move us into the traditional territory of the philosopher, where we are concerned not only with how we treat one another, but with our most fundamental assumptions about the nature of reality. The new questions demand new epistemological containers.

Mind and matter, fate and free will, time and timelessness, good and evil—these are the great eternal quandaries. We may think we have done with them about all we can do, that they are at best topics for a lazy afternoon class on the history of thought.

But such is far from the case. When the cultural snake readies itself for skin shedding, all lies open to question. Our times demand that we give attention once more to these most basic of questions. Our future well-being—and perhaps even our survival—depends on our ability to grasp them in a new light.

We begin this more philosophical inquiry by looking at three pivotal polarities: Subjective and Objective, Rational and Irrational, and Certainty and Uncertainty. Our interest here, rather than academic completeness, is the implications of new insights in these areas. A critical question links these insights: *What is truth in an integral reality?*

Subjective and Objective

> *"The world thus appears as a complicated tissue of events, in which connections of different kinds alternate or overlap or combine and thereby determine the texture of the whole."*
> —Werner Heisenberg

We begin with some historical perspective. Central to the Age of Enlightenment's great triumph was a critical achievement: the establishment of final, clear separation between the inner world of subjective experience and the outer world of objective "fact." It was at once a practical and a conceptual achievement. The scientific method provided a way of separating the physically demonstrable from simple conjecture or personal prejudice. And the accompanying new world view redefined truth so that this distinction stood forefront.

It was a radical step. Always before, these worlds had been intermingled. In the animistic reality of early tribal times, the membrane between inner experience and outer truth was so thin that spirits and dreams traversed it largely unimpeded. For the Greeks, there was not matter without mind. The philosophy of the Middle Ages remained explicitly teleological; material effects had ultimately spiritual causes.[1]

---

[1] The relationship of inner and outer experience is an evolutionary dynamic. Two major themes marked its progression to modern times. First, inner and outer

A powerful victory? Most certainly. An end point in the journey of understanding? Logically it would seem so. How can we be clearer than truth cleansed of all conjecture?

We not only can, but we must. Regarding inner and outer as wholly separate now proves inconsistent with the facts and inadequate to the challenge of addressing our times' critical questions.

The first major blow to this cornerstone of Cartesian dualism came from the very heart of the objectivist world, the hardest of the "hard" sciences—physics. The story is familiar. Albert Einstein had a dream—to bring together in a new synthesis the then major traditions of physics: mechanics and electrodynamics. Making that dream real would overturn some of the most cherished assumptions of traditional science and send tremors through the whole of modern thought. The sacred separateness of subjective and objective represented one of the most pivotal of those challenged assumptions. Reality was no longer fixed and absolute, but relative to the situation of the observer.

Relativity would present only the first in a dramatic series of attacks by twentieth century physics on the stone wall separating inner and outer experience. Quantum mechanics, physics' other major modern voice, went considerably further in daring us to accept how far from impenetrable that wall may indeed be. Princeton physicist John Wheeler put it this way: "One has to cross out the old word 'observer' and put in a new word 'participator.' In some strange sense the universe is a participatory universe." In the words of Freeman Dyson of the Institute for Advanced Study: "…[I]t is true to say that [quantum physics] has brought mind and consciousness back to the center of things—you can't really understand quantum mechanics deeply unless you also understand the nature of mind." The other sciences are only beginning to catch up.

The ultimate interpenetration of subjective and objective is articulated with particular clarity in the emerging discipline of Systems Theory.[2] Central in mature systems thinking is the tenet that

---

grew increasingly distinct. Second, there was a gradual shift of emphasis from inner truth to outer truth.

[2] Creative Systems ideas represent one particular kind of systems perspective.

The new questions demand that we think in terms of the larger reality that objectivity and subjectivity together define. (Pablo Picasso, "Girl Before a Mirror," Museum of Modern Art, New York.)

one can never fully extricate the experiencer from what is experienced. This remains equally so whether the "experiencer" in question is "me" reflecting on my feelings, an individual reflecting on society, or humanity reflecting on nature or the cosmos. We can only reflect on that of which we are a part, but once a part of something we can no more stand back and objectively see the whole of it than we can see our own eyes while watching a sunset.

We must be careful here. I am not suggesting that the subjective is the "real" reality and that "out there" is simply some illusion of mind. In challenging objectivism, we must be careful not to err in the other direction. Do we "create our own reality" as popular psychology claims? Such an assumption represents only a regression to the wishful thinking of the child's magical, self-centered world view.[3]

But what we perceive *is* a function of how we perceive. The unique juxtaposition of rods and cones that forms our visual apparatus makes the world we see very different from that seen by, say, an owl or a jellyfish. And if we move more into the psychological sphere, the effect grows even more pronounced. The ideas presented in the last few chapters provide good illustration. Someone looking for an "other half" in intimacy or an "evil other" politically will experience a very different world than a person holding a whole-person/whole-system perspective.

And more than just our experience is effected by how we perceive. Depending on the sphere of our perceptions—our thoughts, our physical selves, our relationships, our culture, our physical world—to some large or small degree, the act of perceiving links creatively with the fate of what we perceive. Perception is a participatory phenomena, an expression of relationship. When a plant takes in the energy of the sun, not only does the plant change, but in some minute but real way these changes, in turn, affect the real-

---

[3] Actually, hard scientists such as physicists are no more immune to such regressions than more psychologically or spiritually oriented thinkers. Georg Feuerstein expressed it well in his book *Structures of Consciousness:* "Without wishing to deny that certain striking parallels exist between the increasingly *koan*-like world-conception of contemporary quantum physics and ancient Indian and Far Eastern cosmologies, it would be imprudent to ignore the mythologizing trend within the new physics…. At best this trend enhances popular awareness of the fact that the dualistic-mechanistic paradigm of science has been effectively superseded. At worst it signals that the scientific priesthood has merely donned another garb—that of mystagogic visionary."

ity of the sun. When we love another person, if it is real love and not just projection, both ourselves and the person whom we love are changed by that love.

Such musings make fascinating theory. But what about our daily lives? Does bridging "within" and "without" have real practical importance?

In fact, it could not be more practical. A good place to see this is the question of how as a culture we are to "measure" truth in the future. The question of measures is critical. Taken together, our measures are the compass by which we sail the ship of culture.

Throughout our most recent age, in keeping with the triumph of the objective, we have come to measure truth and value almost exclusively in external, material terms. We've equated success with wealth, defense with the size of our stockpiles of arms, education with the accumulation of facts and skills, healing with the defeat of death and disease, artistic worth with value in the marketplace.

Such isolated material measures are simply not adequate for where we need to go. Why? Alfred North Whitehead put it this way: "[They are not enough because] they deal with only half the evidence provided by human experience." The forgotten half is calling to be remembered. Chilean writer Ariel Dorfman said it well in talking of social policy: "How do you measure the amount of dignity people accumulate? How do you quantify the disappearance of apathy?"

The future demands more of us. It requires that we include in our calculations not just "the facts," but inner concerns as well— aesthetic, psychological, spiritual. And it demands that these "softer" concerns be included not just as ornament, things separate and secondary, as has been the case with aesthetic sentiments in our recent past, but as equal, interwoven elements in understanding.

Our present environmental challenges offer good illustration. It is essential that we ask just what kind of language and what kinds of measures best address these challenges. We tend most commonly to think in terms of "resources." The task is to have adequate supplies of raw materials for future generations and a clean environment in which to use them.

Such thinking is a start. It begins to get us beyond the hubris that nature can be ignored. But as a concept, "resources" is not enough. It is handy because it lets us talk in concrete terms, so much of this and so much of that, but it simply doesn't measure all of what is important. Where do we put the feeling of walking alone in an old growth forest, the camaraderie of a neighborhood base-ball game in a city park, the taste of clean water from a mountain stream, or just knowing that other amazing creatures—elephants, condors, whales, penguins, lions—share life on this planet? Making the right choices requires that such supposed "intangibles" hold a solid and central place in our thinking. The task is not just to have a planet a thousand years hence, but to have a planet that nurtures and sustains us. To achieve this, we must base our policies on ideas big enough to embrace these "softer" concerns, and not just as decoration, but as integral parts of the hard data.

When I work with groups from particular professions, this task of redefining truth and value is often where we begin. It is not easy work: It requires a newly personal and vulnerable relationship to one's profession. Yet, there is nothing more critical than engaging in this kind of dialogue.

I often start with some kind of exercise. The following is one example. As you read it, you might try translating it into the spheres that are most central in your life.

> I worked recently with a group of architects and designers. I started by asking those present to make lists of three or four people who had in some way enriched their lives. Then I asked them to write about the qualities in these people that had touched them.
>
> We shared our reflections as a group: memories of the tender bond of a childhood friendship, a person who was willing to speak up even when others thought she was crazy, someone who led with integrity and foresight.
>
> Then I expanded the question. "Let's imagine," I said, "that you could choose the qualities that would be most prominent in people on the planet fifty or a hundred years from now. What ones would you choose? Would some of these you've listed be included? Would there be others?" Again we shared our thoughts.

Finally, I asked the group: "What would it mean if you made these qualities you have just identified the central referents in your work? For a moment, forget all you learned in school about good design, forget what the architecture magazines are saying is the latest thing, forget what you have become known and rightly praised for. What would happen if you made your bottom line that buildings and environments you created would evoke or at least support these qualities in the people who entered them?"

I asked each person to look at projects done in the last few years and to see if making this the referent would have changed decisions he or she had made. I asked them to play with what this might mean for the design of a school...a playground...a government building...a neighborhood.

At one point a member of the group spoke up and challenged me, saying that while what we were doing was fun, it didn't seem very practical. A rich, impassioned discussion opened up in response. The comments of one woman in the group nicely summed up the more general feeling. "Some of the ideas we've come up with may not be immediately practical," she said. "But what we have been trying to do could not be more so. If what we most care about is not our measure, we are hypocrites. And culturally, if we don't act from what most gives life purpose and value, then we are doomed."

These architects had taken an important first step toward establishing a new, more integral determiner for their actions.

A couple observations about such new determiners are warranted before we move on. The first concerns articulation.

Because more integral referents for truth and value bridge usual assumptions, talking about them is inherently tricky. The new measures require that our words honor process as much as content and embrace the elusive and ephemeral equally with things that can be measured with the comforting clarity of litmus paper tests.

I've found a few words and phrases particularly useful in this task of articulation. One is the term "purpose-centered." Integral referents encompass the why of things as much as the how. A second term follows from the earlier observation that new issues in all spheres each ask "questions of life." I often call the needed new referent simply "aliveness." Whether we talk about love, health, or defense, it is "life itself" that we seek to measure, the degree to which an act makes something, as life, authentically more.

The second observation concerns the relationship between different kinds of referents. In an integral reality, the margins separating the truths of different realms of understanding become decidedly "leaky." Bridging within particular domains requires at the same time bridging between domains.

In the old view, the measures that defined different spheres lay like separate columns on a ledger sheet, for all intents and purposes distinct. Facts and skills in education, power in politics, defeating disease in medicine, doing God's will in religion—these, as conventionally conceived, remained quite separate concerns. As we move toward more integral understanding, our various arbiters look less like ledger columns and more like, say, chips in a chocolate chip cookie. They are neither wholly separate nor the same. Actually we need rather gooey chocolate chips to make the metaphor sufficiently dynamic—cells in an organism or facets in a crystal might be a bit closer—but as an image it points us in the right direction.

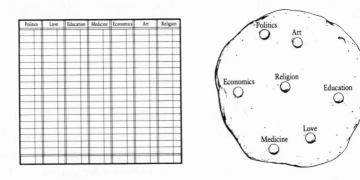

"*Ledger Sheet*" *View*   "*Chocolate Chip Cookie*" *View*

Fɪɢ. 7-1: *Truth and Value in an Integral Reality*

Rational and Irrational

*"He was a rationalist, but he had to confess that he loved
the ringing of church bells."*
                                        —Anton Chekhov

Our next polarity is intimately related to the last, yet different
enough to warrant space of its own. Bridging between the "clear
light" of the objective and the more personal stuff of subjective
reality integrates truth horizontally, linking inner sensings with
what we see as we scan the horizons of our experience. A larger
understanding of truth requires that we bridge vertically as well,
between the various layerings that make up the "above" and "below"
of experience: between conscious and unconscious, mind and body,
thoughts and feelings.

The Age of Enlightenment's grand vision was not just that everything be brought into the light, but into a specific kind of light,
the light of *reason*. The intellect was to wear the crown of final authority. It was a well-meant goal and right for its time. But given
what we have come to know, it was clearly partial. It is not that
emergent reality negates the rational; emergent reality is not irrational. But it is decidedly post-rational. Philosopher F.S.C. Northrop
put it well in *The Meeting of East and West*: "…[A] new type of attitude and a new type of scholarship is being required. We must
bring our intuitions and our imaginations, even our souls, to the
[new] insights."

That the intellect is not enough to describe life is, of course,
hardly new. Poets and mystics have delivered this message since the
first spoken word. What is new is that the nonrational is coming to
sit at the table of hard truth. The needed new understandings in all
spheres require that we bring to them a newly integral view of
"intelligence."[4]

For certain kinds of "thinking," the rational alone serves quite
adequately. Where the concern is wholly form-defined—a math-

---

[4] I use "intelligence" here in its most generic sense, the ability to organize
experience.

ematical equation, a problem in mechanics—it poses no difficulty at all. But for questions that concern life, a category that, as we've seen, includes the pivotal future questions in all domains, more is needed. Limiting our thinking to the rational when addressing this kind of question is like trying to understand a Bach sonata solely by analyzing the frequency of its notes. It is like trying to paint a rainbow using only the color yellow.

The need for more inclusive views of intelligence applies to all domains. It is most obvious for areas where inner concerns are preeminent—the arts, spirituality, psychology—but increasingly thinkers recognize it as pertinent across the board.

In a 1918 speech, Einstein eloquently expressed the importance of this larger view to science. "The supreme task of physics," he said, "is to arrive at the universal elementary laws. There is no logical path to these laws, only intuition."

And the message isn't simply that logic alone is inadequate for discovering the new laws; rather, intuition and the like may be integral to the substance of such laws. Nobel chemist Ilya Prigogine spoke of this further step in *Being and Becoming:* "For most of the founders of classical science—even for Einstein—science was an attempt to go beyond the world of appearances to reach a timeless world of supreme rationality—the world of Spinoza. But perhaps there is a more subtle form of reality that involves [not just] laws but games, [not just] time but eternity."

For me, the need for whole-person views of intelligence stands out with greatest force when we turn to questions of how to manage our ever more complex world. The issue is universally pertinent—to government, business, science, the environment, education. We like to think of our rationality as able to handle great intricacy. In fact, it faces extreme limits in this regard. Even on the best of days, the capacity of the intellect for handling complexity does not begin to approach that needed to manage the functioning of a single cell in our bodies. And life, daily, gets more complex.

More than this, the intellect has a terrible time with things that don't fit into handy compartments. It likes things with square corners and clear distinctions. Unfortunately for this part of us that has prided itself as captain of the cellular ship, life is not only getting more complicated, it is getting more "messy," less and less amenable to simple categories.

We would face a terrible impasse were it not for another quite obvious fact. Other parts of our intelligence can handle complex, relational tasks quite easily. Were this not so, we wouldn't have bodies that worked, relationships that gave pleasure, or art that inspired.

The future will demand that we learn to engage questions of choice ever more subtly with all the multiple levels of who we are. This is being increasingly recognized. Corporate leaders now acknowledge the importance of intuition and "seat of the pants" decision-making. Organizational development experts emphasize the need for flexibility and fluid "process" thinking. Political theorists see how often a leader's ability to relate personally with another leader contributes as much to good international relations as does smart policy.

That intelligence means more than simply intellect is an increasingly "hot topic" in educational circles. For most of this century, I.Q. reigned supreme as the final arbiter of acumen and aptitude. Intelligence was intelligence and that was that. "Not so," says an energetic flock of new theorists.

These new thinkers cut the larger pie of intelligence in a variety of ways. At the simplest level we find popular notions such as "left hemisphere" and "right hemisphere" thinking. Howard Gardner at Boston University School of Medicine delineates seven different intelligences: linguistic, musical, logical-mathematical, spatial, bodily-kinesthetic, interpersonal, and intrapersonal. Yale University psychologist Robert Sternberg uses what he calls a "triarchic" model of intelligence, dividing the pie into componential (analytic), experiential (creative), and contextual (street smarts) intelligence.

More important than the number of slices in the pie or where the cuts are made is the fact that we are starting to acknowledge the whole pie. We are starting to "remember" just how big "living" reality, and with this "living" intelligence, in fact, is.

In *The Creative Imperative*, I put forward a further approach to cutting up the pie of intelligence. It is important in that it offers a way to move beyond simply acknowledging the existence of mul-

tiple intelligences to address both why we should have such different ways of knowing in the first place and how these different ways
of ordering experience work together to make us the living, evolving beings that we are.

This Creative Systems view of multiple intelligences argues
that our various kinds of knowing relate not just as different options
on a menu, but work together as the "mechanism" of creative process. Each stage in the creative cycle can be seen to associate with a
particular way of ordering reality, a particular "mode" of intelligence. Let's take a moment to briefly examine these creative "modes"
of intelligence and the creative realities they define.

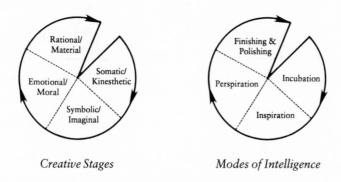

Creative Stages   *Modes of Intelligence*

FIG. 7-2: *A Creative Systems View of*
Multiple Intelligences

The first kind of knowing I call *somatic/kinesthetic intelligence.*[5]
It orders truth during the earliest germinal stage of creation—the
"incubation" stage—that dark time before the appearance of creation as form. In creation's beginnings, truth arrives less as idea
than inner patterns of movement and sensation.

---

[5] To simplify things, we could just call these "intelligences" body, imagination, feelings, and intellect. But, as I outline in *The Creative Imperative*, in fact each
stage and its concomitant "intelligence" includes aspects of each of these four
"languages." One predominates in each stage, but it's the unique creative
relationship between them that defines that stage's conception of reality.

When I work on a new writing project, I often start by retreating to the bathtub. I climb in and fill it almost to the edge. Sometimes I'm there for three or four hours. Thoughts come first less as ideas than as "inklings"—inner movements, kinesthetic sensings of possibility. (For the uninitiated who may be withdrawing in horror at images of shriveled skin, the famed prune effect in fact reverses itself once an hour or so has passed.)

Creative incubation. (Jeff MacNelly, "Shoe," Tribune Media Services.)

In a similar way, somatic/kinesthetic intelligence orders the earliest times in our individual lives. It predominates during the intrauterine period and much of the first year of life—when touch, taste, and movement provide our fundamental knowings. Culturally, it orders truth during civilization's creative beginnings. It represents the intelligence of animism: an aboriginal father teaching his son to catch lizards, not by words, but by himself—spear held aloft—becoming the lizard, and his son in turn behind him—his smaller spear similarly aloft—becoming his father becoming the lizard.

The next kind of knowing, *symbolic/imaginal intelligence*, moves to the foreground during creation's "inspiration" stage, that period when images of the possible first make their appearance. During this time, the primary language of intelligence shifts from the kinesthetic to the metaphoric, to the "magical" language of imagery and symbol.

When I'm working on a new writing project, this stage often occurs in the bathtub as well. During this stage, another bathtub dweller, Archimedes, uttered his now famous "Eureka." Rather than yelling, I am more apt to grab a yellow pad and start drawing pictures and jotting down loose associations or evocative phrases.

Symbolic/imaginal intelligence is the primary language in the child's magical world of make-believe and let's-pretend. Culturally, it steps forefront during civilization's mythically-charged, early "golden" period. It provided the ordering language in early Olympian Greece, during the time of the Meso-American high cultures (Aztecs, Incas, Mayans, Toltecs), and in the classical East.

The third mode, *emotional/moral intelligence*, predominates during that critical time when inspiration makes its impassioned struggle into first crude form, the time Ben Franklin called with grudging respect the stage of "perspiration." Here, instead of sensations or images, feelings most define creation.

When I reach this stage in my writing, the tub will no longer do. Brow furrowed, I dry myself off and sit down at my desk to apply my "heart and guts" to getting my thoughts on paper. I try ideas out in different ways, seeing what in them really matters, tugging them this way and that. Often I work them back and forth with a friend.

In individual development, emotional/moral intelligence moves forefront during adolescence, that period when childhood's magic gives way to the teenage years' ever-vacillating passions, tests of courage, and searches for the heartfelt. Culturally, it holds reign during that stage represented by our Middle Ages, when truth was ordered by the moral laws of the church and the emotional ardencies of feudal struggle.

The final mode, what I call *rational/material intelligence*, steps to the fore during the most form-defined part of creation, the "finishing and polishing" stage. As attention shifts to questions of final manifestation and detail, the logic of simple cause and effect comes to define our primary intelligence.

In that writing project, pen in hand, I lay out my new ideas now with some completeness. I make things as clear as possible, look for inconsistencies, and think through implications. I research the literature. I give what I have written to colleagues for criticism.

In individual development, rational/material intelligence dominates during young adulthood, that period when issues of achievement and finding one's place in the world step to the fore-front. Culturally, it provides the language with which we feel most familiar, that which has dominated from the beginnings of the Age of Reason to modern times.

These four kinds of intelligence interact at multiple levels. They represent developmental variables, both personally and culturally. While we in modern culture define intelligence as rational/mate-rial thought, in many tribal cultures a person described as thinking primarily with his head would be assumed crazy. As well, they de-fine human difference—personality style and learning style. Dif-ferent people can be seen to embody preferentially different balances and relationships of these four basic kinds of intelligence.[6] And they are variables in the important question of what it means to think and act in a timely fashion. At different times—in a learning task, in a relationship, in the life of an organization—various ones and combinations of these types of intelligence may offer the most.

In talking with teachers about the importance of including all our various kinds of intelligence in the educational process, I fre-quently play off one of education's other currently hot topics, the notion that we must teach not just ideas but "thinking skills." I applaud this, then offer that it represents just the first layer of a much deeper challenge.

The critical questions, I argue, demand not just that we learn how to think, but how to think innovatively, in ways that reveal new options. More than this, they demand that we think from the depths of our beings, from our passions and our souls, from the archetypal wellsprings of existence. We are challenged not just to be intelli-gent, but to be inventive—and, in this, not just to be clever, but to be wise, to create not just as caprice or for personal advantage, but as shared participation in life as purpose. For this, we must learn to "think" from the greater whole of all the richly diverse languages that together tell the story of life.

---

[6] See *The Creative Imperative*, Chapter Ten.

Certainty and Uncertainty

"There are said to be creative pauses, pauses that are as
good as death, empty and dead as death itself. And in
these awful pauses the evolutionary change takes place."
—D.H. Lawrence

To be complete in addressing the question of truth in an integral reality, we must confront one additional polarity. Perhaps more than any other, it brings us face to face with the magnitude of what these times ask of us.

Part and parcel with separating "within" from "without" has come a parallel dividing of reality into a world of certainty and a world of uncertainty. Subjective life, the reality of us mortals, is riddled with questions. But counterpoised to this, making such uncertainty tolerable, we have heretofore always found some outer final certainty, some embracing ultimate determinism.

This certainty has served like protective bookends around our personal life stories. At one end has sat the determinism of the sacred. Whether represented as nature spirits, pantheons of mythic deities, or a single patriarchal godhead, throughout time our notions of the spiritual have included an all-knowing and all-protecting presence. "The Lord is my shepherd, I shall not want."

At the other end has sat the determinism of the secular, whether that of philosophical precept or scientific principle. These oft-cited words of Laplace powerfully express its material extreme: "An intellect which at a given instant knew all the forces acting in nature, and the position of all things of which the world consists—supposing the said intellect is vast enough to subject these data to analysis—would embrace in the same formula the motions of the greatest bodies in the universe and those of the slightest atoms; nothing would be uncertain for it, and the future, like the past, would be present to its eyes."

These two certainties may seem contradictory, but most often they have coexisted quite compatibly. For example, the "separate worlds" reality of classical Cartesian dualism finds no necessary conflict. God as divine engineer builds and winds the clock of time.

The laws of science describe the clock's workings: how the spring activates the movement and one gear turns another.

The important recognition here is that whatever we have done with these two hands of certainty—whether we have chosen one, the other, or both—determinism has stayed secure. Beyond our personal insecurities, a larger absolute has always presided.

But what happens when reality begins to bridge? What happens when we start to recognize a larger dance made up of sacred and secular together? And what happens when the once opaque curtain separating subjective perception and external fact becomes diaphanous?

That which once looked absolute begins to become itself part of life's question. All around us this is happening. From countless directions simultaneously, we are confronting the startling possibility that reality *as a whole* may include real uncertainty.

I referred earlier to Werner Heisenberg's "Uncertainty Principle." At a first level, it demonstrates that there are limits to what we can measure. More deeply, it asserts that there is fundamental uncertainty in reality itself. John Bell of the European Laboratory for Particle Physics in Geneva summed up the situation: "What is new," he says, "is the idea that…'muddle' is permanently tolerable. [It is no longer just] a phase in the construction of a theory…."

This new post-determinism is also articulated in mathematics. In 1931, a young German mathematician by the name of Kurt Gödel published a short paper with the forbidding title of "On Formally Undecidable Propositions of Principia Mathematica and Related Systems." At the time, most mathematicians found it unintelligible. It has since become recognized as one of the major modern contributions to logic. Its central thesis states that all mathematical systems include unprovable assumptions. In short, even in mathematics, treated for so long as the model of finely polished truth, some degree of uncertainty is an ever-present companion.

The most important challenges to past absolutes touch us much more personally and immediately. They come not from esoteric formulations, but from the critical new issues that define our time. Effectively addressing the questions before us will demand a kind of maturity and responsibility that can be known only once one has accepted uncertainty as a real part of life.

Concerns that involve threats to our survival—such as environmental destruction, runaway population, the potential for nuclear holocaust—put these dynamics in particularly high relief. Faced with the almost unfathomable potential consequences of such threats, we easily hold even more tightly to final truths. We put our trust in science, blindly hoping that with time new discoveries will take us through the deadly impasses we face. Or we look to spiritual security, thinking, "The Divine would not let that kind of harm come our way." But while such trust has served us in the past, it will not do for the future. The critical questions ahead require us to make choices which can be effectively entertained only after we have accepted the need to leave such secure absolutes behind us.

We enter tricky territory here. What does it mean to accept that uncertainty is part of final truth? Does it mean simply replacing certainty with uncertainty: throwing out science, throwing out the sacred? Such would get us no closer to where we need to go. The task is to move forward into a world in which all of experience is defined by the larger reality that certainty and uncertainty together describe.

Again, we are just infants in our ability to grasp what is being asked. Systems theorist Erwin Laszlo touched on one part of it with these reflections on the workings of evolutionary change: "Evolution is always possibility and never destiny," he said. "Its course is logical and comprehensible, but it is not predetermined and thus not predictable." We hear physicist and philosopher Sir James Jeans playing off another aspect with these reflections on determinism and free will: "If something determines choice, we are back to determinism," he said. "If nothing, [our actions come] from pure caprice, and this leads to a free will which is neither the kind we want to find nor the kind we feel we do find."

Earlier I used the word "meta-determinant" for such a larger, creative relationship with uncertainty. It is just a word, but it helps us frame what we are working with. A simple way to think of meta-determinant truth is that it mates the reality of questions with the reality of answers. In the past, "questions" and "answers" described distinct phenomena. Answers were truth; questions were what one asked to get to the truth. But in a "living" reality, truth is as much process as product, as much invitation as destination.

The most effective tool I've found for grasping the implications of a meta-determinant reality is the analogy, offered earlier, comparing present times in culture with the period of midlife transition in individual development. Midlife is many things, one of the most important being the time when we once and for all let go of parents. We left them physically many years before, but we've continued to carry them as symbols. Sometimes they've played the role of "gods," their specialness affirming our specialness; sometimes "devils," objects of our anger and ready foils for our shortcomings. Letting go of these internalized absolutes is central to successful passage at midlife. It is not always a comfortable thing. As the mid-years approach, one often feels fear, despair, loneliness. Without old securities, things easily seem to have no order at all.

Our present time in culture offers strong parallels. In the past, spiritual and secular absolutes have served as mother and father to our growing. Now, at least as we've known them, they must be left behind. Old secure handholds are crumbling: roles in relationships, cultural images as the chosen people, the forever onward and upward trajectory of progress. Again, the feelings easily bring despair. We may wonder if life has any real order, whether we may live in an essentially random world.

The important recognition is that while the feelings that mark midlife can be strong and disturbing, they do not mark the end of the story.[7] Eventually, they are replaced by a very different sense of things. Midlife, in fact, brings a time of profound renewal. Yes, we must give up our parents. But, at once, in an important sense, we meet them for the first time—now as people rather than as absolutes. In a parallel sense, we come to know ourselves for the first time. It is possible to grasp the full meaning of identity only to the degree one has risked this passage.

---

[7] Not usually. However, midlife is a common time for suicide. We may choose the known unknowness of death over the more personally demanding unknowness of maturity.

The fear and despair we often encounter on first entering midlife comes from seeing just half the picture—the loss of external certainty. As we live through this time of passage, we discover that the dynamic truly makes a bridging, that it goes both ways. Midlife is a two-way dynamic in which absolute order is surrendered in exchange for a more mature, more fully empowered relationship to the workings of order.

The new cultural uncertainty appears to embody a similar paradox. Rather than throwing us into randomness, letting go of scientific certainty is revealing kinds of order much richer than we had imagined before. Instead of leaving us alone and unprotected, surrendering our special status as children of the Divine is opening us up to a new, more empowering spirituality. Uncertainty wears the clothes of chaos only when, in our fear of what it will ask of us, we make it certainty's opposite.

Embracing a reality this big does indeed ask a lot of us. The temptation to find ways to avoid having to grow so much is strong. But I suspect that, given time, as with the passage at midlife, we will find an appreciation for the more mature beauty such a reality holds. We will find that we would not go back if we could.

In the end, the fact of uncertainty in existence simply reflects the fact that truth is creative. Wholeness in any "living" sense requires uncertainty. Uncertainty is the crack in the edifice through which reality breathes. It is the space between the notes through which mere sound becomes music.

Traps

Separation Fallacies:	Final truth is what can be objectively demonstrated. The task of understanding is to bring things fully into the light of reason. Once brought into the light, all will be certain.
Unity Fallacies:	Final truth is that which we know within. The task of understanding is to connect into feelings, intuition, and spirit. All is mystery.

Compromise Fallacies: The task is to be balanced as a person, to be educated both in the sciences and the humanities.

Bridgings

Truth is the larger whole of inner and outer experience.

Full understanding requires all of our "intelligences"—working together and engaged in timely fashion.

"Living" truth bridges determinacy and indeterminacy as we conventionally think of them. It is intricately patterned, but with uncertainty as an essential thread in the pattern.

CHAPTER EIGHT

GOOD AND EVIL: TOWARD A NEW ETHICS OF LIFE

*"[T]he secret that puzzled all the philosophers, baffled all
the lawyers, muddled all the men of business, and ruined
most of the artists: the secret of right and wrong."*
—George Bernard Shaw
Major Barbara

*"If I am not for myself, who will be for me?
And if I am only for myself, who am I?"*
—attributed to Rabbi Hillel
from *The Talmud*

*"I see a kind of intellectual, cultural, and ethical anomie,
a condition where people have nothing to live for, nothing to commit their lives to—no sense of meaningful
activity...."*
—Michael Hooker
Chancellor, U. of Maryland

*"Give and it shall be given unto you is still the truth
about life. But giving life is not so easy. It doesn't mean
handing it out to some mean fool, or letting the living
dead eat you up. It means kindling the life quality where
it is not."*
—D.H. Lawrence

We turn now to a species of question that spans all domains,
though most traditionally associated with religion and philosophy:
questions of ethics—of right and wrong, good and evil.

With increasing frequency, people refer to these as times of
moral crisis. They point to rampant drug abuse, "sleaze" in government, corruption in business, the weakening of the family,
overflowing prisons. The label is, I think, appropriate. But this
crisis, I would argue, represents much more than a crisis of morality in the traditional sense—one of having been bad and now needing to be good. Its implications are far broader, and much more
interesting.

Questions of morality and ethics lie at the heart of the major challenges of our time. Here we explore three related bridgings: between Moral and Immoral, Benevolence and Violence, and Success and Failure. The core question: *What does it mean to act morally in an integral reality?*

Moral and Immoral

"Out-worn heart, in a time out-worn,
  Come clear of the nets of wrong and right;
  Laugh, heart, again in the gray twilight,
  Sigh, heart, again in the dew of the morn."
                                        —William Butler Yeats

Moral crossroads abound in today's life. Take a moment with the following situations. For each, what would you choose to do, and why?

Your child was in an auto accident and has been in a coma for six months. There is extensive, irreversible brain damage and little, if any, chance she will ever regain consciousness. She could be kept in this vegetative state for years. What would you do?

You are an executive for a small local oil company. In order to increase profits, your company is misleading the public about its readiness to respond to potential oil spills. You feel concerned about the environment, but also about the shaky financial situation of your company. If the company collapsed, it would mean the loss of hundreds of jobs in an economically depressed area. On what bases do you decide what to do?

Your sister's husband of thirty years is in a nursing home with Alzheimer's disease. He still recognizes her, but little else. While still married to him, she becomes sexually involved with another man. How do you judge her actions? What, if anything, would you do?

You serve as part of a governmental commission formulating policy toward developing countries in Africa. Plans put forward range from many that would benefit your own country at the ultimate expense of African economies, to others that bring mutual benefit, to some that simply extend philanthropy. If you wish to be most ethically correct, on what bases do you weigh potential policy decisions?

You are part of an international commission addressing the ethical Pandora's Box of new biological technologies: test-tube fertilization, surrogate motherhood, and the potential for such things as creating new species and cloning. What kinds of questions will you need to ask? What policies would you end up advocating?

Once upon a time, questions of ethics and morality looked pretty straightforward. Well...it wasn't always easy to stay on the right side of things. But it was generally pretty clear where the right side lay. The culture, and specifically the church, provided us with codes of appropriate behavior that for most circumstances defined things pretty completely. This is a mortal sin, that a venial one. And here is what you must do if you want your cumulative transgressions not to lead to eternal residence in the hotter half of things.[1]

Today's reality is not so clear-cut. Acting from simple, black-and-white codes often leads to more harm than help.

Some of this results from new kinds of moral questions that just don't fit into the Procrustean bed of traditional moral dictates. The first example above illustrates. With our increasing ability to keep people alive almost indefinitely, the simple rule "thou shalt not kill" ceases to guide us adequately.

But the greater impetus to step beyond blacks and whites, I would claim, results from something even more significant: changes in morality itself. To better understand these changes, let's step back for some historical perspective.

The move beyond black-and-white rules actually began at the time of the Reformation. As the absolute hold of the medieval church came into question, two things took place: God's word opened more to individual interpretation and the primary measure of moral right gradually shifted from avoiding sin to the more personal and flexible measure of doing good deeds.

---

[1] Actually things were never quite this simple. Sincere souls always agonized over moral questions. But the agonizing concerned the interpretation of cultural codes—does this act break that taboo, violate this moral sanction—rather than what the codes themselves should be.

The trend away from the centrality of good and evil got a major boost from the Industrial Age's increasingly individualistic and materialist ethos. The emerging arbiters of truth—science and economics—each defined its sphere as separate from concerns of value. Science was simply objective observation, economics the exchange of capital.

With modern times, we find this trend expressed in the extreme. Popular culture turns the morally defined truth of the Middle Ages on its head. The seven deadly sins—pride, greed, lust, envy, sloth, anger, and gluttony—have now, if anything, transformed into virtues. One could argue that, taken together, they make a pretty good description of the modern American Dream.

We could interpret this in a variety of ways. Many would see it positively: We have reached a point of final moral liberation, they would say, of culminating emancipation from the shackles of churchly dictate. Others would argue that in a fundamental way we have gone astray. They would claim that we stand in the midst of moral crisis for the simple reason that we have abandoned adherence to traditional moral conviction.

I suggest that in the big picture we have not gone astray. These changes have been timely, part of the same story of evolving individual liberty that gave us such things as democratic governance and trial by one's peers. But if out of fear we stop here, our future will not be a bright one.

If *caveat emptor* represents our moral end point, we are in deep trouble. But just as surely cries for a return to traditional values miss how big the questions have grown. We are being challenged to a new morality. It involves a going back in one sense, a "remembering" that issues of value must be kept central. But it also demands that we leave old codes of black as opposed to white well behind us. Setting one part of ourselves against another—personally, the internal "virtuous one" against oneself as "sinner"; culturally, "good" people against "bad"—won't work for the whole-person/whole-system questions that now confront us.

Exactly what is being asked? Again, we must acknowledge that we are but taking the first crude steps. A morality able to circumscribe the either/or of good and evil demands much of us.

Once upon a time, questions of ethics and morality looked pretty straightforward. (Jan van Eyck, "The Last Judgement," Metropolitan Museum of Art.)

Our three criteria for emergent conception can help us begin to approach this new morality. A morality that truly bridges would be a "relational" morality, able to address questions in terms of sensitive weighings of subtly interconnected quantities. It would be an "evolutionary" morality, able to recognize that moral truth is not a fixed quantity—that what is right for one time may not be right for another. And it would be a "meta-determinant" morality, able to address tough decisions in the context of real uncertainty.

To explore more deeply what a larger moral consciousness asks of us, let's look at one specific moral dilemma in detail. An area that cries out for "third space" solutions is the drug crisis. It makes a particularly potent example because, along with requiring a new kind of moral response, it confronts us with the larger systemic challenges that define our times.

Thus far, we have approached the drug question almost exclusively as a crisis of morality in the traditional polar sense: Taking drugs is bad; not taking drugs is good. Consistent with this perspective, we have centered our responses around "attacking" this "evil." We've mounted a "war on drugs"—mobilized offensives against suppliers, punished users, and educated the populace about the evils of drug use.

Whether we look more theoretically or just at the ineffectiveness of current efforts, it is clear that the problem is not that simple. How do we better understand what is going on? What more is the drug crisis than just a question of doing bad?

Our three criteria offer a start. First, the drug crisis is a complexly "relational" question. We can't separate the fact of drug use from a multitude of other critical cultural concerns—education, poverty, the family, fears of living in an uncertain world. As well, it is "evolutionary," a question of its time. Drugs have always been around. The often nearly suicidal attraction we see today is something quite new. And it is "meta-determinant." By all evidence, the drug crisis has no once-and-for-all solution.

The earlier notion that truth ultimately measures "aliveness" helps further expand our perspective. The central fact of the drug crisis is this: Somehow a major portion of our population is choosing to ingest substances that mimic aliveness rather than take the risks necessary to experience the real thing. It can be well argued that the drug crisis is much less about certain people doing wrong than about a larger "crisis of purpose" that affects all of us.

The nature of the drugs themselves adds detail to the picture. Drugs like cocaine and amphetamines provide a way to feel "up." As I see it, their popularity reflects at least a couple of things: first, how much the pursuit of superficial, consumptive pleasure has become our cultural ethos, and second, though we readily deny it, how little hope people today often feel for living a life with real excitement and purpose. Drugs like heroin and alcohol kill pain. Particularly for those who most feel the painful inequities of modern society, they offer an antidote. Hallucinogenic drugs—and also alcohol, though in a different way—evoke feelings of relatedness—with oneself, with others, with the spiritual. Their popularity reflects how such connections are often missing in modern life.

Limited to a good-against-evil, "war on drugs" mentality, we miss the mark on multiple levels. We end up "blaming the victim." We "shoot the messenger" rather than listening to what drug use is trying to tell us. And we turn to, at best, band-aid solutions. Such things as educating about drug use and closing down "crack" houses have some limited value. But in the end, telling our children to "just say no" has meaning only to the degree our children can feel our commitment to a world that deeply and meaningfully says "yes."

A more "relational, evolutionary, meta-determinant" perspective suggests that the "solution" to the drug crisis may lie as much in new ways of being as with doing in the traditional sense of new laws and new policies. The drug crisis challenges us to say "yes" to a new responsibility in the human story.

This challenge has multiple dimensions. We need to step beyond our now impoverishing ethic of "more and more, faster and faster." We need to creatively and committedly engage the multiplicity of factors that combine to make life for many a nearly inescapable dead end: poverty, homelessness, illiteracy, prejudice. We need to address our children's fears that there may not be a future—by saying good-bye to our need for "evil others," by making the well-being of the planet an uncompromisable priority. And we need to give new emphasis to relationships of all sorts—with each other in community, with the natural world, and personally, with our own hearts and souls. In short, the drug crisis demands that we take on the challenge of a new cultural maturity.

Few of today's moral questions hit so directly at the core of the changes required of us as the example of drug use. But all moral questions, however commonplace, ask something similarly new of us. They require that we move beyond simple "good versus evil" polemics and step forward into an at once more liberating and decidedly more demanding moral reality.

The challenge of a new moral consciousness is richly multilayered. Besides bridging good and evil, it involves a second bridging that is at least as big: between questions that are moral and those that are not. It is but a small step from the earlier notion that truth must now be "purpose-centered" to the recognition that choice— choice of all sorts—must now be "ethics-centered." In a critical new sense *all* questions are becoming moral questions. A new moral responsibility permeates every choice we make.

When sacred and secular lay separate, we could rightly say that some concerns were simply practical and others ethical. Bridge, and all questions become both. Just as we have to leave behind simplistic black and white measures, we also have to leave behind expectations of finding any safe questions, safe occupations, or safe roles—actions that do not have moral consequences. What we buy, how we get from one place to another, even what we do with our garbage pose questions intimately connected to concerns of larger well-being. Daily life in an integral world becomes an ongoing process of making whole-person/whole-system—i.e., "moral"— choices.

Benevolence and Violence

"Those whose souls are weak settle for comfort or for violence."

—Erich Fromm

Only a short distance from issues of morality lies the subject of violence. It makes a second powerful entry point into the question of moral right in an integral reality.

We must be ready to step beyond easy polemics if we wish to address the subject of violence at all completely. We saw some of this earlier with the polarity of war and peace. Is war violence? Measured in terms of whether pain is inflicted, few things could be more so. But as we saw, if we reach to a larger definition and ask if at certain times and places in the human story war served a creative purpose, we get a different answer. Determining whether war is violent in the sense of ultimate harm requires asking more questions than simply whether guns and knives were brandished.

Whether a particular act is violence poses a systems question, and more than this, a question profoundly relative in time. What enhances life at one point in the creative life of a system may do obvious harm at another, and equally the reverse.

For example, human sacrifice was a common practice in the earliest stages of cultural development. Was it violence? Practiced in modern culture it certainly would be (and we would assume quite appropriately that the people involved were dangerously deranged). But in its ritual timeliness, I would suggest not. While "terrible" in the poetic sense, it served the essential ritual function of helping to turn the seasons and bring new fertility. The life of the tribe being primary to that of the individual in tribal reality, the act worked ultimately to "make things more."

Another example concerns slavery. If practiced in present times, it would be no less obviously violent. But it was more the exception than the rule in early cultures. Interpretation gets tricky when we try to draw a line. George Washington gave Martha two slaves as a wedding present. Does this mean he was a violent man? If not, or not wholly, what does it say? What, exactly, is violence?

The form of an act alone cannot tell us whether it is violent. The significance of an apparently violent act remains relative to its time and context. If we look closely, we discover that almost any act, given the right situation, can be an act of violence. In an extreme example, nothing appears more beautiful than the closeness of the bond of love between a mother and her infant. But if held past its timeliness, this same closeness strangles and suffocates, becoming no longer love, but a most indelible kind of destructiveness.

These examples spotlight the pivotal question for addressing issues of moral right as a whole and of violence in particular: What, at essence, must be our basis for decision, our guide in making the critical value choices on which our future well-being so profoundly depends? If we can no longer say with finality that killing is bad or that love is good, to what do we turn?

Hints of the answer appear in these examples of the relativity of violence in time. Questions of wrong, questions that we previously would have spoken of in terms of sin or violence, ultimately offer the other side of the coin to the central question of the last chapter: What makes something valuable and true? These questions are the "no" to its "yes." Truth from a "third space" perspective is that which makes something more "alive," larger in creative terms. In a complementary way, "evil" in a whole-system reality means anything that diminishes aliveness, makes something creatively less. The integral "moral" task is to discern when this lessening takes place and how to act so that life can again become more.

Such discerning is not easy. We must bring all of ourselves to the task, bridge on multiple, often extremely challenging levels.

To explore more of what is being asked of us, let's again consider a particular issue. Abortion poses a question often framed in terms of violence—and one that begs for "third space" sanity. The chasm between those who see abortion as the taking of human life and those who see it as a question of individual liberty easily seems unspannable. The following story recounts one person's efforts at addressing the issue in terms of aliveness:

Jean was forty-one, divorced, and the mother of a nineteen-year-old daughter. She first began seeing me about six months ago following cancer surgery.

At a recent session, she arrived quite distraught. In spite of her conscientious use of birth control, she had become pregnant.

"I've hardly slept the last four days," she said, as she set herself uneasily in the chair. "I thought I knew how I felt about abortion. I don't. I've gone from one extreme to the other and everything in between. When I was twenty, I had an abortion. It was so simple then—I wasn't married and wasn't ready. That's all that seemed important to know.

"Logically, having a child makes no sense. I've had enough of being a mother, and the father is not in the picture. And the biggest problem is I have no idea how long I'll live. They think they got most of the cancer, but less than half of people with my kind of cancer live five years.

"And in one sense none of that matters. The fetus is something alive and that is the only thing that is really important.

"You know, I listen to the debates about abortion and what both sides say feels true. Crazy, right? How can they both be true?

"I believe that it is important that the mother be the one to choose. But I can't buy the notion that because a fetus wouldn't live if it was born there is no harm being done. That's a cop-out. A fetus is not a baby, but it would become a baby.

"Is it murder or isn't it, back and forth. Both sides make it so black and white. You know, I don't think they are really asking the right question.

"If I have an abortion it will certainly be a different kind of choice than before. I will have to do it accepting that while it may not be murder, it is a kind of killing, and a killing of something that could be very beautiful.

"But not having an abortion could ultimately be the larger violence. I still don't know what I will choose to do. Whatever it is, it won't at all be an easy decision."

In her inner struggle, Jean was searching for the decision that would support life in the largest sense. To do this she needed to step beyond the polemics of each side of the abortion debate.

Addressing moral questions in the new way being demanded of us usually involves multiple bridgings. The "third space" perspective on abortion with which Jean grappled involved at least four. Each required that familiar form-defined answers be left behind and that truth be measured through subtle weighings of aliveness. The abortion question bridges benevolence and violence, our topic here. (It is a simple fact—abortion involves the ending of a potential life. Is it thus by definition wrong?) It also bridges self and other. (Is the fetus part of the mother or a unique individual? And what about its relationship to life as a whole?) It bridges self and society. (If abortion does have a place, who should make that decision?[2]) And it bridges life and not-life. (This polarity most defines the intractability of the usual polar positions on abortion. If the fetus is alive, abortion is killing and therefore wrong. If not, it is not killing, and therefore not wrong.)

Besides helping us in making moral decisions, the concept of an integral referent can help us as well in the task of articulating moral/ethical positions—in communicating about what we see happening and what we feel needs doing.

The question of articulation is immensely important, for by their nature "third space" positions are tricky to communicate. Traditionally, taking a stand has meant assuming a polar posture, setting one position in opposition to another. The polar tension in this served to get others' "attention," and setting "this as opposed to that" helped us delineate what we claim to be true.

Using a referent like aliveness gives us a way to speak, and to speak with *passion*. We might easily assume that a "third space" moral voice always speaks with moderation, that it balances equally opposing views and expresses from a place of calm composure. This is a compromise fallacy and decidedly disempowering. More than ever before, the cultural challenges require a willingness to speak strongly for what is morally right.

Let me get up on my soapbox for a moment about a kind of violence that I find of particular concern. The following is ex-

---

[2] The person who takes a "pro-choice" position may answer reflexively, "the mother." But what if it was one day prior to delivery?

cerpted from a talk I gave to a group of communications majors. What is important is not whether you agree or disagree with my conclusions, but the question of articulating new moral truth.

If someone asked me to list the most pervasive inflictors of violence in the culture today, I would put television near the top of my list. I don't see T.V. as inherently violent, but violence is often its effect.

I'm not talking here simply about violent programming. Rather, my concern is with the total effect of the medium, as presently utilized, on personal and social well-being.

In part, the function of television is to communicate. But it has another function as well—a function not terribly different from that of an addicting drug. The analogy is worth looking at in some detail.

Most programming includes some useful content, but at least in the offerings of the major networks, content is generally secondary to a more primary function. That function is to divert, to keep us artificially stimulated by bombarding us with "pseudo-aliveness"—car crashes, the knee-jerk melodrama of the soaps, the mindless material fantasies of game shows, endless shootings—safe substitutes for the real aliveness that comes from more vulnerable acts like asking real questions and having real relationships. Even the news, symbol of the modern informed populace, is not wholly exempt from this charge. With its incessant focus on the latest disasters and scandals, it is often more a kind of indulgent, quasi-intellectual soap opera—"info-tainment"—than anything that actually informs.

Actually, the problem is less television itself than television advertising, or, more specifically, what the television environment becomes as a function of being advertisement driven. In the abstract, advertising serves a valuable purpose—to inform people about the availability and benefits of products. In practice it most often works quite differently. Modern advertising's bottom-line purpose is to get us to buy things, whether or not we need them and irrespective of their real value. In advertising classes, one of the first rules taught insists that one never talk logically about what one sells—this gets people to think, with the likely result that they would not buy the product. At essence, then, advertising functions as a form of manipulation—more pointedly, lying. Because substance in programming promotes questioning and discernment, activities mutually exclusive with effective lying, advertising drives the medium in the direction of increasingly empty and consumptive fare.

The problem goes beyond advertising's effect on programming to advertising itself. It would not be so great a concern were its deceptions not so effective. This effectiveness comes from the place advertising speaks to in our psyches. Advertising uses the language of art and spirit: the preverbal—metaphor, image, movement, sound. In terms of money spent, it wins hands down as our time's preeminent "art form." But it takes the traditional function of art, invoking our inner connection with beauty and purpose, and perverts it in quite an ultimate way: Rather than enabling the soul, it seeks to rob and deceive it.

These potent subliminal effects are particularly disturbing when directed at children. This is one of the places where the art of advertising as hypnosis reaches its highest development. I see it here as child abuse of the worst sort; abuse not of the body, but of the heart and soul.

"Coke is it." "Salems are springtime fresh." At no other time in history would such statements be tolerable. Perhaps "God is it." Or "democracy is it." Or "logic is it." But "Coke is it?" And we wonder at the level of addiction and the degree of superficiality and aimlessness that so mark our times.

These are strong words. It is important to hear what I am saying and what I am not saying. Hear that I do not make advertising *the* cause of our cultural anomie. It simply contributes one part of a complex dynamic. And I certainly do not suggest that advertising should be outlawed. It is an important part of a market economy.

I do suggest that television and television advertising are critical focuses of concern—that we need to understand keenly the various levels at which they affect, that we need to educate our children about the dynamics of that effect, and that we need to be willing to speak out strongly when those effects do harm. And I think we should enact safeguards for advertising directed at children, using some of the same boundaries we invoke for other potentially harmful influences such as alcohol and pornography.

For you who will be prime shapers of media in the future, taking significant time with such concerns is imperative. Your willingness to do this will determine the degree to which what you offer with your lives will, in fact, add to life. The future asks of all of us a new kind of moral sensitivity and moral courage. Questions of purpose and effect in the use of media are big parts of that challenge.

The views I expressed were not terribly charitable. Yet, I feel they were relatively integral and important to voice. Framing the issue in terms of "aliveness" allowed me to step beyond polar absolutes yet still speak with force and urgency.

The more that the critical questions become moral questions, the more our world asks that we be willing to take strong stands. Nothing will be more important for the challenges ahead than the willingness to speak strongly against dynamics that make us less and for dynamics that make us more.

Success and Failure

Until 1933, no Rolls-Royce was equipped with a reverse gear. Sir Henry Royce was unwilling to have his car adopt what he regarded as an undignified mode of progression.

It might seem strange that I would include success and failure in a chapter on good and evil, but it is actually quite appropriate. When we moved beyond the Middle Ages' image of truth as an isometric battle between a heavenly above and a demonic below, the "moral" image that replaced it was the "ladder of success." Again, the task was to get from below to heavenly above. Only now, the "above" was material and reachable in a lifetime rather than just in the hereafter.

This image now moves beyond its timeliness as surely as its more strident partner did. The pictures we once used to define both personal and cultural achievement reward us less and less.

In thinking about success and failure, I am often drawn to the memory of the first client I ever worked with. I'll call him Bill:

In our first session I asked Bill what he wanted to accomplish in therapy.

"I want to make more money," he said. "I'm successful, but I could make a lot more. I'm just not motivated like I should be."

Not knowing that a few deeper questions might be in order, I accepted his goal as stated, and we got to work. Sort of. I got to work—he seemed distracted. We were clearly missing the mark. Finally, after several sessions, not knowing what else to do, I started asking more questions.

"Bill," I said, "why do you want all this money?"

"What?"

"What do you want to buy with it?"

"Oh, I think I'd like an airplane," he said.

"Why an airplane?" I asked.

"I'd like to fly to someplace like…oh, Hawaii."

"Hawaii, huh. Why Hawaii?

"Oh, just to hang out on the beaches."

For the first time I sensed just a bit of life in what he was saying, so I kept going. "And why the beaches? Why that?"

A long pause… "Well, maybe I could meet some girls."

With that, he blushed and looked so anxious I was afraid he was going to bolt from the room.

"Have you ever had a girl friend?" I asked carefully. Almost imperceptibly, he shook his head.

"Why don't we work on that?" I suggested. And the real therapy began.

Like Bill, we increasingly find ourselves, both as individuals and as a culture, pursuing goals that miss the mark. The American Dream, its monetary Grail set atop an onward and upward ladder of success, provided an adequate mythic image for the Age of Individuality and Industry. More and more, it ceases to serve.

It is ceasing to serve us on all fronts. It ceases to serve individually: Though we try to hide from the fact, for most people the image of the American Dream no longer satisfies. It has moved beyond its timeliness. Our frenetic pursuit of it, even when we succeed in our efforts, is as apt to bring estrangement and emptiness as fulfillment.

And it ceases to serve us as a species: In realizing their material supremacy, the industrialized nations, as just a small percentage of the world's population, have come to consume the vast majority of the world's resources. This can't continue to work.

How do we better define success? A recent discussion at the Institute helped illumine both this question and a related one: Even if we can learn to think of success in larger terms, how can people be persuaded to live from this new definition?

Our topic was new images for wealth. We started by taking time to explore what had most contributed to a sense of "wealth" in our lives. Some of the things mentioned included close friends, a chance to be creative and effective, a healthy body, the opportunity to learn and grow throughout our lives, a vital and nurturing place to live. A common pattern emerged in our responses. For each of us, the most important things were ones for which material wealth had a secondary relevance. Material things felt important, but ultimately only as tools, as ways to support processes that mattered more fundamentally.

As we talked, we played with delineating a new, more integral definition for success. A couple of themes kept reappearing: separating the concept of wealth from that of material consumption and separating our concepts of status and power from images of the traditional ladder of success. The dialogue was offering useful insights.

Then one of the group members stopped us. Our images sounded wonderful, he said, but there was just no way to get people to make the sacrifices needed for such ideals to be real. A pause followed. He made a good point. Was all our talk just empty idealism?

Then another member chuckled. She asked the group if anyone present made even close to as much money as he could if he put his mind to it. Everyone shook their head. Then she asked if anyone in the group experienced this "living below one's means" as sacrifice. Again people shook their heads...and smiles of recognition came to people's faces. We realized that in major ways all the members of the group already bridged traditional success and failure in their lives. We hadn't done this out of some philosophy of denial, out of some need to be "good" people, but directly as a function of our commitment to enjoying the greatest possible richness in our lives. We recognized an important possibility: The transcendence of onward and upward cultural images of success may be less a moral "should" than part of a natural step in the evolution of culture.

The metaphor of the midlife transition again sheds light. Material achievement is an appropriately central concern of young adulthood, part of the essential task of making one's place in the world. But in the second half of life, with one's place established and one's mortality growing increasingly evident, a new question begins to define success. Most succinctly stated, it asks: "When I stand at the 'pearly gates' and look back over my life, what will I most want to be able to say about my short time on this planet?" Material success comes to have a function only as it serves this larger "goal."

If the cultural dynamic is analogous, it carries major implications not just for how we define personal success, but, as well, for our views on what it means to be successful as a culture. We hear politicians emphasizing the importance of keeping America number one, of holding tight to the reins of world dominance and keeping an upper hand in the world marketplace. My guess is that we will find such images increasingly unsatisfying. They are no more appropriate to cultural maturity than the adolescent-like dreams of a forty-five year old frightened of the second half of life are to personal maturity.

They wouldn't give us fulfillment. And like the often regressive dreams of midlife, they probably aren't even options. There are simply too many places in the world that are just now entering the industrial stage in their development, too many strapping youths. A post-industrial people simply can't keep up, either in terms of the costs of labor or the single-minded motivation needed for extreme material productivity.

We can still be number one, but it must be a new kind of number one. The world cries for mature leadership, leadership that emphasizes things like global cooperation, creativity and quality in the workplace, healthy neighborhoods and communities, and a sustainable relationship with the environment. The question is not how to stay number one, but how to muster the courage and humility to be number one in the new, more mature sense the future will require.

Traps

Separation Fallacies:	Moral laws are God-given, absolute, and eternal: good is good, and evil is evil. Richness in life lies in achieving success and avoiding failure.
Unity Fallacies:	Morality is relative: If it feels good, do it. True richness lies in selfless generosity.
Compromise Fallacies:	No question is black or white; there are always shades of gray.

Bridgings

Questions of morality and immorality, benevolence and violence, success and failure are defined ultimately by the degree to which an act makes existence creatively more.

In the big picture, all questions are moral questions—questions of value and choice in a "living" world.

CHAPTER NINE

ILLNESS AND WELLNESS: HEALTH AND THE WHOLE PERSON

"In the twenty-first century we are going to learn a great deal more about…the human healing system and how to tend it, nurture it, and evoke it, rather than just try to repair it."
—Norman Cousins

"It is as important to know the person who has the disease as to know the disease the person has."
—Sir William Osler

"Whatever happens in the mind influences the body and vice versa. In fact, mind and body cannot be separated independently of one another."
—René Dubos

*"Do not try to live forever—
You will not succeed."*
—George Bernard Shaw

We now step into an arena that has held a particularly central place in my life, that of the physician and healer. Two pivotal questions arise here: *What is health? And how do we best enhance it?* These questions have immense implications not just medically, but philosophically and spiritually as well. Each demands that we engage it in new, fundamentally larger ways.

The Age of Reason was marked by quantum steps in both our understanding of health and our ability to promote it. In the span of but a few centuries, medicine evolved from a relatively crude pursuit to an activity of exalted status. The basis for this leap was a series of dramatic scientific/technological breakthroughs: major advances in our understanding of anatomy and physiology, the discovery of microbes and their effects in disease, such innovations as anesthesia and antibiotics, and, most recently, modern diagnostic technology.

Yet today, signs of stress and perturbation trouble the health care world. We continue to have new medical technologies, indeed at an ever increasing pace. But we are seeing a marked erosion of the high esteem in which medicine was once held. Quality of care is being significantly undermined by spiraling costs. And both the traditional posture of medicine and its traditional arsenal are proving inadequate for many of the afflictions that permeate our times.

These changes can be interpreted in a number of ways. It could be that medicine has reached the apex of its development and is beginning a time of decline. Or we could be seeing a plateau before new technologies return medicine to its previous onward-and-upward trajectory.

Or, as with the changes we have witnessed in other domains, these events may transcend such simple success/failure interpretations. Good evidence suggests that we stand at the threshold of a further quantum step in our understanding of health and disease—one at least equal in significance to that which marked the Scientific Age. This next step will be necessary if we are to be effective at delivering health care in the future, and if our ideas about the nature of health are to be adequate for who we have become.

As with changes in other spheres, the innovations that define this next step will be of a different sort than those that defined the last. The impending challenges in health care require us to re-ask the most basic questions about who we are and what it means to be healthy. Here we will look at three polarities that focus on key aspects of these changes: Mind and Body, Health and Disease, and Life and Death.

Mind and Body

"Of all the objects in the world, the human body has a
peculiar status; it is not only possessed by the person who
has it, it also possesses and constitutes [that person]."
—Jonathan Miller

Some of the most provocative new evolutions in our understanding concern the relationship between mind and body. Both
emerging research and new popular sensibilities are calling into
question well-established assumptions about what it means to have
a mind and a body.

Let's again step back historically. The monumental advances of
medicine during the Age of Reason grew from a then profoundly
new conception of the body. The body, like the universe as a whole,
could be viewed as a machine. René Descartes, in his *Traite de l'*
Homme, described the new "body as machine" in these words: "I
wish you to consider, finally, that all the functions...diges-
tion...respiration...memory...appetites and passions...occur solely
by the disposition of its organs, not less than the movements of a
clock." Modern anatomy developed the study of this machine's
gears and levers, modern physiology the study of how these gears
and levers interact.

A fundamental shift in our thinking about the relationship of
the mind with the body lay implicit in this new view of the body:
Mind became separate and distinct. This remained true whether
one's reference with the word "mind" was mind in the sense of
intellect or mind in the more transcendent sense of psyche or spirit.
A mechanical body had no more ongoing need of such things for its
functioning than would, say, a car or a washing machine. The mind
came to be seen as playing no fundamental role in the workings of
the body; and the body, besides being the mind's locale, was seen as
playing no fundamental role in the functioning of the mind.

This was a radical step. Always before healers had viewed mind
and body as in some way joined. We can see this reflected in our
ideas through time about the etiology of disease. For very early
peoples, concepts of mind and body were inextricably intertwined

and ideas about disease intertwined with them. Diseases, both psychological and physical, were generally considered a product of either the breaking of taboo or of spells cast by disgruntled others. In the early high cultures, we find somewhat more distinction, but body, mind, and spirit remained expressly parts of a single whole. The medicine of the classical East, for example, saw the body as composed of psycho-spiritual "energies." The balance between these "energies" determined a person's well-being. In the West, from the time of Hippocrates through the Middle Ages, we see some further separation, but still significant interplay. Practitioners thought health to be a function of the relative balance of visceral "humors"—yellow bile, black bile, phlegm, blood—emotion-laden inner fluids. Words like phlegmatic and bilious remind us of this time before science so cleanly etched the line between physical and emotional health.

Modern medicine's conceptual foundations abandoned such "superstitious" notions. Separation was now absolute. Disease came to be seen simply as the breakdown of the body as machine; healing, as repair done on its broken parts. One might have feelings about what happened to one's body, and certain diseases, like an illness that caused high fever, could affect the functioning of the mind. But outside of a few carefully circumscribed "psychosomatic disorders," the mind and the body, whether in illness or in health, comprised distinct worlds.

Cleaving mind and body was a momentous step. It ushered in the modern medical revolution. Separating mind and body freed people for the first time to openly dissect the body; cutting into the body no longer risked danger to the soul. And defining the body in terms of mechanical cause and effect opened the door to critical notions like the germ theory of disease with its then radical concept of causation by external physical vectors.

This clear teasing apart of the physical and the ephemeral might logically seem to mark a culmination point in the story of our understanding of mind and body, a final reaching of truth. Instead, it appears that while it may mark the end of one rich chapter, it remains far from an end point. New research calls our present view's most fundamental assumptions into question. Mounting evidence

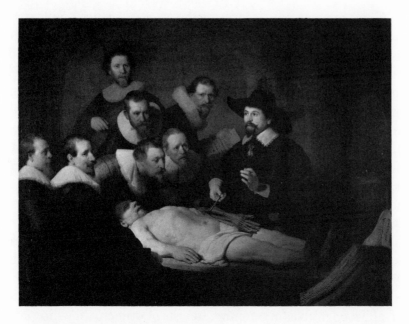

Modern medicine had its foundation in the separating of mind from body. (Rembrandt van Rijn, "The Anatomy Lesson of Dr. Nicholaes Tulp," The Hague.)

suggests that the moat separating mind and body is far from unnavigable; it is a bustling waterway with complex comings and goings.

What are we learning about the larger relationship of mind and body? To start, we are learning just how much thoughts and feelings can affect physiological processes. Some connection was always pretty obvious; when we get scared, our hearts beat faster, we sweat, and we breathe more quickly. Research now shows that these connections work at much more subtle levels than we before imagined.

With simple biofeedback, people can easily learn to do such things as raise and lower skin temperature, alter heart rate, and affect brain wave patterns. With hypnosis we can block pain and alter all manner of physiological responses. In one particularly striking example, a person in a deep trance is told that a pencil touching him is a hot iron. It is not uncommon for a real blister to appear on the skin.

Conversely, we are discovering the degree to which bodily states can affect mood and even intellectual functioning. Much of this discovery results from beginning to bring the language of the body into the "talk" of psychotherapy. We are finding how a relatively small release of held bodily tension often brings floods of long forgotten memories and feelings. We are seeing how much more a person's bodily "posture" represents than merely anatomical mechanics, how it reflects a person's emotional/intellectual "attitude" as well. And we are recognizing the degree to which words like "gut feelings" and "heartfelt emotions" are more than just metaphors, how they express the body's voice in the psyche as a psycho-physical reality.

One piece of research with significant implication in this regard also ties in nicely with earlier topics. Elizabeth Hampson and Doreen Kimara at the University of Western Ontario recently presented the first clear scientific evidence that levels of sex hormones can affect cognitive functioning. In tests of women, they showed as much as a ten percent increase in verbal facility—a trait women traditionally test higher on than men—during periods of the menstrual cycle when blood levels of the female hormone estrogen are high. They found a concomitant decrease in ability to solve problems involving spatial reasoning—a trait at which men traditionally excel. Body dynamics, we find, can affect not just how we feel, but how we think. (Note that these findings—besides having implications for our understanding of mind, body, intelligence, and gender—open up a Pandora's Box of new ethical questions. The timing in one's menstrual cycle could significantly affect scores on major standardized tests, such as the Scholastic Aptitude Test taken by all high-school seniors. Should scores, or when tests are given, be adjusted accordingly? And what about the use of sex hormones to enhance academic achievement in the same manner that anabolic steroids have been used for physical performance?)

As with other bridgings, when we begin to span the separation of mind and body, we find ourselves entering some rather slippery conceptual terrain. What is being asked doesn't reduce to a simple image. Jonathan Miller's words introducing this section help us grasp the scope of the challenge. The body, he suggests, is simultaneously something we have and something we are. This is obviously true, yet also a logical contradiction. In the reconciliation of this creative paradox lies the kind of understanding that the mind/body question asks of us.

We like to think of mind and body as concrete entities. As accurately, we could claim that they simply represent concepts. They are words used to describe a particular kind of dialogue. A dialogue between what? It is not a simple question. Not only has the content of the dialogue evolved over time, but also how we have characterized its participants. The yogi's energy body, the medieval physician's body of bile and phlegm, and the modern Western anatomical body could hardly appear more different.

Once we acknowledge the presence of creative interplay between mind and body, a further question, and a topic of growing interest, logically presents itself. What role, if any, does the mind play in disease?

Expose a group of people to the same germs and some will get sick, some won't. Why? Genetics, diet, and whether a person is otherwise healthy clearly contribute. And evidence is accumulating that psychological factors often play a major role.

A now classic piece of research was done in the 1960s by Thomas Holmes and Richard Rahe at the University of Washington. They measured the amount of life change, both positive (e.g., a promotion) and negative (e.g., the death of a spouse), with which a person had to cope in a given period. Then they compared it with the incidence of disease. They found a high correlation—more life change equalled more disease—and not just for ailments such as ulcers and high blood pressure that we traditionally associate with stress, but for nearly all kinds of afflictions—tuberculosis, leukemia, diabetes, multiple sclerosis. Life change also matched up with things like accidents and depression.

Along with this epidemiological kind of data, we see a significant amount of research relating personality attributes to both illness susceptibility and healing. In a study done over the course of 25 years at the University of North Carolina Medical School, a battery of psychological tests were given to incoming medical students and the results were correlated with later incidence of heart disease. They found that students who measured high in "hostility" faced four times the likelihood of such disease and six times the ensuing mortality. Related work done by Steven Grear at Kings College in England found that, following breast removal for cancer, women with a positive attitude toward the potential outcome displayed better than twice the ten-year survival rate of women who responded with feelings of helplessness and hopelessness.

We also see research that suggests some of the linking mechanisms involved. The work of Janice Kiecolt-Glaser and Ronald Glaser at Ohio State Medical School, for example, demonstrated that exam stress can reduce the effectiveness of "natural killer cells," important players in the immune system. At the biochemical level, researchers are finding a growing number of brain transmitters that communicate directly with the various components of the immune system. Conversely, they are finding receptor sites in the brain for chemicals that immune system cells alone produce. A picture now emerges of mind and immune system linked by a complex, two-way network of cellular processes and informational molecules.

More and more, it appears that mind and matter, brain and body, act together as a coherent, interwoven system to determine our capacity for health.

A recent—and amusing—"blooper" from an Associated Press Wire Service report described an injured football player as being "in a coma of unknown *ideology*." Popular understanding of mind/body interaction in disease has not reached quite that level of sophistication, but we do see a growing cultural acceptance of such notions reflected in the media. We hear Woody Allen in the film *Manhattan* tell Diane Keaton: "I don't get angry; I grow tumors instead." Lily Tomlin gets nods of agreement as well as laughter with her succinct prescription for health: "For fast relief, try slowing down."

These new discoveries elicit excitement. And we should proceed with a certain caution. We must not forget that we are but toddlers in this new territory. As always, ready traps await the unwary.

A common trap leads us to simply fall off the other end of the conceptual teeter-totter, replacing illness as physical with some notion that makes psychological or spiritual dynamics the "real" factors. We say that, in fact, the cause of illness is "stress," or claim that ultimately we "choose to be ill."

Evidence may eventually support the notion that psychological or spiritual factors always at some level exert a causal influence in illness. But in the end, easy psychological or spiritual answers offer no more help than their physical counterparts. They blind us to the complexity of the picture. And they can lead us to cast a most unhelpful kind of blame when compassion is the more appropriate emotion.

As a psychiatrist, I work often with people interested in exploring psychological aspects of physical problems. Time in the trenches has taught me over and over that nothing is more important in working with physical illness than openness to the unique process of each person. A good education for me came from working over the last five years with three men who suffered heart attacks prior to the age of thirty-five. Same sex, same age, same disease—yet the stories that emerged differed profoundly, reaching from one theoretical extreme of causation to the other.

A technique I often use in working with people is to have them enter a dream-like state and "journey" metaphorically to the part of their body where the illness resides. The person then "dialogues" with the illness. The images that emerged for these three men make a useful shorthand language for what transpired in their work:

> Sam described himself as a quiet loner. He had experienced a difficult childhood, one with many losses. He grew up in foster homes and never lived in any one place for more than a few years.
>
> Four years before his heart attack, he met a woman with whom he had his first significant relationship and was married. A year later they had a child. In the six months before his attack, the child was killed in a traffic accident and the marriage dissolved.
>
> Journeying to his heart, Sam saw a small tree in the desert, desiccated and alone. Two branches were broken—one for his wife, one for his child. A crack split the trunk. Sam wasn't sure, but he thought that was the heart attack. Looking at the tree, Sam wept deeply. He said he didn't know if the tree could be saved.

At first it embarrassed Sam to try to talk to the image, but once he did, it came easily. He asked it about the crack. It responded that, yes, that had occurred at the time of the heart attack. He asked what happened. It responded, "Don't you know? I tried to stand strong, but there was just too much pain."

After sitting with this for a while, Sam asked the tree what he needed to do. It answered that he needed to find new ways to nurture and love himself and to find love in his world. This would need to be done quickly, because without help, he wouldn't live much longer.

Over the next year, as Sam worked on these things, he would return now and then to the image. At first he simply saw himself standing by the tree, caring about it. Then in one session he found himself going out in the desert with a small earthen cup, digging until he found water, and bringing it back for the tree. As the months went by, bit by bit, the tree began to recover.

Sam is now doing well. He has done much deep inner work and begun a number of new friendships. Tests show his heart largely recovered.

With Sam, there was little question, at least for me, that psychological issues played a major role in his illness. For a second patient, Peter, the history, the "felt sense," and the images that emerged told a very different story.

Peter described himself as an "average guy." He was married, had one child, and worked as a carpenter. He had often been ill as a child, but had been generally healthy in the years before his attack.

The image that met Peter when he journeyed to the area of his heart was that of an old, lame horse, barely making its way along. Peter asked it what was wrong. Its poignant reply was, "Sorry pal. I'm just worn out. I've tried my best, but I've done all I can do. You drew a weak one. It's not your fault. I was lame and sickly when we started out. I've tried hard not to let you down. I'm sorry."

Six months after we started work, Peter had a second attack and died.

It felt very painful to be with Peter through this work. I realized all I could do was be there as a friend and assist him in getting what help might be of value. As much as I searched for possible underlying dynamics, I never sensed any with Peter. The best I can make of it, Peter was just unlucky enough to get born with a poor piece of anatomy.

The situation with Andrew was different still. Here, psychological factors again seemed to play a role, but in a more general sense.

Andrew was a fast-track executive, a highly driven perfectionist. He worked long hours, ate poorly, got little rest. The image that arose for him was of a car in an auto race that had blown its engine. In one session he asked the car if there was any significance to the fact that it was the engine that had gone. "Nope," said the car, "you drive too hard and don't take care of me. It was only a matter of time until something blew. Could have as easily been the transmission or the differential. And it just might be next time if you don't take it a little easier and bring me in for service now and then."

Andrew faced important questions of goals and life-style, but I never sensed deeper dynamics involved—in spite of my psychiatrist's natural tendency to look for such things.

The lesson? Mind/body dynamics in disease don't fit into simple formulas. At least none have revealed themselves to this point. This awareness is equally critical for those with a more traditional physical bias and those with a more psychological or spiritual bias. We are starting to recognize a few patterns—related to different personality styles, to different kinds of disease. Over time, we will likely tease out a lot more. But a hundred years from now the "answer" for all but a few exceptional situations will most likely continue to lie in our ability to engage the unique process of each person.

In the future, the ability to think in mature mind/body terms will become a health care imperative. When specific infectious diseases provided the primary focuses of medicine, a "broken machine" view of things didn't work too badly. With diseases like polio, typhoid, or tuberculosis, although clearly some people got sick and others didn't, we dealt with afflictions fairly amenable to a "single cause/single cure" approach.

But the major maladies of today are of a different sort. They are what René Dubos has called "afflictions of civilization"—cancer, heart disease, stroke, AIDS, drug and alcohol addiction. These ailments arise from a complexity of factors—environmental, genetic, psychological/spiritual, social. To deal effectively with these ailments that increasingly define health care, we must learn to think about both causation and cure in dynamic, systemic terms.

This new picture presents a much more challenging reality than that with which we are familiar. But if we can be humble to the size of its questions, it has immensities to teach us.

Health and Disease

"Witchcraft, and all manner of spectre-work, and demonology, we have now named madness, and diseases of the nerves, seldom reflecting that still the new question comes upon us: What is madness, what are nerves?"
—Thomas Carlyle

The bridging of mind and body holds implicit in it a second bridging of at least equal importance—that between our traditional concepts of health and disease. In a similar way, this bridging brings many of our most basic assumptions about health and healing into question.

In conventional medical thought, health and disease stand as polar opposites. The physician's job is to promote health and to defeat disease. The particular flavor of this polar relationship has multiple sources. Much of it comes directly from our modern mechanistic view. Health is an intact machine, disease a broken one. Beneath the surface, we also find lingering tastes from a more medieval world view. The relationship of health, disease, and the healing process is not just mechanical, but mythological and moral. Disease is the evil dragon; the physician is the white-coated knight whose job it is to slay the dragon and protect the populace. Deep at its core, modern medical practice remains based in a heroic mythology.

Medicine's heroic posture has worked adequately, indeed often exceptionally, for meeting the medical challenges of our past. But for the future it will not be enough. A brief story illuminates:

Joyce had cancer. We had worked together off and on throughout the eight-year course of her illness, my helping her as I could to adjust to her illness and to explore the many questions that it presented about herself and life as a whole. Few people with her particular kind of cancer live over two or three years. She died recently.

I visited her in the hospital in the week before her death. As I walked into her room, I was struck by how at peace she looked. We talked at length. As I sat there holding her hand, at one point she looked at me and said: "Charley, you know I'm really not sad about dying. I can't even say I regret having gotten cancer. When I look over these six years, I realize I have learned so much. Perhaps I would have learned it all anyway, but I doubt it. Having to deal with this thing in me has been such a teacher.

"If I had my choice, I'd like to live on. But if someone came into the room right now and said 'Joyce, you can take your life as it has been and die now, or give up the experiences of the last six years and continue living,' I think I'd probably choose to die. I feel full. I could not ask much more from life."

As I listened, I reflected over the time I had known Joyce. She was an active, vital woman, someone who saw herself with many good years potentially ahead. She had tried vigorously to deny the cancer's presence.

Finally, following surgery that revealed extensive spread of the disease, she gradually acknowledged what was happening. She began to let her feelings about it grow real. With time, her attitude toward the cancer shifted. She found herself meeting it as simply part of her life—something that perhaps she could conquer, but whatever, something she would need to engage face-to-face.

Sitting there, I realized that in spite of knowing that her body was riddled with disease, I had come to experience Joyce as one of the healthiest people I knew. I shared this with her and saw the warmth of acknowledgment in her gaze.

As I left the room and walked down the hall, I found myself pondering just what in Joyce made me feel this way. It wasn't just that Joyce was a special person. She was, but it had more to do with her relationship to the process of the cancer. What was that relationship? A courageous fight? A spiritual transcendence? It was more encompassing than these things, yet also more ordinary. It had to do with the simple integrity with which she met her illness, her commitment to grappling with it, learning from it, letting it take her to the unknowable edge of who she was. My own life was enriched by Joyce, as was my thinking about medicine.

Joyce and other patients like her challenge past conceptions of health and disease. Seeing health as simply the absence of disease is no longer enough. Neither can we view our task as simply that of "fighting" disease. The old heroic mythologies aren't big enough. They won't hold all that is important in what happens in the healing relationship. And they are inadequate for addressing the immense emergent challenges of health care.

The imperative of bridging health and disease and moving beyond an isolatedly heroic posture is a function of several converging factors. First is the nature of those "afflictions of civilization" that now make up the majority of disease. Often they can be prevented; frequently much can be done to limit their course; but rarely can they be defeated. Conquest either lies far in the future or is simply not the appropriate task.

A second factor arises from the need to face economic limitations. Health care costs already comprise 12 percent of the U.S. economy and are escalating out of control. A heroic mythology views stopping short of doing everything possible as failure. The intransigent nature of modern afflictions and the ever higher price tag of high-tech medical weaponry[1] make this a formula for bankruptcy.

A third factor concerns our new understandings about the place of the mind in disease. Where the mind plays a major role, a heroic mythology is often not only unhelpful, but a significant obstacle. The illness dynamic then more resembles a civil war than an invasion by alien forces. Sometimes when a strong psychological com-

---

[1] The advances that marked medicine's past great triumphs, such things as antibiotics and sterile technique, were all quite inexpensive. New advances have most often been extremely costly.

ponent enters into an illness, the appropriate task is still to "fight" the disease. But as often it is to listen to it, open to what it is trying to say. With nothing but a heroic mythology as guidance, the patient easily ends up like the person who shoots his own image in a mirror believing it to be an intruder. In the name of good health care, time and money get directed far from where the attention needs to go.

We are being challenged in powerful ways to find a larger story. As with other polarities, we find it much easier at this point to say why the old story is inadequate than to make out the new one. Again, we are just taking the first steps.

As a psychiatrist, I have spent many hours grappling with this particular polarity. I might share a few bits and pieces of where these reflections have taken me as they tie nicely into other ideas we've explored here. These ideas most directly concern psychological health and dis-ease. We will look later at their likely pertinence to questions of health and illness in general.

With rare exceptions, the mythology believed by those of us who focus on concerns of the psyche and do our healing with words has not essentially differed from myths for the more physical side of things. There is health—"normality"—and juxtaposed to it, dis-ease—"neuroses," "psychoses," "disorders of personality." Our task has been to defeat disease and restore health.

Significant outcry has risen against applying such a "disease model" to the psychological. But generally this has presented more the left hand voicing its opposition to the excesses of the right than the two hands really getting together. More "humanistic" views have softened the hard edges of the old categories a bit, but if we look beneath the surface, we most often find either that one has thrown the baby out with the bath water—chosen to ignore the sense in which dis-ease remains very real—or simply exchanged old disease words for fancy new ones: blocks, games, addictions.

The challenge requires that we think about psychological process in a way that acknowledges such things as symptoms, but frames them in dynamic, "living" terms. The central notions born from my attempts at finding a more integral perspective complement ideas we explored earlier in looking at new concepts of truth and morality. Again, a story serves as the best introduction.

One of the clients I remember most vividly from my early psychiatric training was a young medical student I'll call John. During his first visit, John said he wanted to work on times when he "got weird."

"Sometimes I get real tense," he said. "Other times I feel down and discouraged."

I asked him when his symptoms tended to occur. His response came with unexpected emotion. "It's not fair," he said. "The things I get uptight about are exactly the things that matter most to me. I lose it around school things, you know, like the big year-end tests that are coming up. And I lose it in relationships, when things start getting too close."

My response took him by surprise and, while on one level obvious, began opening something new for me as well. "Isn't that just how things work," I said simply. "The only things worth getting tense or discouraged about are those that really matter to us."

As we talked, John began to see his symptoms in a new light. He began to see them less as pathology than just as ways he responded when things got a bit too big.

With this new perspective, the focus of the work shifted increasingly away from these "problems" to the question of just what did matter to John. He explored how he felt about himself as someone in training to be a physician. He examined what he wanted out of a relationship. When he did explore his fears, he did it now from a different place, treating them less as things to be gotten rid of than as ways to learn about himself and what was important to him.

Near the end of our work, John said with a teasing smile, "Charley, we've utterly failed. Here I am almost done, and I'm not cured. When I'm ninety-five, I bet I'll still get anxious or depressed when things get too big."

Since his symptoms hadn't changed, I asked what had. "It's funny," he said, "the ways I get weird don't seem like enemies anymore, just ways I protect myself. In a curious sense, I wouldn't want to get rid of them if I could. Two things have changed. I've learned a few other ways to protect myself. And now things can get a whole lot bigger before I need protection. By the time I'm ninety-five, who knows how big they'll be able to get."

Over time, I've come to view almost all psychological "symptoms" in a similar way, less as broken things that need fixing than as creative mechanisms that we use in various ways to protect ourselves. At this point, I frame it this way:

At any one time, as individuals or as social systems, we possess a certain capacity for aliveness. As a function of where we are in our development and who we have uniquely become, there is a finite "volume" of creation that the "vessel" of who we are can hold. "Symptoms" arise when, either acutely or in an ongoing way, we are challenged to more aliveness than we have capacity to hold. Things like intellectualizing, spacing out, or being sadistic lift us safely above whatever is too real. Becoming a victim, getting depressed, or being underhanded drop us safely beneath it. Withdrawing keeps it safely at a distance. Being overly aggressive lets us push safely past it. Symptoms serve to protect the fragile vessel of life from breakage by getting us out of the line of fire.

What "symptoms" we use are a function of a variety of things: our basic personality style, where we are in the stages of personal development, our cultural context, who we've learned from, and what will work in that particular situation. We all have an array at our disposal. When we are pushed to the limits of how much life we can hold, appreciated or not, they will make their appearance.

In this view, "symptoms" go beyond being either good or bad. Symptoms are "good" in that they protect us, and protection is important. Symptoms are "bad" in that they indicate that we are not big enough to handle whatever is happening. Is the task to get rid of symptoms? Yes and no. The task asks that we risk the journey of living life just as fully and honestly as we can. To the degree we engage with this risk, the amount of life we can hold increases, and our need to use symptoms as protection in any particular situation diminishes.

Is such an approach to understanding applicable as well to dealing with symptoms of a more physical nature? One could usefully hypothesize that to the degree a physical illness has a psychological component, a similar creative dynamic is at work. It is consistent with the data cited earlier correlating disease with life change, although this data has several possible levels of interpretation. The data suggests that we tend to get sick when we overfill the "vessel of life," but it doesn't distinguish between symptoms as a function of a simple mechanical "breaking" of the vessel or more specifically creative dynamics. In my experience, each can sometimes best match the evidence.

If a heroic posture toward health and disease is not enough, what should replace it? If illness has all these potential layers—from just showing something broken, to providing a method of protection, to raising a voice of new possibility—how, if we wish to heal, do we best relate to it?

Again, what we can say with any surety is just a beginning. We obviously need to pay attention to all the layers of significance. In addition, we want as much as possible to relate not just to the illness, but to that person as a unique being and to the illness process as something real in the individual's life.

Such a whole-person/whole-system, "third space" posture toward the patient gives the highest likelihood that the patient will, in time, find a similar "third space" relationship with his or her illness. I see the ability to facilitate this kind of relationship with disease—and life as a whole—to be fundamental to future health care.

Life and Death

"[T]o die is different from what anyone [might] suppose."
—Walt Whitman

The heroic mythology of traditional health care has contained two parts. The physician's task has been not only to slay demon disease, but, more fundamentally, to keep us safe from death's dark jaws.

Concomitant with this, the modern healer has viewed death ambivalently. Seeing it as a symbol of defeat, we have tended to keep death at arm's length. We have avoided talking about it with each other. As well, we have not infrequently avoided our dying patients or at least avoided the topic of death when with them.

Our heroic attitude toward death has served us. Seeing death as an enemy provided the driving passion behind the development of much of our modern health care "weaponry." But increasingly, our adversarial relationship with death, like that with disease, ceases to heal. We are challenged to a larger and more mature relationship with the fact of death.

Again, a story brings us to the threshold:

Recently I was working with a client—I'll call her Beth—when she suddenly broke into tears. Over the next hour, in obvious pain, she related the story of the plight of a younger sister.

At the age of three, the sister was diagnosed as having cerebral palsy. Her childhood was one of isolation, wheelchairs, and endless, painful operations to give her minimal use of her extremities. Beth, as the oldest child in a single parent household, provided much of her sister's care.

The sister was a fighter and made it not only through high school, but college. She met a man, got married, and not long after became pregnant.

Then things turned bad. Her body unable to support the child, she miscarried. Soon after, she and her husband separated.

Through all of this, her body gradually deteriorated. Before, with her adolescent spunk and the help of physical therapy, she had managed to keep things working fairly well. Now, her body was beginning to cease functioning.

After long consideration, Beth's sister decided that her life had taken her where it could. She resolved that she wanted to die. At first Beth could not understand this. She tried to talk her sister out of it, but after visiting her in the hospital and listening deeply to what her sister said, she came to see things differently. She saw that what her sister wanted for herself was right, and that it was the most loving and "healing" thing that could happen.

It was not to be so simple. The sister decided she would simply stop eating, but she was told she could not do this. The case went to court, and the court ruled that she should be fed forcibly and that everything should be done to keep her alive, regardless of her wishes.

That occurred two years ago. She remains alive. The intervening time has been a horror story: gastric tubes, insensitive and inadequate care in second-rate nursing homes, and her body putrefying as more and more tissues waste and atrophy.

As Beth spoke, her deep rage and tortured helplessness choked her tears. The words didn't need to be spoken: "How could this happen? They say they are doing the kind thing. How could they be so blind? How in the name of goodness could one stand by and inflict such pain?"

The story of Beth and her sister dramatizes the need for medicine, and culture as a whole, to find a new relationship with death.

Much of the need for a new view of death comes as a direct function of modern medicine's success in defeating it. In the past, when death presented itself with any great conviction, it prevailed. But increasingly, if we wish to avert death, we can do so. As the story of Beth's sister illustrates, with new technologies at our disposal, the old truth is often nearly turned on its head. Rather than death being our enemy and the opposite of life, we often find that promoting life in its living sense requires, when timely, that we ally with death.

Making death a friend presents difficulty for people trained to meet death as an evil other, but for our actions to continue to heal, this most fundamental joining is essential. Otherwise, we will find ourselves increasingly in situations where, in the name of good, our actions in fact do violence.

The importance of addressing issues of death and dying is being more widely acknowledged in the medical sphere. This shift was just beginning when I was in medical school. Now, classes that focus specifically on death and dying are a part of every medical school's basic curriculum, and thanatology—the study of death and dying—is becoming an increasingly accepted discipline (along with gerontology—accept death and the latter years take on quite a different hue). It would be unthinkable today for someone to graduate without being able to recite Elizabeth Kübler-Ross's five stages of reconciliation with death.

I see several layers in the changes happening in our attitudes toward death and dying. The first layer reveals simple acceptance of death as something to be dealt with. It acknowledges that death may sometimes present the most "life giving" choice.

This layer is important, but it is at the deeper layers that things become most interesting. Here we begin to move past simply tolerating the fact of our mortality to engage it as something with the capacity to enrich us.

One can't work long with dying people before being struck by how much death can teach. I am reminded of May Sarton's description of a friend's last days in *Plant Dreaming Deep:* "Every layer of pride and reserve was peeled off one by one, until what was left was nothing but a translucent center, as alive to light and shadow, to a caress, to a passing bird, as is a child or a very old woman of genius."

So often it happens that one enters the room of a dying person with the intent to help and heal, and leaves realizing that it is oneself who has been most healed. Somehow death touches very close to wisdom.

The idea that death might be in some sense "positive" feels foreign to modern sensibilities, but it is not at all new. The power of death and its role in wisdom recall ancient themes. The new task is again one of "remembering" as much as of creating wholly new awareness. In earliest times, places such as burial mounds often served as the primary sites of religious ceremony. Death, as ultimate mystery, was venerated as the entryway into the source place of existence. Both Eastern and Western mystical traditions often view death as an ultimate spiritual teacher. At the center of both Tibetan and ancient Egyptian spiritual practice, for example, we find "Books of the Dead," depictions of the story of realization as a journey through the realms of death.

Zen Buddhism contains a notion that a teacher's most important words will be those uttered when he is closest to death. A favorite story recounts a death-bed lesson on the "ordinariness" of profound experience. It comes from the death of a contemporary Zen master, Roshi Taji.[2]

> As Roshi Taji drew near to the time of his death, his senior disciples gathered around him. One disciple, knowing that the Roshi was very fond of a particular kind of small cake, had traveled much of the day before and searched many shops to find a bit of this confection.
>
> As the time of the Roshi's passing approached, the students gathered closer—the room electric with suspense—and humbly asked if he had any last words for them.

---

[2] The story is recounted in Philip Kapleau's *The Wheel of Death.*

"Yes," he replied.

Leaning forward, ears strained, the students waited in anticipation. Lifting one of the morsels that had been brought to him to his mouth, he turned to those gathered. "This cake is delicious," he said...and died.

Roshi Taji carried on the Zen tradition of teaching wisdom through the moment of death.

I spoke earlier of midlife as the time in individual development when the creative edge of truth begins to shift from knowledge to wisdom. A simple way to understand this is that midlife brings the time when we first begin to really grasp the fact of mortality. Death's visage stands before us and challenges us to ask what matters most. To the degree we let in the question, we surrender our heroic images of identity and move on to the challenges of balance, perspective, sustainability, and integration that define the larger "success" of mature life.

If the notion that present times comprise a parallel point of cultural passage is accurate, we should find them marked by a dual transformation in our relationship to death. At the personal level, we should see, particularly in life's second half, a renewed openness to death as experience, both in the sense of personal mortality and in the sense of the myriad "small deaths"—letting go's, questionings, surrenderings—that comprise such an essential part of a life lived with real depth and purpose. Culturally, we should find this new personal relationship with death, combined with the potential fact of our species' mortality, opening us to the questions of wisdom and responsibility on which a healthy future depends.

Reconnecting into the power, even beauty, of death challenges us not just to reengage the potency of death, but to understand death in new and larger ways. What happens when we die? One might reasonably expect that the second half of the journey, concerned as it is with wisdom, would offer an answer to this question. In the past, in a sense, it did. It brought us close to whatever interpretation of death lay in the spiritual teaching of our cultural time and place. "After death one becomes a part of the spirit world." "After death one is reincarnated according to the laws of Karma." "After death one goes to heaven."

But if that second half occurs not just in one's personal lifetime, but in the lifetime of culture, a much more profound challenge arises. Before, our images of death arrived filtered through the protecting screens of our culture's childhood and adolescent needs to keep its ultimate significance at bay. The new challenge, one we have never before known, is to meet death personally and un-adorned, face-to-face.

What then do we see? Is there an afterlife as spiritual views have always offered? Or do we perhaps return to dust as secular reality would suggest? Bridging suggests that reality is larger than either of these—more demanding and more creative. We are just beginning to be big enough to grasp it at all meaningfully.

With the recent death of my sister, I've been confronted in a very personal way with the demand to be more in my relationship with death. She was in the hospital for over a year with a brain tumor, in and out of a coma. Death has been very present for me of late.

What do I think happens after death?

It was interesting to notice my responses to the various comments that people made after Jody's death: to the minister's assurance that she was in heaven and God was taking care of her; to the aside of a friend with more "new age" leanings that Jody remained present with us and would feel pleased with how we were honoring her parting; to the pained regret of a more secular friend that at one moment Jody could be there, vibrant and alive, and in the next...gone. In each I felt a piece of truth. But none felt big enough to hold how I found myself needing to be to fully honor her passing. I needed to find the courage to let death stretch me, to leave behind familiar explanations, to attempt to be with death in its unadorned immensity.

What does it mean to die? Whitman's words perhaps least vio-late the truth of it: "[T]o die is different from what anyone [might] suppose." Again, we remain infants in these new learnings. The one thing that seems certain is that keeping death at arm's length will no longer serve us. "Aliveness" is not the opposite of death, but the larger whole of life *and* death.

Traps

Separation Fallacies: Mind and body are separate and distinct. Microbes and genes are what cause disease; the mind plays a role only in a few specific "psychosomatic" ailments. The job of health care is to fight disease and defeat death.

Unity Fallacies: The body is not real, just a container for the spirit. Psychological/spiritual dynamics are the real causative factors in disease. Death is ultimately an illusion.

Compromise Fallacies: The mind influences the body and the body influences the mind. All diseases have psychological and physical components.

Bridgings

Mind and body are neither separate nor the same, but the left and right hands of an evolving co-generative relationship.

Causation in disease involves—depending on the person, situation and infirmity—multiple, generatively interplaying factors—genetic, environmental, psychological, cultural, spiritual. Health in its fullest sense is not just the opposite of disease, but something which includes disease. It is a multifaceted, multileveled statement about our capacity for life.

Life as something "alive" is not just the opposite of death, but the larger process that life and death together define.

CHAPTER TEN

HUMANKIND AND COSMOS: TAKING OUR PLACE IN THE BIG PICTURE

"Economic deficits may dominate our headlines, but ecological deficits will dominate our future."
—Lester Brown

"What we want is to reestablish the living organic connections, with the cosmos, the sun and earth, with mankind and nation and family."
—D.H. Lawrence

"Call the world, if you please,
The veil of Soulmaking,
Then you will find out
the use of the world..."
—John Keats

Our focus turns now to the largest sphere of human experiencing, to our felt relationship to planet and cosmos. Here two primary relationships define our place. First is our relationship to nature—we, the conscious beings who stand and make civilizations in relationship to the earth as the ground of our being. Second is our relationship as mortals to the divine—to some concept of a heavenly above and lordly rule within it.

Major tremors mark the recent history of each of these once solidly established hierarchies. The news confronts us daily with stories of the damage we are doing to our environment. Finding a new human relationship to nature will be critical if the planet is to continue as a healthy home for ourselves and the rest of life. Similarly, old relationships no longer satisfy our search for a sense of spiritual home. Both a growing hunger for the sacred and a growing dissatisfaction with traditional orthodoxy mark our times.

For our future to have purpose, indeed for us to have a future at all, we must take on the challenge of engaging each of these relationships in ways beyond what we have known before. The first two sections of this chapter, Man and Nature, and Man and God, explore what these most primary and eternal of relationships seem to be asking of us. The third section examines a further juxtaposition, Consciousness and Cosmos, that encompasses the domains of each. Our core question asks: *If our actions are to serve a vital future, how do we best understand our place in the "big picture" of creation?*

Man[1] and Nature

"I'd like to talk about the environment—after all, where would we be without it?"
—Marc Kasky

A good friend of mine and a member of the Institute is a marine biologist. He takes groups to such far-flung places as the Amazonian rain forests, the South Pole, and the Galapagos Islands to educate them about world environmental concerns. At one of our think tank sessions, he shared that he was feeling quite torn about what to do with a group he would soon be leading. He wanted to know if we had any advice.

The expedition was to Hudson Bay. The major focuses would concern whales and dolphins and efforts to protect them. He had given talks on this topic many times, but felt it was important to do it differently. In the past, he'd mostly presented the available data—about whale populations and world whaling practices. Now he wanted to be more of an advocate for policy.

But he felt tugged between two parts of himself with quite different things to say. One part, feeling deep empathy for and connection with the whales, wanted to be their ally and go to battle for them. Another saw this simple "save the whales" mentality, while "politically correct," as overly romantic and too easily blind to the complexity of factors involved.

In the past he'd dealt with this inner tug-of-war by staying the objective scientist. Now he wanted to do more, but he didn't

---

[1] I use the term "man" rather than the more gender-neutral "humanity" to reflect modern culture's patriarchal bias and to emphasize the polar nature of this relationship.

know how to start. In his words: "I've got to get this inner struggle resolved if I'm going to have anything to say."

We threw ideas back and forth for quite a while. Finally one of the group suggested that perhaps the struggle didn't need to be resolved, that his own conflict might be the most powerful tool he had to help others wrestle with the questions. The more he thought about this, the more right it seemed.

He tried it out, role-playing in front of us. First he improvised a short introductory piece, sharing his own conflict and his sense that neither side was wholly right and that the truth lay in a larger view. Then he "became" in turn each of the parts. He moved "stage left" and talked from the "pro-whale" voice, speaking passionately about the beauty of cetaceans, their intelligence, how some are near extinction, and the barbarism of whaling practices. Then he moved "stage right." From the very different voice of this place, he argued that some species of whales, seals, and dolphins were, in fact, quite plentiful; described indigenous cultures in which hunting them has an important role; shared some of the colorful lore of whaling history; and challenged the "audience" as to why killing a whale was essentially different from other kinds of killing we do for food.

After the trip, returning to the Institute, he shared his excitement about what had taken place. People had grappled with tough questions: whether there should be different policies for different species, issues of cultural tradition, what we know about whales' consciousness and intelligence and how this should affect our choices in relation to them. Often there were more questions than answers, but the right questions were being asked. He felt a deep satisfaction in having found a way to lead strongly from the uncertain edge of his own understanding.

My friend was exploring the creative edge of a most important modern challenge: that we learn to relate to nature in new ways. Although the ramifications of this new way of relating only begin to reveal themselves, we see increasingly that it is not only important, but imperative. This imperative has at least two facets.

First, we must learn to relate to nature differently for the sake of human survival and the health of the planet. Although less dramatic than the specter of nuclear war, the destruction most likely to be humankind's undoing is ecological destruction. The litany of emerging crises goes on and on. Clouds of pollution strangle our cities; unmanaged chemical dumps foul our groundwater; a fourth of the planet's mammals are now endangered, with estimates that a fifth of the planet's total plant and animal species will be extinct by the year 2000; acid rain destroys our lakes and forests; nuclear wastes, deadly for thousands or millions of years, accumulate with no clear plan for what to do with them; depletion of the ozone layer threatens to turn more and more arable land to desert and bombards us with ever increasing doses of cancer-causing ultraviolet radiation. It is obvious that a continuation of present environmental attitudes and policies into the next century would be tantamount to planetary suicide. A person visiting from another planet, on seeing how we relate to our biological and physical home, might rightly ask, "What on earth are you doing?"

Beyond such questions of survival, we need a shift in our relationship to nature for another equally critical reason. We need it for the sake of our souls. John Muir once said, "I only went out for a walk and finally concluded to stay till sundown. For going out, I found that I was really going in." We too are nature. In forgetting nature we, in a very important sense, forget ourselves as well.

What exactly does it mean to "remember" nature in the sense being asked of us? What all does this critical bridging entail? We must keep the questions large, stay humble in them. At this point, we can say one thing for certain: The questions confronting us demand that we be bigger than before we've known how to be.

Our developmental metaphor is helpful here. We are being challenged to a fundamental growing up in relation to nature. In the past, we were like children to the earth. She suckled us, protected us within the skirts of her mountains and forests, and watched as we went about our heroic building and exploring. Now we must accept the challenge of caring for her in return—accept the role of stewards for the planet.

The broad policy implications of this are fairly straightforward. We need to adhere to an ethic of sustainability both in our use of resources and our production of pollutants. We need to pay serious attention to questions of population. We need to give high priority to the preservation of our planet's species diversity. And we need to look at every choice we make in terms of its long-term effect on the planet's well-being.

And more than just better policy is being asked for. The task is not only to protect nature, but to learn from nature. The species challenge requires that we begin a new intimacy with nature, and allow ourselves to be transformed by that intimacy.

In just beginning to understand this challenge, we must be wary as always of easily seductive traps. With the best of intentions we can end up, if not doing harm, at least wasting energy that could well provide benefit. Each of our now familiar polar fallacies stands ready to masquerade as integral thinking. Again, just changing ends on the conceptual teeter-totter or sitting congenially in the middle, however right and pure these things may make us feel, get us no closer to where we need to go. An important personal moment of "ah-ha" comes to mind:

I come from pioneering stock, my ancestors being some of the first to make their way over the Oregon Trail into what is now Washington State. My sense of connection with these people who risked so much has always been very dear to me.

About ten years ago, I was sitting before the fire in a cabin I built board-by-board several years earlier on an island in Puget Sound. I was reading some of the family journals written along the trail and was transported in time. Suddenly I stopped. I knew the feeling, that unsettled mild dizziness that marks a cherished belief beginning to crumble.

I realized that these brave people had had a view of nature quite opposite to that which I, almost as religion, had come to assume as "right." They respected her, but were anything but precious with her. Nature to them was clearly less friend than worthy adversary.

I felt uneasy. I realized that I needed to be bigger to make peace with this, but trying to make sense of it made me feel a bit crazy. My ancestors were not bad people. But if they were not, how could they speak of nature with the kinds of words I saw before me?

A first step in finding that peace was accepting that their posture toward nature, while harsh, had a rightness given the context. Crossing snow-covered mountain passes, rafting the Columbia River with wagons and livestock—these were life and death situations. My more reverent "smell all the flowers" attitude, however righteous I might have felt about it, would, in that setting, likely have been more hindrance than help.

At the same time, I saw that my ancestor's relationship to nature wasn't big enough for today's challenges. I found myself sitting long hours with the question of what it would mean to be a "pioneer" in relation to nature in my time. I saw that it would ask much more than the simple heroic view that to them must have seemed so obvious and right. And I saw that it also would require more than my equally simple-minded reflex allegiance.

This encounter challenged me to see that our modern view of nature represents not how things have always been, but only the most recent chapter in a lengthy story. I found myself fascinated by that larger story, taken with how much it might have to teach.

Let's take a moment with that story. Understanding it can help us frame where we need to go and avoid traps like that to which I succumbed.

The story begins in early tribal times. The view of nature then was far from that of today. Rather than an inert resource to be utilized, she—as mountain, river, forest, and soil—was cherished as the divine source of all life. Mortals stood small in her mysterious immensity. As a Northwesterner, I grew up with the words of Chief Sealth: "The Great Chief in Washington sends word that he wishes to buy our land. How can you buy or sell the sky—the warmth of the land. The idea is strange to us…. Every part of this earth is sacred to my people." By all evidence, a similarly reverential relationship with nature has been at the heart of tribal reality since our species' beginnings.

With the rise of the early civilizations, we saw first real separation from nature. Animism gave way to ascendant pantheons of deities, and man came to inhabit a realm seen fully distinct from the creaturely. But while nature and humanity were no longer one, their relationship was still strong. The early Greek gods were ascendant above nature, but they were born from Gaia, the earth. The Eleusinian Mysteries, while beyond animism, embodied a deep awe of nature, a message of shared consciousness between matter and humanity.

Our relationship with nature first grew overtly contentious in the period identified with early Judeo-Christian times. The rise of monotheism manifested itself in both a more forceful ascendancy of the divine and a new ascendancy of man. The divine now stood as a singular lord on high. And mortals, while respectful of nature's power, saw themselves now as sovereign over her. From the book of *Genesis* come these words: "Be fruitful and multiply, and replenish the earth and subdue it: and have dominion over the fish of the sea and over the fowl of the air and over every living thing that moveth upon the earth."

This voice of dominion would continue to rise in volume, calling with ever greater force for the taming of nature. Nature's wildness became increasingly something to control and conquer. By the early Renaissance, we heard statements such as this by the French poet Bossuet: "May the earth be cursed, may the earth be cursed, a thousand times be cursed because from it that heavy fog and those black vapors continually rise that ascend from the dark passions and hide heaven and its light from us and draw down the lightning of God's justice against the corruption of the human race."

The last centuries have revealed a significant further abstraction from nature. Much of the moral condemnation has subsided, but this has occurred less because we have come to terms with nature's power, than because we have put her sufficiently at arm's length that she no longer threatens. Human consciousness has risen far enough above our creaturely origins that nature seems, for all intents and purposes, inert. Our bodies have become things we have rather than are, animal behavior the product of instinct and reflex, and the earth an assortment of material resources to be exploited for the practical tasks of human achievement.

This might seem to be a final step. But if it is, we are in dreadful trouble. Gregory Bateson said it in no uncertain terms: "If this is your estimate of your relationship to nature, and you have an advanced technology, your likelihood of survival will be that of a snowball in hell." The question is less whether we will find a more integral relationship with nature than how much we will make ourselves and the planet suffer on the road to achieving it. As the Roman poet Horace wrote: "You may chase Nature out with a

During the Middle Ages, nature increasingly came to be seen as an "underworld" to be tamed and conquered. (Umbrian Raphael, "Saint George and the Dragon," National Gallery of Art.)

pitchfork, but she will ever hurry back to triumph in stealth over your foolish contempt."

Recognizing that the story of our relationship with nature is evolutionary helps us not just see where we have come from, but as well, connect into where we need to go. By reminding us of the completeness of our bond with nature in earliest times, it helps us reembrace her richness. By acknowledging experiences like those of my Oregon Trail forbearers, it helps affirm how pushing away from nature is equally a part of the larger story.

The task ahead? We've experienced our beginnings, held close in nature's arms. We've had our time of separating from her, of finding our independence. Now we must find our maturity with nature, remember our connection with her, but do so in a way that fills out rather than diminishes our appreciation for our unique role in her workings.

This evolutionary story can help us as well to avoid stances that may appear integral but which in fact merely polarize off the reality of our most recent stage in culture. The task ahead is very different than just siding with nature against humankind, or more accurately siding with a mythologizing of nature against a mythologizing of humanity. (As writer Landon Lockett succinctly put it: "Anyone who loves nature beyond the level of 'Bambi' recognizes that it has brutality as well as beauty.") It is also different from simply reducing humanity to nature (a mere regression to primitive animism). By recognizing both the original power of oneness and the place and purpose of separation, we can avoid polar dogmas that might keep us short of the needed new maturity.

Yes, we must save our forests. No, we can't do this in a way that ignores trees as an important sustainable resource, that simply says trees are good and loggers are bad. Yes, we need to look carefully at the question of the unnecessary use of animals in scientific research. No, it's not as simple as just waving a banner that says all such research is wrong. Yes, we must find ways to preserve endangered species not just at home but in faraway places, such as the Brazilian rain forests and the African savannah. No, we can't just say this is good so it should be done. Approaches that don't benefit the local people in tangible ways, however much we might want them to work, are doomed to failure.

The new maturity demanded of us requires that we move beyond easy polar answers of all sorts. The critical questions are of a new type. To use our earlier language, they are both relational and evolutionary: They demand subtle weighings between a myriad of interplaying variables. And they don't stand still.

And they require a new, more mature willingness to make choices in the face of often quite immense uncertainty. We like to have answers before we act. But for many of the questions we now face, waiting until we have "the truth" may mean waiting until it is too late. Since ecological questions are systems questions, and questions always in process, the jury is often out on exactly what needs to be done.

The Greenhouse Effect provides a good illustration. Are we seeing something real, or just one of the frequent fluctuations in planetary weather patterns? We cannot know for sure. In a court of law the case would be thrown out, the evidence too circumstantial. In a scientific debate we would conclude more data is needed.

Yet by all appearances we need to act—and act quickly. We need to accept that we are dealing with a phenomenon less akin to a legal brief or a scientific experiment than a game of chance, a deadly one like Russian Roulette. Even if the odds of the Greenhouse Effect being real stood only one in six, it would still represent a revolver at our heads, cocked and waiting for the chamber to spin. The mature person does not take this kind of chance, even if the cost to remedy the situation is considerable. For a mature species, the risk should be similarly unthinkable.

What is being asked of us is not at all easy. From the common person it will ask a major shift in attitude. It will require an ability to embrace a much larger, more demanding, and less certain reality, and a new willingness to sacrifice immediate personal gain for long-term benefit. Politically, it will ask a degree of shared will between nations beyond anything seen before in a time of peace. Negotiations to reduce nuclear arsenals will seem kid's stuff compared to what will be required.

The challenge appears in one sense immense and nearly overwhelming. In another, it is quite simple. In the words of poet Robinson Jeffers: "It is time for us to kiss the earth again."

Man and God

*"Religion will not regain its old power until it can force
change in the same spirit as does science."*
—Alfred North Whitehead

There is a wonderful story about an exchange between Charles
Darwin and the Duke of Argyll that took place in the last year of
Darwin's life. Pointing to some earthworms they had been examining, the Duke told Darwin that "it [is] impossible to look at these
without seeing that they [are] the effect and the expression of mind."
Writing later about the discussion, the Duke commented: "I shall
never forget Mr. Darwin's answer. He looked at me very hard and
said, 'Well, that often comes over me with overwhelming force; but
at other times,' he said, shaking his head vaguely, 'it seems to go
away.'"[2]

Nature and the divine each speak from a certain place of home
and origin within us. Lying close to the essence of things, they are
intimates. And at once they are opposites. Looked at mythically,
nature has served as our cosmic mother, ascendant divinity our
cosmic father.[3]

The relationship of humanity to home and origin in a religious
sense is, as with nature, one of above and below, only now things
stand reversed. God, the all-knowing shepherd, watches from on
high; human beings, the humble sheep of his flock, now inhabit a
world beneath.

---

[2] Recounted in *Coming of Age in the Milky Way* by Timothy Ferris.

[3] In Chapter Seven, I spoke of sacred and secular as the symbolic mother and
father of experience. It might seem that here in talking about the religious in
masculine terms I am contradicting myself. The apparent contradiction resolves
in recognizing the interrelated workings of horizontal and vertical polar dynamics. Horizontally, the "softer" voice of the archetypally feminine takes expression
in the inner world of subjective experience. Religion is part of this, one half of the
horizontal duality of sacred and secular. Within this, vertically, the "below"
expresses more the archetypally feminine reality of source and mystery, the
"above" the light and dominion of the archetypally masculine. Spirituality
involves both, set in evolutionary relationship. Over the course of time, religion
has evolved from an initial emphasis on nature and the feminine, to become
increasingly ascendant and masculine in its representation.

Fascinating rumblings in the realm of the sacred mark our times. For much of humanity in this century, the spiritual has, as it did for Darwin, essentially "gone away." Church attendance has dropped and secular values have supplanted traditional religious teachings.

Some would argue that as a species we have moved beyond the need for what the spiritual offers. Perhaps, as the popular vernacular might put it, "God is dead"—or at least dying.

But a second trend, one primarily of the last thirty years, suggests something more at work. There has been resurging interest in spiritual matters. We've seen both new vitality in traditional religious contexts and a major upwelling of interest in traditions from other times and places. Many would claim that we are seeing the beginning of a major historical "rebirth" of the sacred.

Good evidence suggests that we are indeed at a richly important time in our relationship to the sacred, that the door is opening to a deeper and more complete spirituality than we as a species have previously known. But the evidence also suggests that this rebirth will ask more than we may at first wish to give. It promises a more complete meeting with the spiritual, but realizing that promise will require that we surrender some of the most cherished aspects of traditional belief.

What is being asked? Our developmental metaphor is again useful for getting us started. Risking passage into the second half of an individual life means simultaneously taking final authority in life and coming to understand a much more fluid, creative, and subtly interconnected meaning for authority. The new spirituality appears to challenge us to a parallel passage in existence as a whole. Again, the task requires accepting authority. And again it is authority in a new sense. It is the authority neither just of the personal will, nor just of a collective spirit. It denotes the authority of responsible participation in a new, now more overtly creative and dynamically interrelated reality.

Some historical perspective can again help bring this easily elusive picture into focus. Through time and culture, uttered in a multitude of voices, we can identify a small handful of themes at the heart of spiritual experience. Seeing how these themes have grown and evolved to this point can help us engage with what may lie ahead.

Three primary themes stand out. Spirit has been concerned with *oneness* of all types—inner oneness, the oneness of community and congregation, the oneness of reality as whole. "Religio," the root word of religion, means to reconnect. In addition, spirit has been concerned with the fact of *creation*—"In the beginning...." And finally, it has been concerned with *values*, with questions of right and wrong. The word worship means "worthy."

As culture evolved, three things happened with these themes. First, they moved from being concerns spoken of primarily in the language of the mythically feminine to take increasingly ascendant and patriarchal expression. (In earliest times, nature and the divine were essentially one and the same. By late medieval times they became polar opposites.) Second, the domain they inhabit became more and more only one half of an either/or: the sacred as opposed to the secular. (In our animistic beginnings, all was sacred. In the "separate worlds" reality of Cartesian dualism, sacred and secular comprised two distinct spheres.) And third, as the "softer" half of this either/or, through time this domain and the themes it holds moved from clear predominance to an increasingly secondary role. (In the Middle Ages we saw the first solid challenging of the church by royal dominion. With the Age of Reason, the "harder" sensibilities of science, business, and politics came to overshadow the sacred's less objective and material truths.)

And today? Something different seems to be happening with this story, something at once exciting and unsettling, at once affirming and easily frustrating in the paradoxical nature of what it asks.

Present times suggest that this story may be turning around. If we examine the critical issues of today, we find that each in some way asks that these "spiritual" themes once again take a central place.

Each theme has been a repeated motif in these pages. The importance of reaffirming "oneness" has spoken through the recurring emphasis on thinking relationally, in terms of wholes and interconnections. The centrality of "creation" has been mirrored in the continuing focus on "living" change, and more specifically in the suggestion that reality as a whole may be creation. And the need to remember "values" has come unequivocally to the forefront with the assertion that in our times all the critical questions have transformed to questions of value.

But the challenges of our times call for more than *just* a "turning around." The new spiritual imperatives demand more than a resurrection of past religious forms and doctrines, more even than just a reimmersion in the spiritual wellspring.

The "oneness" of an integral reality, we've seen, is not just the oneness of spiritual unity, but an embrace that holds sacred and secular equally. "Creation" as we have spoken of it represents not only omniscient determination; it speaks the voice of uncertainty as much as it does that of divine order. And as we've explored in detail, simple codes of good set against evil become useless for today's essential questions of "value"; the new questions demand more mature and subtle conceptions of moral right.

In exploring the implications of a "rebirth" of spirit, we are being challenged to keep the questions large. I find it useful in this to look not just at what the new spirituality must include, but also what it must leave behind. Besides themes—recurring motifs—religion has functions—social needs that its practices fulfill. I think of three past central functions of religion which are now growing vestigial. These functions, if held to, will increasingly negate the spiritual as a vital social force, indeed make it a force for violence. Let's examine the first two together, then move on to the third.

First, traditional religion, as much as politics, has served a territorial function. Subtly or not, religions have defined "chosen" peoples. While the spiritual half of us tends to identify with peace, that applies only to one's own. All wars are as much religious as political.

Second, religions have served to reinforce our place in cultural time. They have taken one "slice" in the evolution of culture and made the reality of that slice true and absolute. At best this has given a narrow view. At worst it has offered a justification for oppression or genocide, such as the slaughter of "heathens" in the medieval Crusades or tribal peoples on the American frontier.

When one meets arguments over small distinctions in dogma, usually one of these two functions, rather than theology per se, defines the real question. The person wants to know if you belong in his group. And he wants to know whether you are straying from the slice in the whole that he has made "the answer"—are you a bit too mystical; too fundamentalist; perhaps a bit too modern, too humanist?

A key characteristic of emergent spirituality is that it leaves these two functions behind. Indeed, it turns them on their heads. The central task of the new spirituality, along with bridging sacred and secular, is to embody the larger story of the sacred. This means not just ecumenicalism, a liberal acceptance of beliefs other than one's own, but an embracing of the power of other traditions as ultimate teachers for a larger spirituality. The various ways we have related to questions like "oneness," "creation," and "value" through time represent more than random beliefs. They express the multiple colorations of experience that together comprise the palette of mature spiritual understanding.

The third outmoded function that religion has served is not separate from these two, but defines the clearest break point with past belief. Traditional religion offered us safe refuge as cultural children. Whether manifest in the more embracing maternal imagery of animism and mysticism or in the sterner and more philosophical fatherly images of patriarchal forms, religion has been the symbolic parent to our inner life, an all-knowing, all-providing absolute. Present times challenge us to a more mature relationship with the sacred.

How much this asks came home to me recently while listening to a friend's story about her five-year-old daughter. The daughter had come to her in tears. Her best friend wouldn't play with her any more. It seems the friend had casually remarked that her mother and father knew everything. My friend's daughter had replied that this couldn't be true; parents don't know everything. Her little friend had run home crying and now didn't want to see her. In a similar way, on glimpsing the new maturity being asked of us, we readily flee—into denial or into pat beliefs.

Is God then dead? As always, however paradoxical and frustrating it may seem, neither just yes nor just no adequately answers the question. An integral reality is richly interconnected and decidedly mysterious; this would suggest that God's presence is paramount. But this mystery and oneness is different than before. While it

The cutting edge of spirituality challenges us to step beyond a one-way, parent and child, creator and created, conception of reality. (Michelangelo Buonarroti, "Creation of Adam—Detail," Vatican Museum.)

remains richly ordered and creative, it is no longer omniscient and all-protecting.

How then do we best describe the new, more mature spirituality asked of us? As hard as we try, it won't fit into a single pat definition. We barely begin to grasp what it is about. And even when we know it better, definitions will only help in the most secondary way.

But the tools we've been developing here can at least help us get started in the right direction. First, they can help us identify traps. This new maturity does not mean becoming God, claiming humanity as the new keeper of the final answers. Neither does it mean eliminating God: "Okay, enough of this Santa Claus stuff; it's time to grow up and face the real world." And it differs also from making everything God, simple pantheism. (Although aspects of each of these can be thought of as parts of it.)

And our tools can point us generally where we need to go. If the notion of integration is sound, we can say with some confidence that the new spirituality is a bridging spirituality; it links above with below and below with above in a new way.

From below, this spirituality asks that we mortals assume a new ascendancy, a new authority: It asks that we realize a new capacity to be conscious and responsible in life as creation. This ascendency is both simpler and more profound than things we might confuse it with—the machismo ascendancy of technological God-playing or the narcissistic ascendancy of "create your own reality" wishful thinking. It is the ascendancy of humanity growing up, the ascendancy of a mature acceptance of responsibility in a world where decisions, like it or not, often have God-like consequences.

From above, it takes the divine and brings it more down to earth. It makes the sacred "ordinary," though not ordinary in the sense of mundane. The words "ordinary" and "ordain" have the same root. I am reminded of the words of Walt Whitman: "As to me, I know of nothing else but miracles." The new spirituality, in healing the old iron-clad separation of things divine and things pedestrian, should become increasingly a spirituality of daily life. Rather than emphasizing the separate and transcendent, it should remind us of the magic and mystery inherent in any moment lived from a place of truth.

Along with bridging above and below comes that critical bridging with uncertainty. If Whitehead's challenge is to be met, if the spiritual is to again become a force for change, it must be a spirituality in which uncertainty is not just acknowledged but embraced. It must be a spirituality not so much of beliefs as of fundamental questions—a spirituality of inquiry in the fullest, most courageous sense.

Consciousness and Cosmos

*"Recent conceptual developments...clear the way for a
natural fusion of science and religion."*
—Roger Sperry

With shifts in how we view both nature and the sacred, how do we best understand the "big picture?"

Early on, I asserted that the critical first step, if we wish to develop practical and detailed theoretical perspectives big enough for the new questions, requires that we delineate a new "fundamental organizing image." I shared one I was working with: that of reality as a whole functioning as a creative process. Hopefully, the various explorations in these pages have provided a deepened sense of what I mean by the term "creative" and some sense of how it applies to what is being asked of us.

Since the topics in this chapter have been of cosmological scale, we might take a moment to look a bit further into this way of defining the whole. To do so, we'll explore three questions pertinent to our concerns in this chapter. For each, the implications of a Creative Systems perspective have been at least hinted at previously.

The first question: What is the relationship between science and religion? In modern times, science and religion have served as our primary languages for talking about nature and the sacred. As well, they've provided our primary "whole ball of wax" images for reality. How, ultimately, are they related?

In most recent times, we've tended to deny that there is much of a relationship at all. We've held them apart in the posture of the Cartesian split, regarded them as concerned with essentially separate worlds. But one can't hold this posture with comfort for long. The notion that we live simultaneously in mutually exclusive realities just does not satisfy. Often we've dealt with this by discarding one or the other, but this really doesn't work either. We need them both. Einstein said it well: "Religion without science is blind. Science without religion is lame."

But just saying they both have a place, even if we can somehow justify both, is not enough either. The task requires not just adding science and religion together, but learning to think and act from the larger process that science and religion together describe.

In a Creative Systems perspective, as we've seen, that process is understood to be creation. Framed creatively, science and religion are languages we've used to describe different parts of this single larger process. They are ways that we have given expression to the two counterpoising hands of creation and to their evolving interrelationship. Religion depicts (and invokes) experience close to the essence of life, at the unformed core of creation. Science engages us in the world of more manifest creation, creation realized in form. Science and religion are ways we've described and taken part—at the "big picture" level—in each hand's unique dexterities and each hand's hidden effect on the other.

A second question follows naturally from the first: What is our place in all this? If we are not simply lords over the creaturely realms, who are we? If we are not simply children of the divine, what is our task?

Besides usefully painting a new "big picture" image, a Creative Systems view gives us a lens and a language for seeing and describing detail within that image. At a first level of detail, it frames a more integral picture of the relationship of the various levels of existence: inanimate, simply animate, and us.

Traditionally, we've either viewed these levels as wholly discrete—"humans have souls, animals do not"—or we've dissolved boundaries completely—"we are all just atoms," "humans are simply intelligent apes." The relationship between levels, seen from a Creative Systems perspective, bridges this usual dichotomy of discrete versus continuous. In one sense, our three categories serve simply as points on a continuum: A rock, an elephant, and Brigitte Bardot are each, most essentially, creation. At the same time, these three worlds remain distinct: Although each represents creation, each represents a unique kind of creation.

How are they distinct? They represent different orders of creative organization. Periodically, creation's expanding story has been punctuated by leaps in organization. "Inventions" have appeared that function as "creative multipliers," qualitatively increasing the potential creative capacity of systems.

Between the inanimate and the animate, this invention was reproduction. Before, creative reorganization occurred by happenstance. Reproduction, with its regular turnover of genetic material, introduced the concept of "planned" innovation. Creative reorganization could happen with new regularity and rapidly.

Between the animate and human, the new invention was conscious awareness. With consciousness, the pace and plasticity of creative reorganization took a further quantum step. In conscious systems, only the capacity for new insight limits change.

So what is our place in the "big picture?" In this view, we are simultaneously simply one part of creation and, because we are where conscious awareness has been most developed (as far as we know), the occupiers of a unique niche in creation. The significance of this curious place remains open to interpretation. One could argue that we are creation's ultimate achievement or equally well that we are a mad experiment (perhaps ultimately a failed one).

What we can say with some certainty is that our powerful ability to create gives us unique capacities—for good as well as for harm. At least for life on this planet and for this moment in cosmological time, these capacities imbue our place with a special significance. They bless our role with fascinating potentialities. And they confer a unique responsibility.

The third question raises the eternal issue of meaning. In thinking about our place in the "big picture," I am often drawn to Einstein's response when asked what he thought to be the ultimate question. "Is the universe friendly?" he said. Two questions are imbedded in the word "friendly"—first, does the universe have purpose, and second, is that purpose benevolent. In the past, each has been an either/or proposition. If there is a God, the universe has purpose, and a benevolent one. If not, we inhabit a great soulless machine.

When we frame reality creatively, a third option presents itself. Yes, the universe is "friendly," though friendly in a somewhat different sense than we may have meant the question. It has purpose: An inherent impetus toward creative possibility defines it—atoms beget molecules, ideas beget civilizations. And it is most elegantly ordered. While such is not purpose in the teleological sense of goal or grand plan, it is purpose nonetheless, and some might argue a rather more interesting kind of purpose.

One could rightly say as well that the universe "cares." It is intimately interconnected and it "wants" things to be all they can. Such represents a particular kind of caring, again not the ordinary. It resembles what we've here called whole-person love. It doesn't come with final guarantees. But as with other whole-person/whole-system relationships, however much we might at times wish things to be safer and simpler, it may, in the end, offer the fullest kind of love.

Traps

Separation Fallacies: Man is wholly separate from nature and has rightful dominion over it. The Divine, omniscient and omnipotent, is wholly separate from the mortal and holds dominion over it.

Unity Fallacies: Nature is truth. We are all God.

Compromise Fallacies: Environmentally, the task is to balance the needs of man and the needs of nature. With the sacred, the task is to find the right balance between things such as prayer or meditation that are spiritual, and things, such as talking with a friend or going to work, that are not.

Bridgings

Humans are part of nature, and as conscious beings have a special place and responsibility in her workings.

Our times are asking for a "rebirth" of the sacred; but it is a new, more demanding and mature sacred that is being born.

The task is to manifest, with greatest beauty and integrity, our unique potential in creation.

CHAPTER ELEVEN

CAUSE AND EFFECT: THE DYNAMICS OF LIVING CHANGE

"The world we have made as a result of the level of thinking we have done thus far creates problems we cannot solve at the same level at which we created them."
—Albert Einstein

"Our linguistic repertoire is geared to a one-sided inter-pretation of causality and thus contains no terms to describe paradox and the acausal nature of the inner world. What we need is a multivalent logic, multidimensional figures of speech, and ambiguous concepts capable of giving us a better idea of ambivalences."
—Bertrand Russell

"We need to understand the phenomenon of evolution itself so that we may then, in due course, understand ourselves and the role we play in...our own evolution."
—Jonas Salk

"We cannot wait for the world to turn, for times to change that we might change with them.... We ourselves are the future."
—Beatrice Bruteau

With this chapter and the next, we turn our attention from specific domains of cultural change to the more embracing question of the nature of change itself. I've argued that our times demand that we take a new responsibility in culture and cultural change. Doing this will require a fuller understanding of the workings of change and a whole array of new change-related skills and sensibilities.

Although change has not always been easy to accomplish, in our familiar, mechanistically perceived reality, the "how" of it has been pretty straightforward. Our task has been to be good engineers: to have clear goals and to understand the steps to achieving those goals.

Stepping over the threshold into a post-mechanistic world, we see that this kind of approach, at least used in isolation, will no longer do. It is only adequate for certain kinds of questions. For most, and in particular the "big questions" on which our ultimate well-being rests, it does not begin to be enough. Change in a "living" reality presents a much more subtle and challenging picture.

The changes reordering our reality are monumental in their implications and both subtle and fragile in their dynamics. Whether our efforts help or inhibit their profound evolutionary potential will depend directly on the degree we can learn to understand change in larger terms.

Our core question is: *How does one effect change in a "living" reality?* Juxtaposing Action and Reaction, we will examine more closely the dynamics of "living" change. With the final two sections, Doing and Being, and Structure and Freedom, we will examine further the question of "tools" for evoking such change.

Action and Reaction

"For the material universe, we shall commonly be able to say that the 'cause' of an event is some force or impact exerted upon some part of the material system by some other part.... In contrast, in the world of ideas, it takes a relationship."
—Gregory Bateson

Each major epoch in culture understood the workings of change differently. In prehistoric times, if we wanted to affect, say, the abundance of mastodon, we might do a mastodon dance, enhancing the mastodon's power through spiritual identification with it. Or we might offer a sacrifice to the mastodon, paying it ritual homage. There was little question then that these were the right things to do to effect change.

In modern times, we too have held particular ideas about how change works. Change happens according to the laws of mechanics, through action and reaction—pushing this button trips that lever, which turns that gear. This virus, by that mechanism, causes that disease. This political leader, by making that decision, causes that change in culture. Like the "mastodon dancer," we have assumed our understanding of change is complete.

As should now be clear, the realities of change are larger than this more modern view as well. At one time, a mechanical view of causality enhanced life. It gave foundation to the rise of industry, to the wonders of the scientific revolution, and to the new preeminence of the individual made possible by the establishment of institutional structures—governmental, educational, economic. But now it is moving beyond its timeliness. Used in isolation, rather than enhancing life, it limits life.

For questions adequately reduced to the material—measuring boards to build a bookshelf, following a recipe, starting one's car— a one-billiard-ball-hitting-another world view remains quite adequate. But when dealing with concerns beyond the purely material, issues of causality are less simple. And as we've seen, "beyond the purely material" is coming to include all the major questions of our time. As soon as one moves beyond a reality adequately described in the language of polarity—mind versus body, masculine versus feminine, leader versus follower—a push-pull, action-reaction view of change ceases to serve. To be at all effective, future change agents will need to approach change questions in more dynamic, "living" ways and carry a broad array of new change-related tools in their conceptual tool bags.

We've already made a start at identifying some of these tools. Change agents in the future will need to be skilled at "measuring" in terms of integral referents, not just in terms of data and behaviors, but in terms of all that goes into making something "alive." They will need the capacity to speak and act effectively from a "third space" posture, from a place that embodies the question as much as the answer, the student as much as the teacher, the context as much as the content. They will need to know how to bring all of themselves to the questions they wish to address, not just their ideas and wills, but the whole of their "integral intelligence." And they will need sensitivity to what it means to lead integrally, not just to act with the expectation that others will follow, but to lead in ways that tap the creative potency of all parts of the systems within which they work.

Additionally, future change agents will need a more sophisticated understanding of the workings of change itself. The effective promotion of change in a "living" reality requires a keen understanding of the how and why of "living" change. As this further conceptual tool is of such central importance, let's take one specific change process and use it to examine the inner workings of "living" change more deeply.

A fitting change process to examine might be that which took us from the Middle Ages into the Age of Reason and Enlightenment, that of our last fully "revolutionary" evolution of world view. Our question: What caused the Renaissance? Consistent with the ways of thinking spawned by the Renaissance, we frame our conventional answers to the question mechanistically—it resulted from this new idea, that new invention. I would suggest, however, that something more creative and interesting took place during that dramatic time.

Our three characteristics of emergent conception—that reality is relational, evolutionary, and meta-determinant—can guide us in making a first cut at what more was occurring. With change intrinsic to "living" reality, these characteristics describe not just reality as a whole, but, more specifically, the workings of change.

Extended to questions of change, the notion that reality is relational turns into the essential recognition that "living" causation always works as a systems dynamic. "Living" change involves the interplay of a multiplicity of variously significant factors.

Talk to ten people from different disciplines about what caused the Renaissance, and you will get just about as many versions of the story. An economist will point to the early explorers' opening of global trade and the rise of capitalism. A political scientist will emphasize the emergence of the nation-state and new ideas of individual sovereignty. A theologian will tell about the new concept of "personal" faith, a faith that requires no interceding priesthood. A scientist will emphasize the growing shift from truth as "authority" to truth as "fact," and the discoveries and inventions that followed from this newly "objective" view. An artist will talk of such things as the classical revival and a newly vibrant secular aesthetic.

Who is right? Of these various factors, which is cause and which is effect? The most satisfying and accurate answer seems to say that all are both cause and effect. Each of these factors, to varying and arguable degrees, played parts in catalyzing the changes that we call the Renaissance. And each, simultaneously, expressed those changes. Causation in a whole-systems reality is always a multifactored, chicken-and-egg proposition. Sometimes one factor dominates so thoroughly that for all intents and purposes we can treat it as "the cause," but this is more the exception than the rule.

What lesson can this give the change agent? To be effective, we need to see and act from the big picture. Single-cause explanations and single-cause tactics, while they often garner the greatest fanfare, rarely touch on more than a small part of what is going on. For some kinds of questions they prove adequate. But as the important questions become integral questions, "one-liner" approaches to change will increasingly lead to little if any real change or may even result in the opposite of what was intended.

We've seen this reflected in all the questions we've given attention to in these pages. We fall short if we make the cause of the drug crisis the evil of drugs and the solution a war against them. Effectively meeting the drug crisis requires taking into account a multiplicity of interplaying factors—poverty, our "magic pill" cultural ethos, the general crisis of purpose that marks our time, and more. Similarly, our ecological crisis asks more than just opposing things that harm nature. It requires a sensitivity to the interrelationships of plant and animal populations, to cultural dynamics, to economic variables—in short, to all aspects of the various systems involved.

The second theme—that reality is evolutionary—is more explicitly about change. As we've seen, change in a "living" system doesn't just happen to a system; it is inherent in it. In a mechanistic reality, things sit still until they experience the impact of an outside force. "Living" systems grow and change; that is how we know they are "alive." "Living" causality is "chickens and eggs" not just in the sense that many factors are involved, but in the sense that "chickens and eggs" implies change, new "hatchings."

Translated to culture, this recognition reminds us that it is not sufficient to think of culture as a static edifice that we change through the force of our ideas and efforts. Change is immanent within culture. The various ideas and inventions that marked the Renaissance were direct expressions of that time and place in culture as a creative process. They would not have appeared, nor been taken seriously, if what had come before had not transpired, and if culture at that time had not been ripe for change.

The lessons for the change agent? There are several, but three are of particular importance.

First, the meaningful effecting of change requires as much a process of aligning with change as imposing change. The earlier notion that right action is "purpose-centered" reflects this aspect of "living" causality. One's efforts end up mattering, indeed most often end up working at all, only to the degree they are right and timely in the potential change processes that define their contexts.

With "living" change, a good ear and a sensitive soul become as important as a strong hand. Gardeners may talk of "growing" plants, but ultimately we don't "make" living things grow, we provide them with the conditions they need to grow. The metaphor is partial—in either personal or cultural change we are not just the gardener but also the seed—yet it is pertinent. The effective facilitation of change in a "living" system happens through aligning oneself with change that is right and timely within the system.

"Aligning" in this sense presents a subtle bridging concept. While it asks more than "doing" in the simple willful sense, equally it asks more than just "going with the flow." The aligning of ideas, actions, and inventions that catalyzed the Renaissance went decidedly against the flow, at least of established opinion. It required a willingness to weather significant opposition and conflict. What one aligns with in the meaningful effecting of change is not the flow of past actions and thoughts, but the flow of creative truth.

The second lesson derives from the recognition that "living" change, being evolutionary, is a *process*. In contrast to the situation in a mechanistic reality, what we align with in "living" change is never wholly visible. In a mechanistic reality, one's first task is to have clear goals. In "living" processes, the "goal" in a concrete sense is often the last thing we find out. The Age of Enlightenment did not result from its early thinkers having the goal of getting to modern times. They knew simply that what they were working with felt powerful and right. To be effective forces for "living" change, we must have the courage to engage change as an unfolding process.

A third lesson adds to the second. The key recognition here reveals that what we align with in "living" change may lack visibility not just because it is a process, but because it is a discontinuous process. "Living" change makes leaps. I've spoken of this before in relation to culture, using the analogy of the snake which sheds its skin. The new realities of the Renaissance did not follow logically from those of the Middle Ages. They came from a willingness to re-ask the most fundamental questions and an openness to the qualitatively unfamiliar. The creative change agent must be open not just to change that adds new pieces to the familiar, but as well to change that reorders understanding from the ground up.

The second major change theme, then, its evolutionary nature, provides several interrelated lessons for the change agent. The third major change theme, that "living" change is meta-determinant—patterned, but not predestined—provides a final lesson. Its challenge should now be familiar. The effective facilitation of change in the future will require more and more that we acknowledge uncertainty as something intrinsic to reality.

The question of determinacy applied to the Renaissance asks us whether it was inevitable that things happened as they did. My hunch is that, given time, something recognizably similar would have taken place. Cultures appear to follow a predictable maturational course, go through a predictable sequence of "skin sheddings." But lots of major unknowns remain.

Although cultural change has predictable direction, it is not inevitable on multiple fronts: in terms of *when* it will happen, *whether* it will happen, or *what* it will look like if and when it does happen. Sub-Saharan Africa was by all evidence the birthplace of our species. Yet until very recently most of its cultural groups remained at early stages of cultural development. The Anasazi of the Southwest United States and the Maya of Central America evolved well into the "inspiration stage" of culture and then for unknown reasons disappeared. And while I would put ancient Egypt, the early Meso-American cultures, and more recently the traditional cultures of Bali or Tibet within the same big cultural slice, in terms of the particular forms by which we recognize them, they could hardly be more different.

Creation's "leaps" involve real uncertainty. Indeed, even the parts that don't leap involve uncertainty. To align with the creatively true is not a dogmatic alignment, but a humble one in which the questions always remain as large as the answers.

Our three criteria for emergent conception, then, can be used to paint the major contours of a "big picture" view of the workings of "living" change. With the next two sections, we will use the interplaying roles of our two hands of truth to examine the hows and whys of change at a further level of detail and to extract additional tools for the future change agent.

Doing and Being

"If we are always arriving and departing, it is also true that we are eternally anchored. One's destination is never a place, but rather a new way of looking at things."
—Henry Miller

"Living" change is always "two-handed." We can fully describe mechanistic change in the language of truth's right hand, in the archetypally masculine language of actions done and things visible. In contrast, "living" change always involves as well the left hand's softer, more mysterious, archetypally feminine side of reality.

If one looks at the factors I listed as "causal" for the Renaissance, one sees that they are not all nice, solid and uniform, Newtonian apples. We've got an apples, oranges, and kumquats assortment of factors—and some of this added fruit is decidedly soft. Things like new inventions and the opening of trade routes look like objective, solidly definable notions. But "personal faith" and "a newly vibrant secular aesthetic" are not solid at all.

In "living" systems, each of our two hands of truth plays a role in causation. "Living" change involves both causation from "without," from the world of forms—an idea, an invention, a governmental dictate—and causation from "within," from the world of nuances, essences, and germinal potentials. Mechanical systems are homogeneous, material within and without. Creative systems are creative precisely because they are not homogeneous.

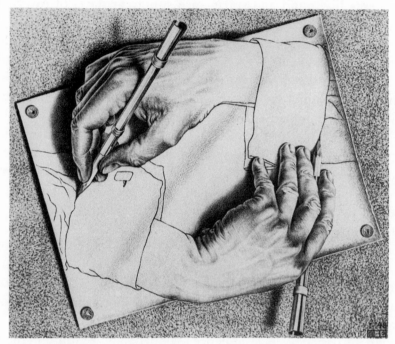

"Living" change is "two-handed." (M. C. Escher, "Drawing of Hands," Cordon Art.)

Recognizing the interplay of the two hands of truth in "living" causality leads us into one of philosophy's eternal quandaries. Which hand is primary? We might take a moment with the question, as it offers useful insight for what is being asked of us.

This question marks a fundamental parting of the ways in traditional understanding. It provides a major point of distinction, for example, between science and religion. Theologians, while coming at the question from a great plurality of perspectives, see action as a function ultimately of reality's less visible left hand. The ephemeral is primary.

Those of a more philosophical or psychological bent can end up choosing either hand. Aristotle said that action ultimately followed from what he called "final causes"—purposes internal to action such as health, beauty, or success. A rational positivist or a behaviorist, to the contrary, would say that such things—along with concepts like mind and spirit—are simply artifacts of external physical factors like conditioning and biology.

At the extreme of the argument for the right hand, for material primacy, most scientists do their best to cleanse their language of even hints of the theologian's teleology, going so far as to avoid potentially leading statements such as a crab has a claw "in order to" pinch, or a human a nose "in order to" smell.

Which view is true? If the notions here are accurate, all and none. Bridge science and religion, subjective and objective, masculine and feminine, and we get a reality in which causality's two hands are each valid and have equal significance. From an integral perspective, if we make either hand primary, we grab but one half of life's causal wishbone.

Understanding that "living" causality involves both hands of truth is critical to the task of being an effective change agent for times ahead. We must learn to appreciate the unique dexterities of each hand. More than this, we must learn to approach questions of change in ways that are consciously "two-handed."

In the past, if we gave credence to both hands, we still kept their functioning separate. We prayed or meditated, exercising the causality of the left hand. We went to work or took political action, exercising the right. The new questions ask something more: that we address change in terms of the larger causality that unites our two hands.

As proposed earlier, one way of framing this larger causality is to see it as the causality of creative process. Creative process—the story of how things come into being, grow, mature, and evolve—inherently combines the "separate realities" of causality's two hands. In it, essences evolve into forms and new forms in turn give us new, more mature essences. A creative reality is explicitly "co-causal."[1]

---

[1] To the question of which hand is primary, a Creative Systems perspective decisively says "both." In addition it says, "And it depends on when you look." Early in generative processes we experience essence, then the much larger force, as causal. Thus the causal reality of the "mastodon dance." Later, as the newly created form comes to dominate the picture, our perspective flips. The manifest then seems to be the "real" power. More material concepts of causation, like Newton's Laws of Motion, then step to the fore.

This notion that causality is creative can help us take a further important step in identifying tools for the new change agent. Most of the tools we have so far, things like keeping a "third space" perspective and using "aliveness" as a referent, include all aspects of the creative whole equally. But for certain situations, we also need tools that emphasize one hand or the other.

To help delineate and keep track of these additional tools, I like to "map" them in terms of their points of effect within the whole of creative process. The change agent's tools can be thought of as lying along a continuum bridging the dexterities of our two hands. The following diagram outlines this way of ordering our "tool bag":

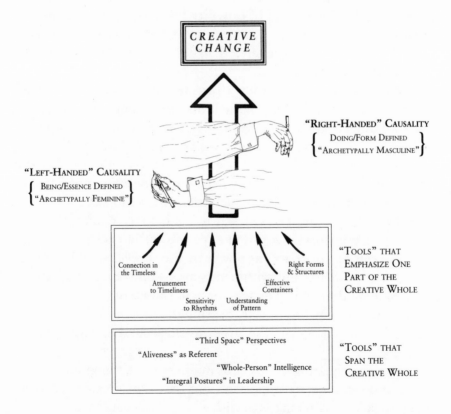

FIG. 11-1: *The Creative Change Agent's "Bag of Tools"*

In the remainder of this section, we'll examine a few tools from the left side of the bag, and in the next section we will do the same for the right.

Starting farthest to the left, we find tools that transform by bringing to bear the power of the creatively unformed—the power of mystery and timelessness. Talking about this kind of power is inherently tricky. As Bertrand Russell said, our language "contains no terms to describe…the acausal nature of the inner world." Here we deal with "power" that is by nature not visible, actions that often appear quite the opposite of action, and effects that often seem to follow not at all logically from what preceded them.

But however elusive this left hand of causality might seem, we must find a new kind of relationship with it. In our times, we have largely forgotten it. But ultimately, this softer, more allowing, archetypally feminine hand of causality holds equal transformative power to its more pointed complement. Indeed, because it has been forgotten, today it is more often than not where the greatest power for meaningful change lies.

Words do a little better if we focus less on the power itself than on ways to open to it. One of the most simple and obvious ways is one we often acknowledge, yet rarely take time to do—simply to pause. I am reminded of the words of Georgia O'Keeffe: "Still—in a way—nobody sees a flower—really—it is so small—we haven't time—and to see takes time, like to have a friend takes time." In our fast-food rush up the ladder of achievement, we forget the importance of taking time. The renewal available to us requires remembering the transformative power of pauses and latencies.

We can also open to this power by the simple act of listening. This may mean listening within ourselves—reflecting, meditating, noticing our dreams and images, or being aware of the language of our bodies. It may mean really hearing the soul of another. It may mean listening deeply to the larger world around us, to nature, to culture.

Someone hearing these words might say, yes, things like taking time and listening are important, but they don't "cause" change. They just help us get in touch with what needs changing.

I would differ. In pausing and listening within I am not just noticing what is within; I am, in ways I can never fully comprehend,

participating in creating what is within. In deeply receiving another, I not only hear how to respond to further our relationship, I
live in the connection that is that relationship, am changed by it,
and in turn change it.

These less visible change dynamics are equally fundamental in
the social/political sphere as in the personal. What is most important in bringing the leaders of two superpowers together or in getting together as citizen-diplomats of those countries? Is it the ideas
we exchange, the policies we debate? At this point, what is probably
most important is simply that we risk being together. Reagan and
Gorbachev's early meetings accomplished little in terms of policy,
but the personal chemistry that developed between them moved
the world a small but significant step towards becoming a safer
place.

A favorite poem by Juan Ramon Jimenez touches close to the
essence of this kind of transformative power:

> I have a feeling that my boat
> has struck, down there in the depths,
> against a great thing.
>
> And nothing
> happens! Nothing...Silence...Waves...
>
> Nothing happens! Or has everything happened,
> and are we standing now, quietly,   in   the   new   life?[2]

You might take a moment to reflect on the role such things as
listening and pauses play in your life and on the place of mystery
and the timeless for you.

If we move a bit from the world of essences towards that of
form, we encounter a second, equally important, tool. This is the
power of sensitivity to time*li*ness. Again, this is a largely forgotten
power. Today we tend to mark our calendars as if each hour, each
day, and each month were much the same.

It was very different in earliest culture. Back then, attunement
to timeliness lay at the heart of life. Great attention was paid to
daily ritual, to the turning of the seasons, to times of passage. Find-

---

[2] Translated by Robert Bly.

ing a new sensitivity to timeliness, to the pulses and patterns of life, is a further important piece of cultural "remembering."

This new attention to timeliness will contribute on multiple levels. It will be increasingly important for our daily health and well-being. Learning to stay more in touch with rightness in time—when to sleep, when to awaken, when to be alone, when to be with others—offers one of the most reliable antidotes I know to the ravages of "stress" that so mark our time.

And we will more and more recognize the importance of timeliness in facilitating change. As anyone knows who has tried either to open a walnut or to open another's heart in love, "living" change is always as much a question of "when" as "how." At the wrong time, one's efforts will be to no avail no matter how deft one's technique. At the right time, one can often blunder unmercifully and it matters not. Machines can do most anything anytime, but "living" change has its seasons. To effectively facilitate it, we must possess a keen sensitivity to timing—when to push, when to wait, when to assert, when to question.

The notions that catalyzed the birth of the Renaissance, offered a few years earlier, would likely have been ignored (and likely were). With the timing right, one idea sparked another, and that another, setting off a chain reaction that explosively transformed the whole of understanding.

Take a moment with this aspect of change as well. How good are you at sensing timeliness in relationships with others—when to be together and when to be apart, when to speak and when to listen, when to push and when to let go? How deeply do you feel connected in your sense of timing in your relationship to yourself? Are there ways you might want to enhance these sensibilities?

The last major tool on the left side of our diagram is related to the first two, but includes more of the sensibilities of form. This is the power not just of moment-to-moment timeliness, but of stepping back and having perspective on life's rhythms.

One of the things that most marks our age is the requirement that we begin to take personal responsibility for the rhythms of our lives. In the past, culture determined our major rhythms. Gender roles and cultural prescriptions for dating, marriage, and child rearing defined the major rhythms of love—how much time we'd spend together, what we would do when we were together, the "right" course for a successful relationship. And the nine-to-five framework of the industrial workplace defined the rhythms of the working day and the appropriate trajectory of a successful career. Today we find ever greater choice within these rhythms. Along with new freedom, this confers a profound new responsibility. For our lives to be effective and fulfilling in the future, we will need to be more in touch with our unique rhythms and more willing to make choices that honor them.

You might take some time to reflect on how you structure the major rhythms of your life. How do they express your unique nature? Are there ways you might want to try things differently?

If the concept of bridging, and with it a renewal in the archetypally feminine, is accurate, we should find these "softer" sorts of tools—connecting in the timeless, a sensitivity to timing, being more conscious and pro-active in the rhythms of our lives—increasingly important in how we approach questions of change in all spheres. They ask different things of us than we usually associate with "making" change—sensing and intuiting more than analyzing, allowing and being more than doing. And they are not as easily pinned down and defined. But the sort of power to which they give access will be increasingly critical if we are to succeed in addressing the questions on which the future depends.

Structure and Freedom

"Not the autocracy of a single stubborn melody on the one hand. Nor the anarchy of unchecked noise on the other. No, a delicate balance between the two; an enlightened freedom."
—Johann Sebastian Bach

Approaching the question of tools for change from the more form-defined end of creative process, we start on more solid and familiar ground. The change language of a materially defined world—having goals, "making" change happen, achieving the kind of progress defined by material structure and acquisition—largely defines our modern reality.

Although, this makes our task different, it makes it no less challenging. Whereas the challenge from the left side of creation asks that we connect integrally with forgotten sensibilities, the challenge from the right side presents the equally tricky task of taking things we think we know well and grasping them in new ways.

Let's start at the far right-hand, most form-defined side of our diagram, since there we meet the challenge most directly. The integral question for this most concrete part of creation asks what the role of the material becomes in our now post-material reality. If things like hierarchies, roles, and beliefs as rigid structures no longer serve, what becomes the place and purpose of form?

Unity fallacies lurk nearby to lead us astray. Popular thought often equates emergent understanding with the elimination of form, with a world cleansed of hierarchies, boundaries, institutions, and belief structures.

The task clearly requires much more than just willy-nilly getting rid of forms. But if post-material doesn't mean antimaterial, what does it mean?

Our earlier analogy between present cultural times and the midlife transition in individual development is again helpful. Midlife involves a parallel shift to a newly post-material identity. The various forms we previously created in our lives—our professions, our relationships, our beliefs—come increasingly into question. We see more and more clearly that none of them, by themselves, define either truth or fulfillment.

Upon realizing this, we often respond by suddenly abandoning our old forms and trying all sorts of new ones—midlife is a common time for divorce, major job changes, trying on new philosophies. But while changes of form may be appropriate, changing forms alone misses the point. The change that most fundamentally reorders experience and brings new meaning at this time requires the recognition that forms alone, old or new, will no longer work as answers. The creative edge, what makes something alive, has moved on.

If we succeed in traversing the passage of midlife, gradually we find ourselves seeing the forms we have created in a new light. The fact that we are doctors, artists, or architects, ceases being, in and of itself, of great importance. But the fact that these forms and their attached skills may serve as tools for enhancing life grows increasingly important. We do some adjusting—toss out some trappings that really don't serve, add new skills that will help fill out what is possible—then shift our attention to the bigger picture and to how our knowledge and skills can serve it.

How can these observations help us with the task of being integral change agents and specifically with developing tools for change that tap creation's more right-handed sensibilities? They suggest that form-defined things—goals, beliefs, structures, possessions—and the more "doing" reality associated with them, very much have a place. We need simply to recognize that indeed they are tools. They aren't truth in and of themselves. But they can serve us richly in the tasks of making reality more true.

You might use this first piece to reflect personally. Look at the "things" you've accumulated in the course of your lifetime: skills, beliefs, possessions, relationships. How do each of these serve aliveness and purpose for you? Which seem most important and why? Have some outlived their usefulness? Do others need updating or repair? Should some new ones be added if the future is to be most richly engaged?

Then use it as well to reflect culturally. Look at the material things we associate with wealth in our culture. Which of them make us richer? Which less rich? Then look at defining cultural beliefs: nationalistic, moral, religious, political. Are there some that have outlived their usefulness or need updating? New ones that might better guide us?

The second, more form-defined tool is related to the first, but requires more of reality's left hand. A further creative power of forms is that they function as "containers" for new creation. The forms created during any one creative process provide living contexts for new creation in the next. I've spoken previously of context primarily in terms of its archetypally feminine elements. But context possesses equally strong and essential archetypally masculine aspects. Creation's vessel has both an inner and outer surface. The inner surface holds and nurtures; the outer surface gives structure and protection. There are few more powerful tools of "creative management" than skill at discerning the kinds of containers best suited to different kinds of creative processes and to different points in those processes.

I spend a lot of time taking stock of and care of the containers I've created for my life: the physical places where I work and where I live, the commitments that define the relationships in my life, the kinds of things I choose to do. I find that, to a remarkable degree, if I just care well for the containers, what happens within them takes care of itself, growing and unfolding in ways that surprise and gratify.

The concept of creative containers offers a nice conceptual bridge for one of life's trickiest polarities, Structure and Freedom. We tend to make structure and freedom opposites, envision freedom as a life unbridled by limits. But such a vision blinds us to the full power and beauty not just of structure, but of freedom as well.

At best, such a vision presents freedom in only the most trivial sense. It offers the freedom of the anarchist or of the self-centered hedonist, a freedom that gains its power to do anything by being related to nothing. At worst, such freedom gives no freedom at all. Look behind the surface of movements that too strongly wave the banner of freedom, and you will most always find a hidden autocracy.

Freedom in its full creative sense results not from the absence of constraint, but from right relationship between "containers" and their "contents." In only the most trivial sense does a bowl of soup become more free by removing the bowl. Real freedom gives not just the power to act independently, but the power to act purposefully and creatively.

In reflecting on the relationship between structure and freedom, I am often drawn back to a memory of taking part in a local conference on the arts and mental health some years back. What transpired both reminded me of the importance of structure and boundary and confronted me with the challenge of using structures and boundaries in new, more dynamic ways.

The structure of the conference, the container, had workshops in the morning and early afternoon, then later in the day a time for the various groups to get together to share some of what they had done. On hearing the plan, I knew I wasn't wholly happy with it, but didn't give it much further thought.

I co-led an afternoon workshop with a friend, doing an exercise designed to help people get in touch with something that was a "creative edge" in their lives. People imagined their lives as journeys along some kind of "pathway." Then each drew his journey, moved as his creative edge in it, and explored the excitements and fears that it presented.

As people shared their experiences in doing the exercise, I saw that for many it had been extremely powerful. I realized I didn't feel comfortable having agreed that, in a couple of hours, we would share this very vulnerable and personal material with a large room full of people. The container wasn't right. As I listened, feeling the potency of people's images, I pondered what I should do.

Failing to come up with something that felt right, I asked the group for their thoughts. I told them I felt I had made a mistake and was prepared to tell the larger group that sharing our experience just didn't feel appropriate.

Several people agreed that it would feel like a violation to do a "presentation." Then one man suggested that maybe we could just move the circle into the larger room and keep working. We had only had time for ten or so of the twenty-five people present to share their experiences. Rather than preparing something to present, he suggested, we could just keep sharing with each other. If people found it felt safe enough, they could speak up. Otherwise, there would just be silence. We decided to do this.

Back in the larger group, we were the last of the workshops to present. I stood and introduced what we would do and why. I explained that it would be an experiment and invited their attention in it. I also explained that because of the safety needed for that experiment to work, we would, in effect, ignore the larger group.

As I spoke, I felt a palpable change in the feeling tone of the room. The atmosphere had been playful and open. It was pleasant, but not terribly conducive to depth in people's work. The strength of the boundary I needed to set offered a marked contrast in tone.

As I spoke, I realized a kind of ferociousness rising in myself. In my mind's eye I saw the ancient mythic figure of the guardian gatekeeper. With these feelings I realized just how central this role of guarding the creatively significant was to my life. As we started to work, a woman yelled from the audience, "I can't hear." The quickness of my response—"that is for you to deal with"—startled me and removed any lingering doubts in the room about the solidity of the circle's boundary.

The sharings in the small group were even more powerful than earlier, each building on the one before. It felt like our fifteen minute time elapsed before we started. Many people commented at how struck they were by what had happened and by the obvious fact that it was able to happen because of the rightness and the integrity of the container we had made for the work. This was something, they said, they would not soon forget.

The experience reminded me in a most personal way of the importance of choosing containers carefully. And it reminded me once again of the critical importance of not falling for the fallacy of equating freedom with "soft" containers. Arriving at our new container involved making traditional boundaries more permeable— the boundaries of authority in the small group, the boundaries around how decisions would be made for the conference as a whole. But my willingness to ferociously assert the boundaries of that new container, to make them clear and absolute, was essential to the freedom we felt together. The art is not to choose between freedom and structure, but to understand their larger creative relationship.

You might take a few moments to look at the containers that play roles in your life—your commitments, where you live, where you work, the groups of people you spend time with. How effective is each of them in supporting the things most important to you in your life? Are there things you would like to change? New containers? Boundaries softened or made more solid? Larger containers, simpler or more selective ones?

With the third more right-hand tool, we find that we are but a short distance from the most delineated of our more left-hand tools. This tool is the capacity to discern pattern in change. Both the sorts of forms that effectively make things more alive and the kinds of containers that enhance freedom in the largest sense change in characteristic ways through time. Whether we talk about it in the more left-hand language of rhythm or in the more right-hand language of pattern, there are few more powerful skills available to the change agent than the ability to describe and predict these changes.

The notion that human experience is ordered creatively offers one useful way to think about rhythm and pattern. We've seen some of the power of this approach—with the concept of evolutionary stages in culture and the notion of creatively related "modes" in intelligence. In the next chapter, we'll look more generally at how a Creative Systems perspective can help us delineate patterns in change. But a brief story might be useful here, both to give a better feel for the value of thinking in a "living" pattern language and to illustrate how notions of creative patterning are practically applied.

Recently a friend and I were talking at lunch. He was about to lead a workshop for high school students on leadership and wanted my reflections on likely group dynamics. I told him that I didn't have much to offer in the "do this, then do that" department, but that looking together at the different creative processes involved could offer useful insights. We talked about the stages that groups commonly go through in their development. We looked at adolescence as a creative stage in individual development. And we explored some of the implications of present cultural transitions, both for adolescent identity and for adult/adolescent interactions. Then we put all of this in the context of my friend's particular personality style—how, given who he is, he would be expected to respond, helpfully and not so helpfully, to the various creative challenges that might present themselves. No easy formulas. But this understanding of the various change patterns involved and how they might intersect helped my friend walk into a challenging situation feeling creatively open and prepared.

None of the new tools we've added to the change agent's tool bag in this chapter provide final answers or infallible guidance for how to proceed. But these are the kinds of tools that work in a "living" reality. This is true personally. Planning one's life is great—

but only if one is willing to get out of the way so that life in all its flesh-and-blood unexpectedness has a chance to happen. And it is equally true culturally. Schools can't provide all the necessary facts and skills for a world still years in the future. They *can* serve as powerful laboratories for learning the art of world creating. In the end, governments can't define the direction of a populace. They *can* provide formidable vessels for empowering a populace in the task of seeking right direction.

Traps

Separation Fallacies: Change is a product of simple cause and effect. The way to get something done is to do it. The goal of action is achievement.

Unity Fallacies: Cause and effect is an illusion of mind. The timeless is the real truth. The goal is freedom, to be without boundaries and constraints.

Compromise Fallacies: There are two kinds of causality; sometimes one applies, sometimes the other. Life should be ___% spiritual and ___% material, ___% being and ___% doing, ___% freedom and ___% responsibility.

Bridgings

Causation is participatory and creative—a function of evolving, "living" systems interaction.

Matter and spirit, time and timelessness, structure and freedom are "co-causal." The task is not to choose one over the other, but to learn the art of using them together in the service of what is most alive and true.

CHAPTER TWELVE

BEYOND POLARITY: TOWARD A REALITY OF "LIVING" WHOLENESS

"The big news of the twenty-first century will be that the world as a whole has got to be managed, not just its parts."
—Norman Cousins

"The times when scientists could distrust theories in direct proportion to their breadth and dismiss integrating research as 'meta-physics' are past. The age of analysis has done its work; the age of synthesis has begun."
—Erwin Laszlo

"I surrender to the belief that my knowing is a small part of a wider integrated knowing that knits the entire biosphere of creation."
—Gregory Bateson

"Welcome, O life! I go to encounter for the millionth time the reality of experience and to forge in the smithy of my soul the uncreated conscience of my race."
—James Joyce
A Portrait of the Artist as a Young Man

We turn now to look at the phenomena of bridging in more theoretical detail. Thus far, we've kept a generic view of bridging, treating one polarity like another. And we've focused more on the simple fact of bridging than on its underlying dynamics. We will conclude by examining questions of polarity and bridging with a finer theoretical lens.

We will do this two ways. First we will look historically, examining how polar assumptions have evolved through cultural time. And we will chronicle the progression of ideas that through this century have engaged the challenge of a "new world view." On first encounter, the various contributions, coming as they do from wide-ranging domains and disparate or even antagonistic schools of thought, can easily seem a crazy-quilt of unrelated notions. This brief historical journey will help put these ideas in perspective.

Then we will look at Creative Systems thinking as one specific tool for bringing detail to our understanding. Creative Systems ideas confront the critical task of delineating rhythm and pattern in "living" organization. In doing so, they offer possible answers for each of the pivotal why's of polarity: why we think in terms of polarities in the first place, why polarities take the forms they do, why these forms change as they do over time, and why now we may be moving beyond the need to think in isolatedly polar terms.

In presenting a few similarly theoretical notions near the book's beginning, I emphasized that one need not necessarily agree with them to make good use of the book's contents. This remains true. My purpose in writing *Necessary Wisdom* will have been realized if the reader departs moved by the importance of transcending outmoded polar perspectives and possessing some tools for making sense of the larger reality ahead. The theoretical notions in this chapter offer one way to begin mapping the workings of that reality in greater detail. But they are only a map, and just one map.

Either/Or's and Both/And's

"[E]very matter has two handles, one of which will bear taking hold of, the other not."
—Epictetus

Taking a great kaleidoscope of forms, polarities have played a part in human understanding since our beginnings. A brief historical journey can offer insights both for better grasping the role of polarities in understanding and for making sense of today's challenge to bridge in that understanding.

Let's begin in earliest times. It is sometimes argued that thinking from the first few stages of culture more closely resembles the needed "new world view" than does the greater portion of today's thought. This is true in only the most limited sense, but the sense in which it is true is worth examining. Early views do have curious similarities with emergent conception. Polar juxtapositions, then, were seen less as opposites than as siblings. And polarities were commonly linked to a recognition of life's generativity.

Fundamental truth in Stone Age reality is revealed in the tribal myths. Most important among such myths are the myths of creation. In some way, all creation myths tell a single story—an explicitly polar story—of "how the one became two." The creation story of the Maori of New Zealand provides a good example. It begins with Tane-mahuta, the first human, pushing to separate the sky-father Rangi and the earth-mother Papa to free himself from the womb. At this stage in culture, images of "twoness" hold a most important place, but they always remain very much secondary to those of "oneness"—oneness with nature, oneness in mystery. There is separateness, but only in the sense that a mother and her infant are separate. Opposites exist, but only in the sense that intimates in deep embrace are opposites.

The most colorful depictions of the interplay of the two hands of truth appear in the next stage of culture, that spanning from the early civilizations to the beginnings of monotheistic dominance. Again, notions of polarity and creation were intimately tied, but the emphasis shifted from creation as a single event to creation as simply what life was about. We see the creative poles represented in a variety of ways. They may manifest themselves as mythic figures, such as Apollo and Dionysus from the Greek pantheons, Shiva and Shakti from stories of classical India, or Horus and Set from early Egyptian belief. Or they may take more abstract form, as in the interplay of yin and yang in Chinese Taoism or the intertwining serpents of the Greek caduceus, today our symbol of healing in medicine.

The poles at this stage were seen as more separate, but still complementary. People of these times saw opposites as working together to create the ongoing magic of existence. From 500 B.C. Greece we hear these words from the philosopher Heraclitus: "There is harmony in the tension of opposites, as in the case of the bow and the lyre." From the same period in China come these words from the sage Chuang-Tzu: "Those who would have right without its correlative, wrong; or good government without its correlative, misrule—they do not apprehend the great principles of the universe nor the conditions to which all creation is subject."

Through the rest of the course of culture, polarity held just as much a place, but the relationship between poles was thought of less and less as complementary or, with this, generative. Exceptions occurred, most specifically in more mystical traditions. The central theme in medieval alchemy, for example, was quite specifically the resolution of opposites and through this the realization of integral truth in the image of the Philosopher's Stone.[1] But for the most part, from the beginnings of monotheism to present times, we find polarity framed in quite different terms. In contrast to the words spoken from the previous stage, we hear these from the book of Matthew: "Let not your left hand know what your right hand doeth."

Through the Middle Ages, we find polar pairs increasingly regarded as polar opposites: good set against evil, man against nature, the crown against the church, lords against the peasantry. In the Age of Reason this tension relaxed somewhat—juxtapositions such as art and science, subjective and objective, while still opposites, were less overtly contentious. But this easing of conflict signified less an expression of resolution than the mutual safety afforded by greater distance and distinction.

Given this perspective, it is easy to see why the needed "new world view" is sometimes popularly equated with early cosmologies—the new physics with Eastern philosophy, the needed new ecological sensibilities with the spirituality of our tribal beginnings. Early views, in a limited but important sense, bridged. They regarded the relationship between polarities as both complementary and generative.

And, as should be obvious by now, the kind of thinking our times demand is much more than a restatement of forgotten truths. The new story is "bigger" in three primary ways.

First, it more fully embodies what I have called the creative whole. Early notions, because they speak from the first few stages in culture as creation, held an inherent bias toward the unformed

---

[1] We call certain medieval traditions mystical because their primary emphasis remained with "the one" in contrast to the more general cultural movement toward distinction.

and the unitary, toward creation's left hand. Listen to these lines from the Turkish mystic Rumi:

> "This piece of food cannot be eaten,
>   nor this bit of wisdom found by looking.
> There is a secret core in everyone
>   not even Gabriel can know by trying to know."[2]

These are beautiful words, and words of wisdom, but they are biased toward the more creatively germinal truth of early times. The critical tasks of today demand a broader wisdom, one better able to address the whole of creation: the food that *can* be eaten equally with that which cannot, the periphery equally with the core, that which we can know only by trying equally with that which comes to us through surrender. Thus, unless carefully expanded for modern times, ideas from early cultural stages can lead to distorted conclusions. These ideas are particularly limiting for questions that require any degree of strong archetypally masculine presence—for example, questions of governance, economics, or defense.[3]

Uncertainty's new role defines a second way in which the new story is bigger. Early views eloquently addressed the task of maturity and wisdom in the story of an individual life and with this the task of coming to terms with personal uncertainty. But they came from very young times in the lifetime of culture, times when cultural/cosmological truth still lay in the safe embrace of parental omniscience—God Kings and gurus, taboos and divinely ordained codes of conduct. As we've seen, the new understanding demands not just personal maturity, but cultural maturity, and with this an acceptance of uncertainty in reality as a whole. To provide help in any complete sense, earlier concepts must be expanded to include this next layer of maturity. Otherwise, instead of enlightening us, they can end up hiding us from the new responsibility our times demand.

---

[2] From *Unseen Rain*, translated by John Moyne and Coleman Barks.

[3] Wise utterances from earlier cultural stages often explicitly emphasize balance between extremes, between "oneness" and "twoness," feminine and masculine, yin and yang. But this is balance in the context of a conceptual reality itself strongly weighted toward "oneness."

The third way the new story is bigger relates to our emerging capacity and imperative for perspective in the whole. In past world views, one's time-specific and place-specific cultural polarities *were* truth: Rangi and Papa or Shiva and Shakti were seen not just as metaphors for truth, but truth itself. As conceptions, they included no recognition that other cultures might live by equally valid conceptions or that they represented just one slice in the larger story of cultural time. Today's imperatives demand the capacity to see time- and place-specific experience within its larger "living" context. This new capacity perhaps best sums up the challenge of the new world view: to be not only creators of culture, but conscious in the larger process of culture as creation. Unless carefully expanded for modern times, ideas isolated from early stages leave us short of this critical capacity as well.

Let's turn now to the modern story of bridging. It includes contributions from most every field. I think of the story beginning about a hundred years ago and involving three "waves" of innovation. Each wave bridged at a deeper level and revealed an increasingly dynamic view of reality and our place in it.

The first wave crested around the turn of the century. Ripples arrived earlier, but this initial wave brought the first truly revolutionary breakthroughs in understanding. The key figures were Charles Darwin, Sigmund Freud, and Albert Einstein.

While Darwin's seminal works were published some forty years earlier, it took new discoveries in genetics for his ideas to gain credence and begin to have broad impact. The concept of evolution by natural selection confronted the clean distinctions of his cultural time with a dual bridging, at once of humanity and nature, and humanity and the divine. In this new view, the human species no longer stood wholly separate from the creaturely, and creation no longer looked like just the once-and-for-all handiwork of a separate divinity. Creation became ongoing and intrinsic to life.

Freud's thinking involved a parallel bridging with the creaturely, but here the creaturely lay within us rather than outside us in nature. His concept of an unconscious and his interest in the reality of dreams made powerful statements of "remembering." They bridged the inner workings of the psyche and radically challenged the prevailing ideal of the supremely rational man.

The first wave of the new understanding crested around the turn of the century. ("Einstein and His Wife in Chicago," The Bettmann Archive.)

Around the same time, Einstein's contributions bridged on multiple fronts, most notably between energy and matter, time and space, and the observer and the observed. Not only did his thinking usher in a new era in physics, it came to symbolize for the whole of humanity the possibility of a radically new kind of truth. No longer could we rest comfortably on old absolutes. From this time on, truth would be relative, a function of relationship, in time, in space.[4]

---

[4]Breakthroughs at the threshold of passage into a new world view can often be looked on equally well as comprising the exciting first chapter of the new story, or the culminating chapter of the old. For example, while in one sense natural selection is a bridging concept, it can be described with equal validity as a final cry of victory for the material, a reduction of man to biology and of creation to the sterile machinations of competition and genetics. The ideas of Freud can be seen, with equal accuracy, as offering material consciousness entry into the one domain from which before it had been excluded, that of the soul and psyche. The theory of relativity can be similarly depicted as the ultimate deterministic cosmology.

The second major wave crested about a third of the way through this century. In science, the major event of this second wave was the emergence of quantum mechanics, its primary figures Max Planck, Niels Bohr, and Werner Heisenberg. Quantum mechanics not only bridged matter and energy and the observer and the observed, but joined certainty with uncertainty and cause with effect as well. Over time, a growing recognition emerged among the thinkers of quantum mechanics that their ideas held major philosophical as well as scientific implications. Niels Bohr once commented: "Those who are not shocked when they first come across quantum theory cannot possibly have understood it."

At about the same time, Kurt Gödel's similarly provocative innovations in mathematics appeared. His demonstration that the comprehensibility of any theory depends on factors outside its assumptions—in short, that we can never have the whole truth—provided further evidence that traditional notions of fact and fancy, certainty and uncertainty lay in the past.

The bridging concepts put forward by the next generation of major thinkers in psychology and psychiatry added further depth to our understanding of the psyche's creatively paradoxical workings. The ideas of Carl Jung presented a new, less forbidding and more generative picture of the unconscious and offered important new insight into the interplay of masculine and feminine elements in the psyche. Wilhelm Reich argued that often the most direct way to affect patterns in the mind was through the body. Bridging themes have a place in the contributions of many other major psychological thinkers of this period—Harry Stack Sullivan, Alfred Adler, Otto Rank, Viktor Frankl.

Important related threads appeared in philosophy at this time. Georg Hegel's major works were published nearly a hundred years earlier, but they came to new attention during this period. Hegel's formulations had their origins in an attempt to reconcile the opposed rationalist and romantic perspectives of his day. He proposed that history was dialectical, an evolutionary process that happened through the ongoing creation and synthesis of opposites. Whitehead's process philosophy effectively bridged on multiple levels—being and doing, rational and irrational, determinate and indeterminate—and was explicitly creative. From a different direction, that of language, Alfred Korzybski contributed his principles of General Semantics, elucidating how the confusion of language with reality creates false securities. Existentialism, with its rejection of both poles of traditional surety, both mechanically structured reality and conventional theism, played an important role in this wave of innovation. While existentialism's conclusions were often not integral, it served to effectively propel understanding toward the paradigmatic threshold. Two further figures, Swiss cultural philosopher Jean Gebser and German psychologist and philosopher Erich Neumann, have particular pertinence here. Each saw history as an evolutionary phenomenon and framed the emergent evolutionary task in expressly integral terms.

Movements in the arts during this time—Cubism, Surrealism, Abstract Expressionism—expressed similarly integral themes: the surrendering of the literal, the bridging of reason and intuition, the importance of a new comfort with uncertainty. Picasso once remarked: "Art is not truth. Art is a lie that makes us realize truth." We hear these words in André Breton's *Second Manifesto of Surrealism:* "Everything leads us to believe that there is a certain point in the spirit from which life and death, real and imaginary, past and future, communicable and incommunicable, are no longer perceived as contraries."

The swelling of the third wave in this sequence has been a phenomenon of the last twenty to thirty years. Along with continuing breakthroughs in specific domains, we see three major themes: new bridgings between disciplines, the elucidation of more comprehensive perspectives, and a growing consciousness in the mass of culture of the importance of integral concerns.

In specific domains, we've seen a multiplicity of contributions. Ilya Prigogine's Nobel prize winning elucidation of self-organizing processes in chemistry is of particular note as it challenged a previously untouched domain. Numerous other contributions brought new research in the role of mind/body interaction, new concepts in management and organizational theory, more inclusive models for intelligence, and more dynamic perspectives for education.

Between domains, we've seen a growing recognition that the richest territory for discovery has moved from within established disciplines to the creative boundaries that previously held them separate. New movements across fields increasingly discover their creative impetus in some such interlinking. The last decades contributed a proliferation of hybrid disciplines—biophysics, organizational psychology, sociobiology. The major new movements in psychology in the second half of the century—humanistic psychology and transpersonal psychology—each expressly bridges traditional domains. Humanistic psychology, born from the thinking of Abraham Maslow, Carl Rogers, and Rollo May, bridges psychology, philosophy, and social consciousness. Transpersonal psychology, its major early threads spun from the thinking of Jung, Maslow, Italian psychiatrist Roberto Assagioli, and the philosophies of the East, attempts to bridge the psychological and the spiritual.[5]

With this we've begun to see the appearance of more comprehensive perspectives. Many of the ideas most pertinent here fall into the category of what I have called generically "systems" frameworks. While much of systems thinking is highly mechanistic, in its best formulations it quite directly takes on the challenge of bridging. Ludwig von Bertalanffy, formal systems thinking's first major figure, defined systems thinking as "the exploration of 'wholes' and 'wholeness,' [concerns] which not so long ago were considered to be metaphysical notions transcending the boundaries of science." The systems ideas of Eric Jantsch and Erwin Laszlo are noteworthy because they focus specifically on evolutionary dynamics.

We see perspectives with big picture implications on a variety of fronts. The cybernetic concepts of Gregory Bateson eloquently framed the challenge of new understanding. The ideas of Chaos Theory, while still basically mechanistic, are helping science move past the constraints of traditional determinism. And constructivism in philosophy is bringing new attention to the inherent relativity of belief.

---

[5] The best of thinking in humanistic and transpersonal psychology has bridged, while the worst has simply flipped poles: humanists identifying with feelings and rejecting the intellect, transpersonalists identifying with spirit and rejecting the material.

Central to this third cresting has been the increasing prominence of integral themes in the thinking of the mass of culture.
This has had two parts: the appearance of social movements that
reflect major cultural bridgings and a newly popular recognition of
integral dynamics and issues.

Three major social movements born out of newly integral sensibilities mark the last decades: the civil rights movement, the
women's movement, and the environmental movement. While each
has, often as not, been reduced to polar rhetoric, none, I would
suggest, would have come to prominence without a new potential
for bridging in the "psyche" of culture: between haves and have-
nots in civil rights, between male and female in feminism, and between humankind and nature in environmentalism.

At the same time, bridging concepts have begun to penetrate
popular thought. Most frequently they are used superficially, even
in ways that negate what they are really about, but the simple fact
that they are becoming part of common discourse is significant. We
hear people talking about "shifts in paradigm" (drawing on science
historian Thomas Kuhn's notion of quantum steps in evolutionary
change), about dealing with questions "holistically," about finding
"win/win" solutions to conflict, about the importance of using "both
sides of the brain." With challenges that require us to bridge in our
understanding becoming imperatives of daily life, we are seeing
integral concepts and sensibilities beginning to form the core of a
new "common sense."

Creative Causality

"And, as imagination bodies forth
The forms of things unknown, the poet's pen
Turns them to shapes, and gives to airy nothing
A local habitation and a name."
—William Shakespeare
A Midsummer Night's Dream

With this section, we turn more specifically to Creative Systems ideas. It is most important that the reader not interpret this,
coming as it does near the book's conclusion, as me doing a drum
roll and asserting, "Okay, now here it is: *The Answer.* Here is how to

think integrally." Naming any particular perspective as "the answer" would violate everything the book has been about.

This material is included because it provides an important further level of detail for our exploration of polarities, and because it
usefully frames what is required if we seek to move fully into the
territory beyond our conceptual threshold. As well, it provides *one*
practical and powerful approach to "new world view" understanding.

I like to think of the challenge of "new world view" understanding in terms of our now familiar conceptual threshold and three
related but distinct steps beyond it. I call these steps "initial bridging," "defining the big picture," and "mapping the territory." Most
of the thinking in the three waves of innovation described above
addresses primarily the first step, though some goes considerably
further. Quantum mechanics, for example, concerns itself exten-
sively with "mapping the territory," though specifically within the
domain of physics. Creative Systems thinking offers a comprehensive approach to understanding that begins to address each of these
three steps.

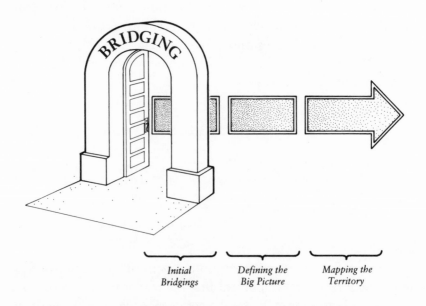

| Initial | Defining the | Mapping the |
| Bridgings | Big Picture | Territory |

FIG. 12-1: *Stepping Beyond the Threshold*

The first step, "initial bridgings," brings the simple recognition that either/or understanding is not enough for the new questions. Much of this book has been concerned with this step. We've looked at the imperative of bridging in our understanding and identified traps that can leave us short of the doorway's threshold.

The task of the second step, "defining the big picture," is to make some crude sense of the new reality to which bridging opens us. Where do we find ourselves when we step over that conceptual threshold? My assertion that emergent reality is "evolutionary, relational, and meta-determinant" represents a start at making this second step.

To complete this step, however, we need more than just a listing of characteristics. We need some concept of why reality should display these characteristics. I spoke of this need earlier in emphasizing the importance of finding a new "fundamental organizing image."

Here a Creative Systems perspective begins to make its specific contribution. Emergent conceptions are "evolutionary, relational, and meta-determinant" it claims, because reality is, most fundamentally, a creative dynamic. A Creative Systems perspective views reality as a multilayered, creatively self-organizing process.

The notion that reality is creative is original in this particular formulation, but the heart of it enters into all ideas that successfully traverse our conceptual threshold. If we got all the contributors mentioned in the previous section into the same room, most would have some related notion to share: Darwin would talk about natural selection; Freud, the evolving interplay of id and ego; Hegel, the ongoing dialectical story of thesis, antithesis, and synthesis. Whitehead would tell about creation itself, his "Universal of Universals"; Prigogine, "order by fluctuation"; and Bateson, life as a stochastic process, alternatively random and selective. The idea that reality is creatively ordered, while not before explicit in this sense, lies embedded in most all successful emergent conception.

The third step past our threshold presents another order of challenge. The new "big picture" provided by the second step gets us oriented in the right direction, but leaves us short of any real ability to think integrally. New thinking requires not just defining a new whole, but, as well, new ways of discerning parts. The question of parts is critical. Differentiation, the capacity to separate one thing from another, to say "this is this and that is that," is what makes understanding of any practical significance.

But here we find ourselves in a pickle. Differentiation in any customary sense means dividing atomistically. It throws us immediately back into a machine world. The dilemma could not be more central: How do we think in terms of parts and at the same time honor the "living" nature of reality? Approached conventionally, the question presents a seemingly intractable Catch-22.[6]

A Creative Systems perspective offers one solution. It addresses the question of differentiation by radically reframing the nature and relationship of parts.

From a Creative Systems perspective, reality is creative not just in the "whole ball of wax" sense of being interconnected and generative, but is, as well, *creatively patterned*. In a Creative Systems perspective, these patternings in the whole serve as the needed parts for our thinking.

"Parts" in this sense represent a new kind of concept. Rather than atomistic bits as in mechanical models, parts become principles of creative organization, ecologically related statements of "living" relationship. We got glimpses of this very different approach to differentiation earlier with the image of cultural "skin-shedding" and with the notion that our various intelligences might be better seen as creatively related organizational processes than as static, discrete faculties. By framing parts creatively, we open the door to a wholly new human capacity: the ability to think with detail about life and have our descriptions of detail not only acknowledge but highlight the central fact that life is indeed *alive*.

Let's begin to look more specifically at this notion of creative patterning. In briefly introducing these ideas near the book's beginning, I offered that Creative Systems thinking provides possible answers for two of the most pivotal and puzzling questions about polar dynamics: why we tend to think in polar terms and why

---

[6] Differentiation has presented the major stumbling block in attempts to develop really practical "new world view" concepts. More often than not, we've seen either notions that are, in fact, only elaborate ways of saying "all is one," or ideas that are ultimately no less mechanical than those they sought to replace.

bridging concepts are now coming to prominence. The notion of creation as necessarily dialectical, a process that can't happen without separating the new creation from its context, offers one intriguing explanation for the central place of polarities in human understanding. And the notion of a "second half" in creation, the idea that formative processes involve not just creative differentiation, but integration as well, provides a fascinating possible explanation for the sudden proliferation of more integral views at the current cutting edge of our understanding.

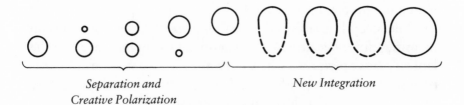

Separation and
Creative Polarization

New Integration

FIG. 12-2: *Creation as Pattern*

The concept of creative patterning provides a way to address a further essential question about polarities, one that if ignored would leave an inexcusable hole in our discussion: Why are different polarities different? The question deserves examining in some detail.

I've claimed that all polarities represent, in the end, variations on a single theme: the "procreative" dance between form and the formless, between the archetypally masculine and the archetypally feminine, between creation's right and left hands. While this notion seems generally consistent with the evidence, huge differences do exist between polarities. Some of these differences result from where one is looking—for example, "teacher and student" versus "doctor and patient." But many are more fundamental. If we compare the polarity of "subjective and objective" with that of "moral and immoral," for example, we find not just different content, but a marked difference in feeling tone—"subjective and objective" feels clinical, "moral and immoral" feels stern and unforgiving. How do we best understand such differences? The question is critical. If it can't be adequately addressed, the whole notion that we are dealing at essence with a single theme comes into question. A Creative Systems perspective offers one way to both understand and map these differences.

From a Creative Systems perspective, three types of variables play roles in making different polarities different: domain, the defining creative rhythm, and the defining creative stage. It is the last of the three, creative stage, that most helps us as a tool for differentiation, but each serves to fill out a creative perspective.

The first variable, "domain," is pretty obvious. As in the example of "teacher and student" compared to "doctor and patient" above, some polarities differ for the simple reason that they deal with different realms of activity.

The second variable is the "defining creative rhythm." Certain polarities differ because they are defined by different layers in the larger creative picture of who we are: the creative story of culture as opposed to that of our individual development, or the creative story of our individual development as opposed to that of a particular interpersonal relationship or a particular creative task. Actually, our experience of a polar pair is never limited to just one layer. Like colored transparencies, one placed upon the next, the various layers of creative experience combine with varying emphasis to establish the defining hue of any particular polarity. But certain polarities take primary expression from particular creative rhythms, for example, "government and governed" from our stage in culture, "parent and child" from our stage in personal development.

The third variable is the "defining creative stage." Each stage imbues polar dynamics with particular qualities. Some polarities connect specifically to particular stages. More often, polarities span the stages, but take on unique characteristics as a function of the stage that is most dominant. Our experience of a particular polarity at any moment is a function of the stage we occupy in each of the various creative rhythms that make up the reality of that moment.[7]

Since the concept of creative patterning comes most directly to bear with this third variable, it is worth examining in greater detail.

---

[7] Add to this our particular personality style. As I present in *The Creative Imperative*, personality differences can be understood as expressions of the different places in the creative whole from which we preferentially live and act.

Over the course of any creative rhythm, how we experience any particular polar pair can be seen to undergo characteristic changes. These changes represent several types: changes in the images and feelings we associate with each pole, changes in the felt relationship between the poles, and changes in the relative dominance of the poles.

Our experience of nature through time illustrates these interrelated change processes. Our *images* of nature have changed over time—nature in earliest culture appeared divine; in our modern view we see it primarily as a resource. Similarly, our *felt relationship* with nature has changed—over that same time we moved from feeling essentially at one with nature to feeling increasingly distant and estranged from her. And our *dominance relationship* with nature has changed—in earliest times, we saw ourselves as tiny and nature as immense; with modern culture, humanity looms large, and nature often goes nearly forgotten.

Let's explore these change processes more closely. To do this, we'll take a brief journey through one creative cycle, looking at how polarities evolve over the course of several different kinds of creative dynamics: work on a creative project, a lifetime, and the story of culture. A quote from poet John Ciardi nicely sets us on our way: "Nothing is more powerful of man than the fact that he naturally gives off forms, and is naturally enclosed by them. To acquire knowledge of aesthetic form is to acquire knowledge of man."

Creation tells the story of how we are simultaneously created as form and act as the creators of form. It begins "In the beginning...."

Creation's first stage, what I have called the stage of incubation, arises prior to polarity in any overt sense. The whole of original unity remains as yet unbroken. We begin in darkness, in a womb-world. The feeling tone is of mystery. The language is creaturely, timeless. Life presides here, but it is the life of latencies and potentials, not yet the life of one thing set against another.

In a creative project, whether a poem or a new scientific discovery, we start in the world of John Livingston Lowes' "surging chaos of the unexpressed." In individual development, this is the womb world of the fetus and the young infant's world of mother's protecting arms, a world of taste, touch, and deep bodily rhythms as yet unchallenged by the demands of task or time. In the story of culture, we reside in the time of the tribal circle, a time when nature felt all-defining—at once mother and father—and truth spoke through the eternal turning of seasons; the chant of the healer; the voice of bear, eagle, mountain, river.

At this point, when we encounter polarities, what most marks the relationship of the two halves is the oneness that securely holds them. There is difference here, but more as texture than difference in any absolute sense. While mother and fetus are not wholly the same, if we separate them the relationship—as life—ends. The tribal sky differs from the earth, and the seasons come one after the other, but these are only intonations in nature's timeless song.

What is the primary quality here? One could say peace, but language is tricky in these realms. We could as well say wildness. The special beauty here is as much the "terrible beauty" of the untamed as the quiet beauty of serenity. This is the peace, simply, of a world yet without "other."

With the next stage, what I've called the stage of inspiration, polarity begins to take on a quite different quality. Here, for the first time, we encounter real separation. The new creation has broken through the circle of original wholeness, opened its eyes to the light, and taken its first steps toward independent existence. The felt quality is one of magic and new possibility. The language is that of symbol, myth, and imagination.

In a simple creative act, that poem or discovery, this time brings the "ah-ha." Beethoven wrote, "From where do I get my ideas? That I cannot with certainty say. They come uncalled, directly and indirectly." Developmentally, we are in childhood, our truth ordered by the mythic causality of make-believe and "let's pretend." Culturally, these times encompass the early civilizations, times when cosmic order was understood through the epic dramas of deities, when art spoke as loudly as science or politics, and when numbers and words, while often used with great complexity, were as much things of magic as matter.

In this stage, we tend to give our attention to the numinosity of the new creation. In fact, new form remains small compared to the less visible immensity of its context and is still deeply dependent on it. New creative inspiration enchants, but it is still fragile, naive, and easily harmed. The young child, taking its first steps, doing its first drawings, ventures out fearlessly and claims the center of attention. But its new consciousness is still small compared to the matrix of home and nature that gave it birth.

Whatever sphere of human creation we concern ourselves with—from a creative moment to the story of culture—and whatever kind of polar relationship we wish to examine—from conscious and unconscious to consciousness and cosmos—the basic characteristics at this stage remain the same. Here the felt quality of individual poles is magical; they are like loci of variously colored energy. The felt relationship between poles is collaborative; while we have moved beyond simple oneness, relatedness still predominates over distinction. And while the more archetypally masculine pole often receives greatest attention, here the archetypally feminine, the pole of source and context, contributes the far greater force.

Only with the next stage, what I have called the stage of "perspiration," do polarities manifest fully as opposites. New inspiration, numinous but frail, here begins making its struggling way into solid form. Without this stage, creation is never more than a dream. Schiller said it well: "If the manifold potentialities of man were ever to be developed, there was no other way but to pit them one against the other." The central quality here is tension, polar opposition. The language is moral and visceral, the grammar of heart and guts.

In a creative project, whether writing a poem or seeking a scientific answer, this stage has us first grapple with potential obstacles to realization, both limitations in our own abilities and obstacles presented by our world. In taking them on, our abilities grow, our visions mature, and in some small way our world is changed. In a lifetime, this is adolescence. With childhood receding, the task here requires us to challenge external limits and to establish inner ones. Emotions run strong. The prize for taking on this challenge is the realization of crude but independent identity. In western culture, this period spans the time from the Roman Empire through the Middle Ages. These were times of struggle—historians often speak of major parts of them as the Dark Ages—

but also important times. In Europe we saw a new solidification of organization under kingly rule, the church stepping forward as an organized power, and the increasing establishment of formal structures of commerce.

Whatever the creative rhythm, the poles here display a consistently different quality. They are firmer, more visceral—the force needed to cut a piece of stone with a chisel, the ardencies of an adolescent, the moral posture of the medieval church. The relationship between poles has similarly evolved. Increasingly, it manifests itself as a kind of isometric: the sculptor struggling against the limitations of what a stone can be made to do, the adolescent's ambivalence about authority, the inherent tensions and turmoils of medieval feudal structure. This ambivalence and struggle has its source in our third variable; each pole now possesses equal power.

In the next stage, the last in the first half of the creative cycle, that sense of struggle is gradually replaced by a new excitement and a new finer focus. Creation is now sufficiently established that we need no longer fear that it might fall back into chaos. Finishing and polishing, finding completion as form, now defines the central task. Truth with this stage grows increasingly material and rational, defined in terms of things that can be seen, measured, and analyzed.

In our creative project, we now shift attention to issues of detail and final appearance. Crude form has been established; the job now is to refine that form and to make it shine. In a lifetime, this is young adulthood, the period when we take the crude identity garnered from the struggles of adolescence and step forth to make our place in the world. The tasks are again ones of form: finding a mate, establishing a lifestyle, making it up the ladder of success in a profession. In the evolution of culture, this period came during our most recent age, our Age of Reason and Enlightenment. The moral and blood-bound truth of the Middle Ages fell away and was replaced by an increasingly material reality—a physical reality of actions and their concomitant reactions; a personal reality of individuality, intellect, and achievement; and a social reality of industry and economics.

With entry into this stage, again consistent changes transform the defining polar dynamics. The felt quality of poles is less viscerally charged—more concerned with surface, and more refined. The relationship between poles grows less contentious. Juxtapositions like control and chaos, moral and immoral are replaced with pairings such as success and failure, intelligence and ignorance. Paralleling these changes, we find the more form-defined pole increasingly taking preeminence. In a creative act, creation's left hand remains important, but now as a voice in questions of aesthetics, no longer as the awesome power of mystery. Our twenties and early thirties bring times of hubris, times to act, to leave doubt in the past. At the core of thought in our Age of Enlightenment has been the belief that it is only a matter of time until, through reason and the light of consciousness, all of life's mysteries will be elucidated and all of humanity's problems solved.

While the story of creation may seem complete with this last, most form-defined stage, as we've seen, we are in truth barely approaching its midpoint. The new object of creation (an artwork, individual identity, culture as institution and structure) has found realization as form, but the tasks of maturity lie yet ahead. The second half of creation is marked by the gradual reconnecting of what has been newly created with the original context of that creation. The amnesias that before served to keep the new form from falling back into the safety of old realities are no longer needed and begin to dissolve. Increasingly, we become able to see the new creation within the larger process of which it is, and in truth always has been, a part. Polarities begin to bridge, and gradually a new, more integral whole comes to life.

The motifs of the second half of the creative cycle have been key themes in these pages. A new kind of perspective comes to define reality; we find ourselves more able to step back from the task of creation, to see it as a process, and to take mature responsibility in that process. Truth grows increasingly post-material, no longer just that newly created object, but that which is new in a more and more integrated relationship with the living world that gave birth to it. And uncertainty comes to have a newly positive role.

In a simple creative project, this stage often takes one by surprise. Having finished a piece, one easily assumes the task to be complete. But in fact, the journey of creation remains far from over. The piece has yet to be placed in the world, to reengage its social context. What will happen to it? Will it do good, harm, be ignored, be destroyed? As well, in an important sense it has yet to be placed in the person who has been creating it. A creative act is always as much an act of creating the creator as of creating an object. The conscious focus in the first half of creation concentrated on the manifestation of the new object. In the second, the focus shifts more and more to the larger whole of that object set in living relationship with its contexts, to the new creation's significance in the life of the person who gave it birth and to its significance for the cultural time that gave birth to both of them.

In the story of a lifetime, we experience that now oft-remarked period of the midlife transition. In a similar way, our apparently secure ideas about truth and identity begin to reveal themselves as, in fact, only a part of the picture. Big new questions—ones that can't be answered in the old ways, questions of purpose, of life—present themselves. "Yes, I'm successful, but to what degree is what I do really me? And does it really contribute, make the world a better place?" The second half of life challenges us to a larger perspective and with this a larger responsibility. More and more we come to see our life as a process, and not an isolated process, but one intimately interwoven in its living contexts. Identity shifts increasingly from something we measure with accomplishments and define within the either/or of self versus world to something we measure in terms of purpose and define by the integrity of our relationships, of self with self, and of self with world. Truth as the surety of knowledge gradually gives way to the more humble but ultimately more powerful reality of truth as wisdom.

The thesis that we may be at a parallel point in culture is now familiar. It can only offer a hypothesis, but if it is true in any significant sense, even if it provides but the crudest of metaphors, it carries immense implications.

What lies ahead for our culture and for the planet? None of our customary "stories" satisfy.

In God's kitchen

The thesis that we may be moving into the "second half" of culture as creation has powerful implications. (Gary Larson, "The Far Side," Universal Press Syndicate.)

Will we see a continuation of our onward and upward spiral of materially-defined progress? We recognize with increasing clarity that this is not an option. Given time, it would turn into a sure formula for disaster.

Or perhaps we will see a fall of civilization. This is certainly possible. It has happened to particular civilizations, and other species have disappeared from the planet after much longer reigns than ours. But one would hope for other options.

Some would argue that what lies ahead is some kind of spiritual Armageddon, a time of destruction followed by a joyous "second coming" and the rise of some "chosen people." But this comes no closer to satisfying. If our eyes see with any maturity, we know that unless all of life is "chosen," none will be chosen.

If we need a "new story," of what should it tell? Concepts like "bridging polarities," "creative integration," and "cultural midlife" are crude notions, newly born. But these, and others kindred with them, offer a useful start for putting together a new picture.

What evidence supports this kind of "story?" A first piece of evidence is not the sort that stands up well to rational scrutiny, but it brings its own persuasiveness. In contrast to most images we entertain, this kind of story is realistically consistent with survival, indeed with new possibility, with future health and fulfillment.

The nature of the challenges that mark our time provides the more direct evidence. These challenges are what this book has been about: the all-pervasive need to think in more "living" terms; the imperative of a new kind of wholeness in relationships of all sorts; the importance of bringing a new kind of perspective and relativity to our understanding; the need to take a new, more conscious responsibility for the welfare of the planet; and the importance of "remembering" things like the sacred, the feminine, and the power of relationship.

It could very well be that each theme has its own explanation. But given the pervasiveness of these themes and how often they are closely juxtaposed, it seems most likely that they reflect one, or at most a few, common underlying dynamics. The thesis that culture is a creative process, and with this, that the cutting edge of culture as creation lies in the dynamics of integration, is particularly intriguing in that it offers a single coherent explanation. Its appeal is amplified by the fact that it so directly frames and puts forward the human capacity—wisdom—which so clearly must order our future.

The Challenge of Integral Culture

"Always the more beautiful answer, who asks the more difficult question."
—e. e. cummings

The theoretical concerns of this chapter have taken us very much into the world of conjecture. Only time can tell what will be the best explanation for the history we now see. And particular approaches to understanding, like the Creative Systems ideas I've outlined, must prove themselves through their utility.

But the core concerns this book has addressed are not at all conjecture. Very real crises mark our time. And as much as we might like it to be otherwise, it appears that doing what we've always done, only harder, will not solve them.

My basic argument in these pages has been a simple one. Ideas big enough to meet the crises ahead appear to share a common characteristic—they bridge. I've suggested that by understanding what it means to bridge we gain a powerful compass for the journey ahead, one that can serve us by pointing the way and by helping us recognize when we have lost that way.

While the basic argument is simple, as we've seen, thinking and acting in ways that effectively bridge is not so simple. Stepping beyond the journey's threshold and accepting its challenges asks a great deal of us, not just conceptually, but personally. It demands that we leave behind familiar hand-holds of all sorts—ways we have defined ourselves, ready formulas for success and for relationships, once reliable codes for telling us how good people act. And it demands that we find new, more dynamic ways to understand and speak, ways that more fully honor our "living" natures.

It demands another step as well, something easily missed at first, but which in practice often presents one of the most difficult parts of the challenge: that we forgo easy allegiances. Just as most stands are polemical, so are most all traditional orthodoxies and mass movements. This is not to say that traditional orthodoxies and mass movements don't have within them many people capable of mature thought. But at this time, at least on the popular level, one is much more likely to find bonds predicated on shared easy answers than on the kind of courage now required. To speak from integral positions, one must be comfortable with feeling alone sometimes, with not always having the security of popular support or understanding.

To almost all of our familiar "isms," a position that effectively bridges says, "Yes, in part. And things are bigger than just that." To the peace activist it says, yes, there are few things more important than re-owning our cultural "shadows" and stepping beyond our need for conflict. But we must remain very careful not to confuse simply being antiwar with the larger challenge of peace. To the fundamentalist it says, yes, our times are indeed ones of profound moral crisis. But a simple resurrection of old moral absolutes will not give us the kind of mature morality our times demand. To the New Ager it says, yes, we need to reconnect with the spiritual and with the magical in life. But we must carefully distinguish between the magic of childlike dreams and magic as a voice in mature wisdom. To the political conservative it says, yes, competition and freedom in the marketplace are important. But unfettered, these same things merely provide euphemisms for exploitation. To the political liberal it says, yes, supporting the downtrodden and the common good is critical. But doing this solely through government as good and generous parent is both exorbitant and ultimately ineffective. To the scientist it says, yes, few things have contributed more than the new clarity and precision made possible by the scientific method. But that method alone is not adequate to the task of addressing the increasingly purpose-centered questions that now confront us as a species. To the artist it says, yes, our times ask of us a profound renewal in the aesthetic and creative. But this renewal does not cry victory for art over science or art over technology. It asks, rather, that in a way not before knowable or possible, we work together to make our presence on the planet a work of art.

Our times challenge us to be large. It is a "good news/bad news" deal. The "good news" is we get to be pioneers. The "bad news" is that being pioneers is not at all easy. There are no guarantees, often one feels alone, and many of the rewards are not to be reaped in our lifetime.

Our times challenge us to a whole new kind of maturity. On that the future depends.

"INNER" BRIDGINGS

To address questions of war and peace integrally, one must first have a solid start at finding peace with one's inner warrior and inner peacemaker. To address questions of gender in a creative way, one must find some degree of creative marriage between the masculine and the feminine within. And to address issues having to do with authority, the inner leader and follower, teacher and student, or doctor and patient must have begun to learn to work together.

Below is a simple yet sophisticated exercise for beginning some of this inner work. Since the intellect alone can't bridge, it is designed to engage all of one's "integral intelligence." It is best done with a guide—that way you can keep your attention on the work rather than having to keep looking back to the instructions—but it can also be done alone. It has four steps: 1) identifying the polarity, 2) setting the stage, 3) engaging the dialogue, and 4) reflecting.

1) Identifying the Polarity:

Pick a polarity that in some way feels charged or pivotal for you. It could be any polarity: work and play, masculine and feminine, thoughts and feelings, good and evil, success and failure, parent and child. Most people, if they do a lot of inner work, find that one or two polarities arise again and again for them irrespective of the issue they are exploring. (Note: It is not necessary to have words for this polar pair. They can just as well be feeling qualities or sensations in the body.)

2) Setting the Stage:

Now find a comfortable place to sit, close your eyes, and turn on your imagination. Imagine there is a stage before you, like for a play. And imagine that the poles you have chosen are two characters on that stage. Let the images just come to you. They don't need to make any logical sense.

Notice everything you can about the setting for the play—is it out-of-doors, in a room, on a bright day, on a cloudy day—and about each of the two characters—what they wear, how old they are, how they move, how they seem to relate or not relate to each other. Let yourself be surprised by what you experience. The images may be remarkably clear and distinct or they may be cloudy or confusing. However they come, take them as they are.

Now open your eyes and bring two more chairs into the room, one for each character. In your imagination, offer each character a chair (some may rather stand, lie down, what-have-you). Find the spatial relationship between the chairs that feels right for who they are.

Once they are present, take some time to notice your feelings about each of them. As well, reflect over the last year and get in touch with situations where one or both of them played a strong role. Notice if you find yourself siding with one or the other, making one good, the other bad, making one important, the other not. Commonly, we identify with one half of a polar pair then disown and project the other half, seeing it as an attribute of others or of the world in general. Also notice how the two characters relate to each other. Are they friends, strangers, antagonists?

Notice the degree you feel in a "third space" relationship with the two characters. The hallmarks of a "third space" relationship are that you neither identify with nor disown either character and that you feel at least a beginning sense that it's possible to work together consciously as a team. To start, you may feel only the faintest inklings of "third space" possibilities.

Take some time to solidify the "third space" feelings you do feel. One simple way to do this is to identify both positive and negative attributes of each character, ways that in certain situations each can contribute and ways that each can get in the way. Another is to imagine how, most ideally, the two might work together. (This doesn't necessarily mean being friends. Worthy adversaries can be a quite creative kind of relationship.) What would it look like if you were all relating in the most creatively potent way?

3) Engaging the Inner Dialogue:

Now turn to your two characters and speak to them, sharing your reflections. Share with each the roles you see it playing in your life, what you like and dislike about those roles, and thoughts you have about changes that might make things more rich and alive.

Then pick one of the characters, go over to its chair, and sit in its place. (It usually works best to start with the character you least identify with.) Let yourself really become the character—sense its body posture, feel its feelings, notice what the room looks like through its eyes. Now, as this character, respond to what you said. Let the words that come out of the character's mouth surprise you. Frequently, what it feels like to be a particular character and what a character will say are very different from what one expects.

Return to your chair and take a moment to again become yourself. Respond to what the character has said, both acknowledging things that feel true and challenging the character where you disagree.

Then do a similar dialogue with the second character. Again take time to fully become the character and let yourself be surprised by what it has to say. Then once more return to your chair and respond.

You may wish to do a number of further exchanges as the feelings and content warrant. The process is a dual one. The dialogue itself opens creative, "third space" connections. And the act of going back and forth between the chairs helps one learn in an immediate, visceral sense the difference between being in a whole-person "third space" place and being in a polarity.

4) Reflecting:

After completing the exercise, summarize what you have learned, either verbally to your guide or in writing to yourself. Reflect on what you have learned about the difference between the experience of being in a polarity and being in "third space." Reflect on the place and purpose of this particular polarity in your life. And reflect on what your "creative edge" is in relation to this particular polarity, how you can most use what you have learned to enhance your life.

"OUTER" BRIDGINGS

When I work with groups from different domains, I often begin by having the group make a list of the polarities that have in the past most defined that domain. Then we break up into small groups, with each group taking one polarity.

Within the small groups, people do a sequence of things with their particular polarity. I have them start by caricaturing the polarity so they have a solid feel for the polarity's extremes. If the domain were education and the polarity teacher/student, such a caricatured image might depict a teacher lecturing from a lectern with the students at their desks writing down everything said. Then I have them reflect back on experiences they have had where this polarity was bridged in a way that somehow made the situation "more." I have them share stories, then for each story reflect both on what became "more" and on what aspects of how the situation was handled made it "more." For example, in that group working with the polarity of teacher/student, we might hear the story of a teacher who, by responding to the unique interests and gifts of each student, made each student feel special and empowered. Finally, I ask them what kinds of changes in approaches to this particular domain would most support realization of this bridging. For a group working with the teacher/student polarity, it could be all manner of things: more emphasis in teacher education on the art of creative facilitation, making schools smaller to provide a greater sense of community, greater student involvement in decision making, more use of students as mentors for other students, and so on.

Then I bring the groups back together. Each group shares the most important awarenesses that came out of its work. Then we examine what happens if we combine the various bridgings the different groups have worked on. For the educators, this might be a combining of this bridging of the teacher/student polarity with polarities like intellect/feeling, school/not school, right answer/ wrong answer, administration/faculty, or young/old. We look at the interrelationships between these various bridgings. Then we look both at how this combination of bridgings could increase purpose and effectiveness within that domain and at the kinds of changes needed within the domain as a whole to manifest these various bridgings.

Below are some of the polarities most commonly listed by groups from different domains. You might want to try the above with the domain or domains most central to your life or even gather a group of people who share interest in a particular domain and try it together.

Education
teacher/student
right/wrong answer
intellect/feelings
school/not school
young/old

Religion
God/humankind
virtue/sin
body/spirit
sacred/secular
us/them

Business
management/labor
profit/loss
logic/intuition
work/play
private/public sector

Art
artist/audience
creative/not creative
art/craft
artistic/political
artistic/psychological

Science
humankind/nature
objective/subjective
certainty/uncertainty
science/religion
science/art

Psychology
therapist/client
conscious/unconscious
sanity/insanity
self/society
fact/fancy

Relationships
male/female
parent/child
friend/enemy
self/other
love/friendship

Politics
left/right
government/governed
ally/enemy
haves/have-nots
public/private

Medicine
doctor/patient
health/disease
mind/body
life/death
personal/
  environmental health

One of the things which most marks "third space" understanding is that, in spite of how big things often are, humor prevails. A friend recently gave me this photograph, claiming it to be the first ever taken of a fully integral "polar" bear. ("Two Heads are Better than One," Wide World Photos.)

Resources

(The following sources in some way address bridging themes.)

Chapter Three

Anshen, Ruth Nanda (1947), *Our Emergent Civilization*. Freeport, NY: Books for Libraries Press.

Arieti, Silvano (1976), *Creativity, The Magic Synthesis*. New York: Basic Books.

Bridges, William (1980), *Transitions*. Reading, MA: Addison-Wesley.

Brown, Lester R. (1989), *State of the World*. New York: W.W. Norton.

Ferguson, Marilyn (1980), *The Aquarian Conspiracy*. Los Angeles: J.P. Tarcher.

Fromm, Erich (1955), *The Sane Society*. Greenwich, CT: Fawcett.

Ghiselin, Brewster (1952), *The Creative Process*. New York: Mentor.

Harman, Willis W. (1976), *An Incomplete Guide to the Future*. New York: Norton.

Johnston, Charles M. (1986), *The Creative Imperative*. Berkeley: Celestial Arts.

Land, George T. (1973), *Grow or Die*. New York: Delta.

May, Rollo (1975), *The Courage to Create*. New York: Bantam.

Mesarovic, Mihajlo and Pestel, Edward (1974), *Mankind at the Turning Point*. New York: Signet.

Mumford, Lewis (1966), *Technics and Human Development*. New York: Harcourt Brace Jovanovich.

Prigogine, Ilya and Stengers, Isabelle (1984), *Order Out of Chaos*. New York: Bantam.

Theobald, Robert (1987), *The Rapids of Change*. Indianapolis: Knowledge Systems.

Toffler, Alvin (1980), *The Third Wave*. New York: Bantam.

Chapter Four

Bellah, Robert N. (1985), *Habits of the Heart*. New York: Harper and Row.

Bolen, Jean Shinoda (1989), *Gods in Every Man*. San Francisco: Harper and Row.

Gilligan, Carol (1982), *In a Different Voice*. Cambridge, MA: Harvard University Press.

Goldberg, Herb (1987), *The Inner Male*. New York: Signet.

Hall, Nor (1980), *The Moon and the Virgin*. New York: Harper and Row.

Harding, Esther M. (1970), *The Way of All Women*. New York: Harper and Row.

Johnson, Robert A. (1983), *We: Understanding the Psychology of Romantic Love*. San Francisco: Harper and Row.

Klein, Edward and Erickson, Don, eds. (1988), *About Men*. New York: Simon and Schuster.

Leonard, Linda Schierse (1986), *On the Way to the Wedding*. Boston: Shambhala.

Singer, June (1977), *Androgyny*. Garden City, NY: Doubleday.

Smith, Kenwyn K. and Berg, David N. (1988), *Paradoxes of Group Life*. San Francisco: Jossey-Bass.

Spretnak, Charlene (1978), *Lost Goddesses of Early Greece*. Berkeley, CA: Moon Books.

Stone, Hal and Winkelman, Sidra (1989), *Embracing Each Other*. San Rafael, CA: New World Library.

Tannen, Deborah (1990), *You Just Don't Understand: Women and Men in Conversation*. New York: William Morrow.

Vitale, Stein, Hillman, Neuman, and Von der Heydt (1973), *Fathers and Mothers*. Zurich: Spring.

Welwood, John, ed. (1985), *Challenge of the Heart*. Boston: Shambhala.

Zolla, Elemire (1981), *The Androgyne*. New York: Crossroad.

Chapter Five

Bok, Sissela (1989), *A Strategy for Peace*. New York: Pantheon.

Egendorf, Arthur (1986), *Healing From the War*. Boston: Shambhala.

Foell, Earl and Nenneman, Richard A., eds. (1985), *How Peace Came to the World*. Cambridge: M.I.T. Press.

Keegan, John and Holmes, Richard (1986), *Soldiers, A History of Men in Battle*. New York: Viking.

Keen, Sam (1986), *Faces of the Enemy*. New York: Harper and Row.

Kidder, Rushworth M. (1987), *An Agenda for the 21ˢᵗ Century*. Cambridge: M.I.T. Press.

Macy, Joanna (1983), *Despair and Personal Power in the Nuclear Age*. Philadelphia: New Society Publishers.

Mueller, John (1988), *Retreat from Doomsday*. New York: Basic Books.

Newhouse, John (1989), *War and Peace in the Nuclear Age*. New York: Alfred A. Knopf.

Satin, Mark, ed., *New Options.* Washington, DC: New Options.

Schwitzer, Albert and Jack, Homer J., eds. (1988), *On Nuclear War and Peace.* Elgin, IL: Brethren Press.

White, Ralph K. (1986), *Psychology and the Prevention of Nuclear War.* New York: New York University Press.

Chapter Six

Adizes, Ichak (1979), *How to Solve the Mismanagement Crisis.* Santa Monica, CA: Adizes Institute.

Ginzberg, Eli and Vojta, George (1985), *Beyond Human Scale.* New York: Basic Books.

Hawken, Paul (1987), *Growing a Business.* New York: Simon and Schuster.

Hickman, Craig R. (1990), *Mind of a Manager, Soul of a Leader.* New York: Wiley.

Kanter, R. M. (1983), *The Change Masters.* New York: Simon and Schuster.

Kopp, Sheldon (1972), *If You Meet the Buddha on the Road, Kill Him.* New York: Bantam.

Ouchi, W. (1981), *Theory Z.* Reading, MA: Addison-Wesley.

Peters, T.J., and Waterman, R.H. (1983), *In Search of Excellence.* New York: Harper and Row.

Schon, Donald A. (1983), *The Reflective Practitioner.* New York: Basic Books.

Toffler, Alvin (1985), *The Adaptive Corporation.* New York: Bantam.

Chapter Seven

Alexander, F. Mattias (1969), *The Resurrection of the Body.* New York: Delta.

Bachelard, Gaston (1958), *The Poetics of Space.* Boston: Beacon Press.

Barrett, William (1986), *Death of the Soul.* New York: Doubleday.

Berman, Morris (1989), *Coming to Our Senses.* New York: Simon and Schuster.

Bettelheim, Bruno (1977), *The Uses of Enchantment.* New York: Random House.

Campbell, Joseph (1972), *Myths to Live By.* New York: Bantam.

DeBono, Edward (1969), *The Mechanism of Mind.* New York: Penguin.

DeMille, Richard (1967), *Put Your Mother on the Ceiling.* New York: Penguin.

Dewey, John (1929), *Experience and Nature.* New York: Dover.

Eliade, Mircea (1952), *Images and Symbols.* Kansas City, MO: Sheed Andrews and McMeel.

Feinstein, David and Krippner, Stanley (1988), *Personal Mythology*. Los Angeles: J.P. Tarcher.

Gardner, Howard (1983), *Frames of Mind*. New York: Basic Books.

Hannah, Barbara (1981), *Active Imagination*. Santa Monica, CA: Sigo.

Hofstadter, Douglas R. and Dennett, Daniel C. (1981), *The Mind's I*. New York: Bantam.

Huxley, Aldous (1954), *The Doors of Perception*. New York: Harper and Row.

Keleman, Stanley (1975), *The Body Speaks Its Mind*. New York: Simon and Schuster.

Lowen, Alexander (1958), *The Language of the Body*. New York: Collier.

McDermott, John J., ed. (1973), *The Philosophy of John Dewey*. Chicago: University of Chicago Press.

Medawar, Peter (1984), *The Limits of Science*. Oxford: Oxford University Press.

Montagu, Ashley (1971), *Touching*. New York: Harper and Row.

Morris, Desmond (1985), *Body Watching*. New York: Crown.

Moustakas, Clark (1967), *Creativity and Conformity*. Princeton, NJ: Van Nostrand.

Piaget, Jean (1963), *Play, Dreams and Imagination in the Child*. New York: W.W. Norton.

Polanyi, Michael (1958), *Personal Knowledge*. Chicago: University of Chicago Press.

Reik, Theodor (1964), *Listening with the Third Ear*. New York: Arena Books.

Rogers, Carl (1969), *Freedom to Learn*. Columbus, OH: Charles Merrill.

Salk, Jonas (1985), *Anatomy of Reality*. New York: Praeger.

Samuels, Mike and Samuels, Nancy (1975), *Seeing with the Mind's Eye*. New York: Random House.

Sternberg, Robert J. (1989), *The Triarchic Mind*. New York: Penguin.

Todd, Mabel Elsworth (1937), *The Thinking Body*. New York: Dance Horizons.

Whitehead, Alfred North (1929), *The Aims of Education*. New York: Mentor.

Chapter Eight

Bok, Sissela (1979), *Lying: Moral Choice in Public and Private Life*. New York: Random House.

Brown, Lester (1981), *Building a Sustainable Society*. New York: W.W. Norton.

Elgin, Duane (1981), *Voluntary Simplicity*. New York: William Morrow.

Frankl, Viktor (1946), *The Doctor and the Soul*. New York: Bantam.

von Franz, Marie-Luise (1974), *Shadow and Evil in Fairytales*. Zurich: Spring.

Hampshire, Stuart (1983), *Morality and Conflict*. Cambridge: Harvard University Press.

Hawken, Paul (1983), *The Next Economy*. New York: Holt, Rinehart and Winston.

Kopp, Sheldon (1978), *An End to Innocence*. New York: Bantam.

Lappé, Frances Moore (1989), *Rediscovering America's Values*. New York: Ballantine.

Maslow, Abraham (1971), *The Further Reaches of Human Nature*. New York: Viking.

May, Rollo (1973), *Man's Search for Himself*. New York: Dell.

Neuman, Eric (1990), *Depth Psychology and a New Ethic*. Boston: Shambhala.

Nietzsche, Friedrich (1973), *Beyond Good and Evil*. New York: Penguin.

Peck, M. Scott (1978), *The Road Less Traveled*. New York: Simon and Schuster.

Russell, Bertrand (1987), *On Ethics, Sex and Marriage*. Buffalo, NY: Prometheus Books.

Schumacher, E.F. (1973), *Small Is Beautiful*. New York: Harper and Row.

Sperry, Roger (1985), *Science and Moral Priority*. New York: Praeger.

Stout, Jeffrey (1988), *Ethics After Babel*. Boston: Beacon Press.

Wachtel, Paul (1989), *The Poverty of Affluence*. Philadelphia: New Society Publishers.

Williams, Bernard (1985), *Ethics and The Limits of Philosophy*. Cambridge: Harvard University Press.

Chapter Nine

Anderson, Robert A. (1987), *Wellness Medicine*. New Canaan, CT: Keats Publishing.

Borysenko, Joan (1987), *Minding the Body, Mending the Mind*. Reading, MA: Addison-Wesley.

DeSpelder, Lynne Ann and Strickland, Albert Lee (1987), *The Last Dance*. Palo Alto, CA: Mayfield Publishing Company.

Dossey, Larry (1984), *Beyond Illness*. Boston: Shambhala.

Foss, Laurence and Rothenberg, Kenneth (1987), *The Second Medical Revolution*. Boston: Shambhala.

Justice, Blair (1988), *Who Gets Sick*. Los Angeles: J.P. Tarcher.

Kapleau, Philip (1971), *The Wheel of Death*. New York: Harper and Row.

Kramer, Kenneth (1988), *The Sacred Art of Dying*. New York: Paulist Press.

Kübler-Ross, Elizabeth (1969), *On Death and Dying*. New York: Macmillan.

Levine, Stephen (1984), *Meetings at the Edge*. Garden City, NY: Anchor Press.

Locke, Steven and Colligan, Douglas (1986), *The Healer Within*. New York: New American Library.

Luria, A.R. (1973), *The Working Brain*. New York: Basic Books.

Lyons, Albert S. (1978), *Medicine, An Illustrated History*. New York: Harry N. Abrams.

Mathew-Simonton, Stephanie (1978), *Getting Well Again*. New York: Bantam.

Meltzer, David, ed. (1984), *Death*. Albany, CA: North Point.

Miller, Jonathan (1982), *The Body in Question*. New York: Vintage.

Ornstein, Robert and Sobel, David (1987), *The Healing Brain*. New York: Simon and Schuster.

Pelletier, Kenneth R. (1977), *Mind as Healer, Mind as Slayer*. New York: Delta.

Rossman, Martin L. (1987), *Healing Yourself*. New York: Walker and Company.

Sarton, May (1968), *Plant Dreaming Deep*. New York: W.W. Norton.

Thomas, Lewis (1983), *The Youngest Science*. New York: Bantam.

Chapter Ten

Augros, Robert and Stanciu, George (1987), *The New Biology*. Boston: Shambhala.

Bateson, Gregory (1979), *Mind and Nature*. New York: E.P. Dutton.

Davies, Paul (1983), *God and the New Physics*. New York: Simon and Schuster.

Dubos, René (1972), *A God Within*. New York: Charles Scribner's Sons.

Fuller, R. Buckminster (1981), *Critical Path*. New York: St. Martin's.

Gilman, Robert, ed., *In Context*. Bainbridge Island, WA: The Context Institute.

Griffin, David Ray and Smith, Houston (1989), *Primordial Truth and Postmodern Theology*. Albany, NY: State University of New York Press.

Huxley, Aldous (1944), *The Perennial Philosophy*. New York: Harper and Row.

Lovell, Bernard (1985), *Emerging Cosmology*. New York: Praeger.

Teilhard de Chardin, Pierre (1959), *The Future of Man*. New York: Harper and Row.

Watts, Alan W. (1951), *The Wisdom of Insecurity*. New York: Vintage.

Whitehead, Alfred North (1926), *Religion in the Making*. New York: Macmillan.

The World Commission on Environment and Development (1987), *Our Common Future*. Oxford: Oxford University Press.

Chapter Eleven

Alexander, Christopher (1977), *A Pattern Language*. Oxford: Oxford University Press.

Bernstein, Richard J. (1988), *Beyond Objectivism and Relativism*. Philadelphia: University of Pennsylvania Press.

Harman, Willis (1988), *Global Mind Change*. Indianapolis: Knowledge Systems.

Hofstadter, Douglas (1985), *Metamagical Themas*. New York: Basic Books.

Kierkegaard, Søren (1986), *Either/Or*. New York: Harper and Row.

Levinson, Daniel J. (1978), *The Seasons of a Man's Life*. New York: Ballantine.

Luce, Gay Gaer (1971), *Biological Rhythms in Human and Animal Physiology*. New York: Dover.

Russell, Bertrand (1961), *Religion and Science*. Oxford: Oxford University Press.

Watzlawick, Paul (1976), *How Real is Real*. New York: Random House.

Chapter Twelve

Assagioli, Roberto (1965), *Psychosynthesis*. New York: Viking.

von Bertalanffy, Ludwig (1968), *General System Theory*. New York: George Braziller.

Bohm, David and Peat, F. David (1987), *Science, Order and Creativity*. New York: Bantam.

Capra, Fritjof (1982), *The Turning Point*. New York: Simon and Schuster.

Einstein, Albert (1961), *Relativity*. New York: Crown.

Feuerstein, Georg (1987), *Structures of Consciousness*. Lower Lake, CA: Integral Publishing.

Frankl, Viktor (1969), *The Will to Meaning*, New York: Meridian.

Gebser, Jean (1986), *The Ever-Present Origin*. Athens, OH: Ohio University Press.

Gould, Steven J. (1988), *Time's Arrow—Time's Circle*. Cambridge: Harvard University Press.

Hartstone, Charles (1984), *Creativity in American Philosophy*. Albany, NY: State University of New York Press.

Jantsch, Erich (1975), *Design for Evolution*. New York: George Braziller.

Jung, Carl (1964), *Man and His Symbols*. Garden City, NY: Doubleday.

Korzybski, A. (1950), *Science and Sanity*. Lakeville, CT: International Neo-Aristotelian Publishing Co.

Kuhn, Thomas S. (1970), *The Structure of Scientific Revolutions*. Chicago: University of Chicago Press.

Laszlo, Erwin (1987), *Evolution, The Grand Synthesis*. Boston: Shambhala.

Lukav, Gary (1979), *The Dancing Wu Li Masters*. New York: William Morrow.

May, Rollo (1953), *Man's Search For Himself*. New York: Delta.

Neuman, Erich (1954), *The Origins and History of Consciousness*. Princeton, NJ: Princeton University Press.

Prigogine, Ilya (1980), *From Being to Becoming*. San Francisco: W.H. Freeman.

Watzlawick, Paul, ed. (1984), *The Invented Reality*. New York: W.W. Norton.

Whitehead, Alfred North (1978), *Process and Reality*. New York: Macmillan.

INDEX

CREDITS

Grateful acknowledgement is made to the following for
permission to reprint previously published material:

Robert Bly: For poem by Juan Ramon Jimenez from *News of the Universe*, edited by Robert Bly,
Sierra Club Books. Copyright 1980 by Robert Bly.
John Moyne and Coleman Barks for poem by Rumi from *Unseen Rain: Quantrains of Rumi*, edited
by John Moyne and Coleman Barks, Threshold Books. Copyright 1986 by Threshold
Books.

Illustration Credits:

Chapter 1: (Bridge) "Footbridge in Central Park." Photo—Thomas Schworer, 1982.
Chapter 3: (Dancers) Jeff Bickford and Lori Vadino. Photo—Thomas Schworer, 1987.
Chapter 4: (Gable/Leigh) Still from *Gone with the Wind*. Turner Entertainment Co. Copyright
1939 Selznick International Pictures, Inc. Ren. 1967 Metro-Goldwyn Mayer Inc.
Chapter 5: (Elkin) Sergei Elkin, USSR–USA Cartoon Exchange, 1988. (Wiley) David Miller,
San Francisco Examiner, USSR–USA Cartoon Exchange, 1988.
Chapter 6: ("Upstairs/Downstairs") *Seattle Post-Intelligencer*, Feb. 10, 1988. Photo—Robert
DeGiulio.
Chapter 7: (Picasso) Pablo Picasso, *Girl Before a Mirror*. 1932, Collection, The Museum of
Modern Art, New York, gift of Mrs. Simon Guggenheim. Oil on canvas, 64 x 51-1/4 in.
(MacNelly) *Shoe Cartoon*. Tribune Media Services. Copyright 1979 Jefferson
Communications Inc.
Chapter 8: (van Eyck) Jan van Eyck, *The Last Judgement*. Metropolitan Museum of Art, New York,
Fletcher Fund, c. 1425-1430. Tempura and oil on canvas, transferred from wood, 22-1/4 x
7- 3/4 in.
Chapter 9: (Rembrandt) Rembrandt van Rijn, *The Anatomy Lesson of Dr. Tulp*. Mauritshuis, The
Hague, 1632.
Chapter 10: (Michelangelo) Michelangelo Buonarroti, *Detail—Creazione dell'Uomo Cappella
Sistina*. Musei Vaticano, c. 1508-1512. (Raphael) Umbrian Raphael, *Saint George and the
Dragon*. National Gallery of Art, Washington, D.C. Andrew W. Mellon Collection,
c. 1506, Oil on wood, 11-1/8 x 8-3/8 in.
Chapter 11: (Escher) Maurits Cornelis Escher, *Drawing Hands*. Copyright 1989 M.C. Escher
Heirs/Cordon Art, Baarn, Holland.
Chapter 12: (Einstein) *Einstein and his Wife in Chicago, 1933*. The Bettmann Archive, New York.
(Larson) Gary Larson, *In God's Kitchen:* The Far Side. Copyright 1985 Universal Press
Syndicate.
Appendix: (Polar bears) *Two Heads are Better than One*. Hazenbeck Zoo, Hamburg, Germany.
January 27, 1988. Wide World Photos, Inc.

ICD Press is the publishing arm of the Institute for Creative Development, a non-profit think tank and educational center dedicated to exploring and addressing the critical issues of our time. Information about the Institute and about other Institute publications may be obtained by writing:

The Institute for
Creative Development
ICD Press
PO Box 85631
Seattle, WA 98145-1631